The Emperor's Clothes

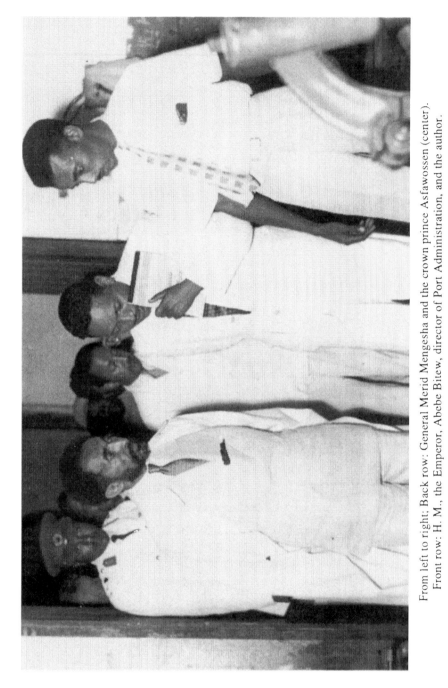

From left to right; Back row: General Merid Mengesha and the crown prince Asfawossen (center). Front row: H. M., the Emperor, Abebe Bitew, director of Port Administration, and the author.

The Emperor's Clothes

*A Personal Viewpoint on Politics
and Administration in the Imperial
Ethiopian Government*
1941-1974

By Gaitachew Bekele

Michigan State University Press
East Lansing
1993

All Michigan State University Press books are produced on paper which meets the requirements of American National Standard of Information Sciences—Permanence of paper for printed materials ANSI Z23.48-1984.

Michigan State University Press
East Lansing, Michigan 48823-5202

Printed in the United States of America

01 00 99 98 97 96 95 94 93 1 2 3 4 5 6 7 8 9 10

Library of Congress Cataloging in Publication Data

Gaitachew Bekele.
   The emperor's clothes : a personal viewpoint on politics and administration in the imperial Ethiopian government, 1941-1974 / by Gaitachew Bekele.
          p.   cm. — (African series ; #3)
   Includes bibliographical references and index.
   ISBN 0-87013-325-X (alk. paper)
   1. Gaitachew Bekele. 2. Ethiopia—Officials and employees—Biography. 3. Haile Selassie I, Emperor of Ethiopia, 1892-1975. 4. Ethiopia—Politics and government—1889-1974, I. Title. II. Series: African series (East Lansing, Mich.) ; #3.
DT387.92.G35A3   1993
963'.06—dc20
                                                                    93-19273
                                                                       CIP

African Series Editor: Harold Marcus

Other African Series Titles:

#1 *"Bonds of Silk" The Human Factor in the
   British Administration in the Sudan*
   by Francis M. Deng and M.W. Daly

#2 *The Development of Higher Education and Social Change
   An Ethiopian Experience* by Teshome Wagaw

CONTENTS

INTRODUCTION   1

1. FAMILY BACKGROUND   5

2. ITALIAN INVASION (1936-1941)   23

3. STUDIES   43

4. EARLY CAREER   51

5. DEPARTMENT OF MARINE, Addis Ababa (1954-1957)   65

6. ASSISTANT MINISTER (November 1957-December 1960)   79

7. ATTEMPTED COUP D'ETAT   101

8. GOVERNOR OF BAHR-DAR   125

9. AMBASSADOR (1963-1969)   143

10. MINISTRY OF POSTS, TELECOMMUNICATION, AND
    TRANSPORT   161

11. CABINET RESIGNS (February 1974)   171

12. EPILOGUE   191

    INDEX   197

INTRODUCTION

It has been said that clothes make a man. While such an over-simplification cannot be wholly true, the clothes which a man chooses to wear can sometimes be a clue to his inner-thinking, how he perceives himself and those around him. I remember when I first went to London, I visited Madame Tussaud's Waxworks and felt enormously proud to find a statue of His Imperial Majesty Haile Selassie dressed in the traditional costume of Ethiopia.

It is my contention that tradition and culture are vitally important elements in the identity of a nation. Especially one which can allow its people to undergo great hardships and then reestablish themselves after periods of social, military or political upheaval. Tradition and culture have sustained my nation of Ethiopia through the centuries, and I was proud to see a statue of my leader dressed in clothes which to me were the embodiment of our culture. Imagine then, my bitter disappointment when I visited the same exhibition some years later and found the same statue of Haile Selassie bedecked in the uniform of a British Field Marshal. In my estimation, he had slipped from the image of an Ethiopian emperor to the shadow of a rather tawdry commissioner in borrowed finery.

Haile Selassie's change of costume was an outward symbol of his rejection of Ethiopian culture and values. He chose to claim the title of Emperor and the privileges which went with it without taking on all of the responsibilities the office entailed. I know many people believed Haile Selassie was a symbol of Ethiopian resistance to Italian rule. On the contrary, he lost the war before it was fought and brought about the defeat and downfall of Ethiopia when he lost faith in his heritage and cultural values and thus suffered from an inferiority complex and subordination. I feel he first lost the affection and respect of the Ethiopian people when he went into exile. A true ruler of Ethiopia in the traditional mold would have rather died fighting to drive an invader from his sacred soil than go into exile as a figurehead.

1

The Emperor's Clothes

I am not oblivious to the great things His Majesty accomplished, particularly in the field of external affairs. He deserves credit for the admission of Ethiopia into the League of Nations and he undoubtedly played a leading role in the establishment of the Organization of African Unity. In the field of education, I was one of those fortunate enough to benefit and I ought to be grateful for His Majesty's special attention and favor in promoting me within his government. However, I wish the personal concern he demonstrated to individuals whom he thought important to impress could have been extended to the general public of the nation he ruled. Had this been the case, the benefit of education could have been spread throughout Ethiopia, instead of resulting in the pitiful illiteracy rate of 90 percent which was evident at the end of half of a century of his rule.

But the important question here is: Why did all these great accomplishments come to nothing in the end? The answer is that the changes, although apparently progressive, were made with the wrong motives, with the wrong objectives in mind. His Majesty was motivated by self interest rather than the interests of those whom he had a sacred duty to serve. He violated the cardinal principle which had always been followed by great leaders of the Ethiopian nation, that the supreme leader had no personal property, so that no self-interest could impinge upon his public duty.

Having been brought up in the court of Menilek, Emperor Haile Selassie must have been quite aware of the example of one of Menilek's judicial decisions. Menilek was the rightful heir to his mother's {a commoner's} land, but ruled that it must be inherited by the tenant who farmed it. His reasoning was that since the Almighty God had seen fit to grant him the whole of the country, he had no right to claim a small part of it.

Many people make excuses for Haile Selassie because of the barbarism of the regime which grew out of his overthrow, saying: "Haile Selassie maregni" or "Forgive us, Haile Selassie." It is wrong to compare His Majesty, from royal lineage and brought up in the court of Menilek with a man of obscure background who did not have the benefit of a traditional Ethiopian upbringing. Haile Selassie must be judged by higher standards, those of the rulers whom he succeeded.

The present chaos in Ethiopia is the legacy of Haile Selassie because it is the inevitable result of the policies which he introduced and allowed to flourish. By systematically removing born leaders and surrounding himself with sycophants, the Emperor created a situation which could only lead to chaos after his death.

The diverse tribes of Ethiopia were bound together for centuries as a single nation by a proper appreciation inculcated in every individual of the glorious history of independence and social justice which were symbolized by the

Crown. When the traditional standards of the Crown were debased, no one any longer wished to be associated with a downgraded and lawless leadership. It is little wonder that Ethiopia has disintegrated and the various tribes now wish to assert their tribal identity. I record here what I know of Ethiopian traditions and culture and what I saw of the decline and disintegration of the Ethiopian nation in the belief that a return to traditional values and democratic principles can be the only salvation of what remains of my country.

1

Family Background

My grandfather Zewdu was born in 1863 in Bulga/Tcdla-Mariam. His father, Wolde-Hawaryat, was a native of that area, a middle class farmer married to the daughter of a prominent highland (Terra) family of the soldier-farmer class. Zewdu and his younger brother Wolde-Selassie were their children. As a young boy, Zewdu did not show much interest in the farming activities in which his family was engaged. He was not keen to go out into the field with the other boys to tend the livestock. On the occasions when he did, he usually lured the other boys away to play games and the livestock ran astray. The only interest he showed was following his father when he went on trips or to public meetings, local courts or other errands. He liked to sneak away to the nearby river to swim; he was an excellent swimmer as well as a good horseman.

These tendencies of their older son made the parents worry about his future. They wanted to discuss their concern about Zewdu with a close relative in government circles who would be able to advise them on what measures to take. They realized it was important that he should be directed early in life so that his natural abilities could be encouraged and developed. The man Zewdu's parents had in mind to help them solve the problem was his uncle Aladeneh, the elder brother of Zewdu's mother. Aladeneh had grown up in the court of Menilek and had become his personal treasurer at the time he was King of Shewa. Aladeneh was delighted to help his sister and brother-in-law by taking his ten-year-old nephew to Court as a page boy. However, after Aladeneh had brought his nephew to Court and arranged for him to be attached to the Court institution which had been his own alma mater, Aladeneh resigned from the service of the Imperial Court in a dramatic manner that madc a lasting impression on his nephew of how justice could prevail over even the power of the emperor.

Aladeneh had been one of the young retainers who had accompanied Menilek when he was taken prisoner by Tewdros to Meqedela. Later, when Menilek became King of Shewa and Aladeneh his treasurer, the King one day sent a page boy to Aladeneh. The page boy was to ask Aladeneh for a certain item from the treasury which Menilek wished to present to somebody. When the messenger did not find Aladeneh at the treasury, he picked up a similar article and ran back to the palace with it thinking that he understood what the emperor wanted.

The article he had been brought was not the one Menilek wanted. Assuming that it was Aladeneh who had made the silly mistake, he sent for him; and as soon as he saw Aladeneh approaching, he flew into a rage. Without waiting for an explanation, Menilek tried to strike Aladeneh with his fist. Aladeneh remained calm and asked Menilek for an explanation of his behavior. The king abused him, saying how foolish he had been to send him an item for which he had not asked. Realizing that he was being unjustly accused, Aladeneh in turn became furious and rounded on the king, asking him:

> Is this the way a king is expected to use his God-given authority and power, abusing it as an instrument to the dictates of his emotions instead of using it to administer justice? Such a king does not deserve my service. From this moment I have resigned my position in the service of the king and I also curse my children if they should enter the service of this king.

He left the palace, never to return.

Menilek, realizing too late that he had blundered, confided to two of his officials what had happened between him and Aladeneh. He sent them to the house of Aladeneh to beg his pardon and to offer compensation for the wrong. The two officials found Aladeneh at his house and told him the king was contrite, offering him compensation for the moral wrong he had suffered and urging him to forgive the king. Aladeneh obliged the two officials by giving them his solemn word of honor that he would not bear any grudge against Menilek, saying that he had already forgiven him for losing control of his emotions. He added, however, that he had sworn an oath never to return to the Court: "Even my children I have cursed them if they enter the service of the King." Menilek compensated Aladeneh by granting him one gasha of land in Bishoftu near Qajima Georgis and Aladeneh never again set foot in the palace.

My grandfather would sometimes recount the story and, when he had finished telling it, would declare that Menilek had been a great and God-fearing leader; genuinely kind, free from pretension suspicion, and intrigue with his main preoccupation being the welfare of his people, the proper administration of justice, and the development of his empire.

6

1. Family Background

So it was that Zewdu was formally admitted into and grew up in one of the Imperial Court institutions, known as Yenjera-Assalafiwotch Denb, an order which literally means "The Food Waiters' Establishment," but which was a court and military unit comparable with the Catering Corps of a modern army. Joining such an Imperial Court institution did not automatically entitle a young person to paid employment but offered an opportunity to train on the job, opening avenues for further advancement, while at the same time providing subsistence at the table of the Imperial Court. Such a system maintained the continuity of family ties by encouraging the young person to continue to look to his family for economic assistance. However, it was not an easy system for an independent-minded and resourceful young person to accept if he wished to establish a household of his own. It was a spur to devising a way of becoming self-sufficient.

Zewdu would go back to Bulga to visit his parents for two or three months every year to exchange experiences and to remind his parents of their obligations toward their son. They gave Zewdu a half-gasha of land (20 hectares) in Minjar, on the plateau. He started developing and built a house for a relative who would stay there and continue with the development. Zewdu's parents also arranged for him to marry Woletehana, the only child of a farming family in Shenkora/Bocan, also on the plateau. Since Bulga was crowded and the subdivision of individual holdings of land between children made farming uneconomical, the strategy to overcome the problem was either to buy land on the plateau or to develop marriage ties with the neighboring highland families.

In the meantime, war on the northern frontier of the empire against the invading colonial force of Italy became imminent and Zewdu was called to arms. He was ordered to join his unit to march to the front at Adwa. His young wife Woletehana was pregnant with their first child. As Zewdu was preparing to leave, Woletehana insisted that she accompany her husband to the battle-front and share his fate. Nothing could make her change her mind. She was so determined that she said she must accompany him as his wife or he could go alone after divorcing her. So Zewdu divorced the mother-to-be of his only child and left for the front.

Four months after the divorce in 1896, Woletehana who was living with her parents in Shenkora/Bocan, gave birth to a baby boy whom she named Bekele Zewdu, which means Zewdu reborn. Because of the victory of Adwa, 1896 was a year of great significance in Ethiopian history but in the life of Bekele it also reminded him of two other events, his birth and the divorce of his parents.

Zewdu survived the battle of Adwa and returned to Addis Ababa. He went straight to Shenkora/Bocan, to see his son Bekele. Although he was welcomed with great emotion and rejoicing by Woletehana, she was adamant regarding their divorce, so Bekele was brought up by his mother until he was four and then went to his father at Addis Ababa and from there to Wollamo where he grew up, married and lived until the Italian invasion in 1936. Bekele was the only child of Zewdu, who had no issue from his subsequent marriage, but Woletehana remarried and gave Bekele two half brothers, Teshome and Lema Tekaligni.

Zewdu built his residence in Addis Ababa at Arat-Killo close to the Imperial Palace on the plot allocated to him by his unit. This was expropriated in 1931 for a historically worthy cause. The first Ethiopian parliament building at Arat-Killo stands on the exact spot where Zewdu and his son Bekele built their residence in Addis Ababa.

Soon after his return from Adwa the government felt the need for administrative reform and reorganization of the central institution known as Mehal-Sefari, hence Zewdu's unit was allocated Gebar in Wolayta. gebar was a system by which, instead of the government collecting tax from its subjects and paying salaries to its servants, the servants would be allocated a group of subjects from whom they would collect tax on their own behalf for their personal use. Zewdu was promoted to the rank of Basha and put in charge of one of the three units of the Yenjera Assalafiwotch Denb. As the head of his unit he went to Wolayta to take up residence among his gebars and he took along with him his son Bekele.

As this arrangement was going to affect the working schedule of the institution regarding the service at the palace as a whole, it called for a complete reorganization that took into account the physical distance between Addis Ababa and Wolayta, the available means of transportation, the time requirement for the new settlers to manage the development activities as well as the official responsibilities of enforcing law and order in their area and then the duty in Addis Ababa. This was achieved by arranging for the three units of the organization to take turns for duty in Addis Ababa which meant that the officers and men of one unit would be in Addis Ababa for four months of the year and for the remaining eight months would be devoted to meeting their economic and cultural needs and to overseeing law and order in their area. This arrangement was referred to as Wor-Tera, which means monthly turn.

The new settlers were referred to as Denbegnotch, which translates as customers or regulars, among the Wolayta people. The Denbegnotch, with their Christian culture, in time earned for themselves respect and a good name in the administration of justice and the fair treatment of their gebars. This should not be surprising when we consider the fact that they had been brought up under the strict discipline of the Imperial Court system where justice and honesty were the cardinal virtues, along with the ability to fill a position of leadership. It has been said that the need for this quality of leadership was recognized and insisted upon during Menilek's regime. The relationship

8

1. Family Background

between the gebar holders and he gebar having been well-defined as a rule, there was very little room for friction as the former mainly depended on the latter for revenue. The consent of the gebars to be ruled depended on the reciprocity of protection and reasonableness on the part of the gebar holders in their exercise of authority.

By keeping groups small, the gebar system was structured to resolve a social and political problem of the time so as to bring the parties concerned closer and afford them direct communications for understanding the circumstances of each other while allowing individual needs to be met easily and to promote unity between the two communities. The system which replaced it, inherited from the Italians, failed to take into consideration the local aspect of the problem; therfore, there was no mutual interest to draw the parties closer, the taxpayer and the collector had no chance to cultivate a friendly relationship and remained strangers which encouraged corruption and oppression.

The unfounded criticism of Menilek's rule and the condemnation of the gebar system as feudal are based on the superficial impression received by European observers who generally ignored local aspects in their analysis and failed to perceive anything but stagnancy and backwardness. They found it difficult to believe in the existence of a unique sociopolitical dynamism and in the political fluidity which characterized the long course of Ethiopian political history. The most damaging and humiliating aspect of the matter was its acceptance by our leaders and the educated generation without questioning its validity, which revealed their confusion and bankruptcy. If the sociopolitical system had not been flexible and pragmatic, how could the nation have been able to stand the test of external threats and internal fragmentation? Unfortunately, today we are witnessing this very situation take place only five decades after Ethiopia surrendered to alien values.

As evidenced by later developments, the relationship that developed between the gebar holders and the gebar in Wolayta was genuinely harmonious and based on mutual respect and interest. For example, during the Italian invasion the propaganda used to incite former gebars to take revenge against former gebar holders failed completely; there was hardly an incident worth mentioning of any attempted retaliation. Even a show of disrespect for the former gebar holders was absent. My grandfather Zewdu, who had retired a few years earlier and was living among his gebars, continued living there throughout the occupation without experiencing any change of attitude on the part of the Wolayta community. His servants remained in his service voluntarily until he left Wolayta to go to Shewa in 1950 because of old age. He needed the close attention of his son who was at that time a provincial judge at Wollisso. Zewdu passed away in 1953 at the age of 90.

9

Even though his parents had divorced, Bekele grew up in a big household in Wolayta. Zewdu's house was full of children. Some came from the Wolayta family, or were Zewdu's or Bekele's godchildren. The servants' children were also there. The big household, which was considered essential as a status symbol for a government official, provided the right atmosphere for Bekele to be brought up in Ethiopian culture. The child was immersed in the crowd and participated in household activities just like the rest without any special consideration for being the son of the master. He was expected to serve at table, to collect forage and to look after mount animals, to follow the master when he was traveling and to attend to visitors, which gave him the opportunity to engage in conversation, to cultivate friendships with interesting personalities, and to attract attention.

The only special attention the master's son received was to be sent to school while the children of the servants remained on household duties. Other than that, they all ate from the same mesob, table, slept on the same earthen floor and dressed in the same cotton cloth. When the servants got married, they established a household on land provided by the master and worked there to support their families. Their children took the place of their parents in the household of the master. On the other hand, the children of the master were free to follow in the footsteps of their father or to find another profession, to attach themselves to the household of Mekuanent [nobility or government officials] or to the Imperial Court, to take up farming, to join the clergy, or to establish themselves in commerce.

Bekele went to church school at Zaba-Selassie and every year he followed his father to Addis Ababa where he was exposed to the workings of the Imperial Court institutions and was able to familiarize himself with the Court environment including the profession of his father. After school while in Wolayta, he accompanied his father to the open courts, to public meetings, and on inspection tours of the area. He also served as secretary to keep records of the court proceedings or accounts of the income of the gebar. At the age of 25 he married Assegedetch Biru, who was 12 years his junior. Assegedetch went to Wolayta with her mother Yimegnushal Ayele at the age of six and, like Bekele, grew up there in the household of her stepfather Aberilet. Yimegnushal had married Aberilet after divorcing her first husband, Biru Asferatchew, the father of Assegedetch. She took with her the second youngest of her six children. The last born, Mulugeta, was a male and his father Biru would not part with him. Both Biru and Yimegnushal were from Qinbebit, which is about 120 kilometers northeast of Addis Ababa in the direction of Debre-Birahn. The grandparents of both Biru and Yimegnushal originally came from Menz.

Normally the marriage between Assegedetch and Bekele would not have taken place because Assegedetch's father Biru was so conceited of his lineage

1. Family Background

that he would not have allowed his daughter to marry a commoner. But it did because her mother went to Wolayta with her second husband taking Assegedetch with her. They lived there among a liberal-minded community and my grandmother was a very kind person, very different from her former husband (my grandfather Biru). When Bekele asked for the hand of her daughter, Yimegnushal did not bother about his lineage; she was satisfied that he was a good match for Assegedetch in all respects. He was a handsome young man and his social status in the community was high, so she agreed to the marriage. When Biru was told of the marriage, he fumed and almost disowned his daughter. For quite a long time he refused to recognize the marriage and would not accept Bekele as his son-in-law. Eventually he acknowledged the marriage after Assegedetch had borne five children.

I do not think there was much love lost between my father and Biru. I remember one day when I was about four and was being brought up by my grandmother (Yimegnushal), who was living in Qinbebit at this time with her relatives on the family land after her second husband died in Wolayta. My grandfather Biru who lived close by on his big property asked for me to be brought to his house to spend the day playing with his family. I spent the day playing with them, but when I saw dusk falling, I wanted to go back to my grandmother. I started crying to draw attention, saying that I wanted my grandmother. My grandfather got angry with me and called one of the servants in the house and said, "Come and take back this Yegud-Liji," which means the child of low birth. In spite of all that, Bekele and Assegedetch remained happily married and were blessed with 9 living children and 35 grandchildren.

Bekele formally joined the same Court service institution as his father at the age of 18, serving with the same unit under his father. When his father retired, Bekele went to the Maichew front at the head of his unit. From Maichew he went directly to Bulga to join the resistance movement and was awarded the title of Kegnazmatch by Melake Tsehay Eyasu (the great-grandson of Menilek who was proclaimed emperor of Ethiopia in 1937 by the leaders of the resistance movement in Shewa, and who at that time awarded the title of Ras to Abebe Aregai, the resistance movement leader).

During the postwar period, Bekele served as a provincial judge in Wolayta and in Shewa: Wollisso/Debre-Sinna/Nazret and Addis Ababa. He was awarded the title of Fitawrari by Haile Selassie and retired from government service at the age of 64 in 1960 and settled in Addis Ababa. But, by nature, Bekele was a very agile person and could not sit idly and waste time. Habitually, he left the house early in the morning at six. This habit continued after his retirement; he was busy developing his land in Bulga and Wolayta, and was always on the road until the revolution. Then he was restricted from performing his constructive daily activities, and forced to spend his time idly at home.

11

That caused a duodenal ulcer to flare, and he had a major operation at the age of 80 in 1976. The first operation was not successful because the surgeon, considering the advanced age, thought it would be wiser to carry out a modified operation instead of completely cutting out the affected part. Unfortunately it did not work.

After two weeks the patient, having been on glucose only, was a living skeleton. The surgeon sought my consent to reopen and perform the second surgery. I asked the surgeon whether the patient would survive the operating table. His response was that the patient in any case was going to die as it was. He would like to try if he could save him by reopening and performing a normal surgery. I gave him my consent. The operation took four hours and it was a delightful surprise to everyone concerned, including the surgeon Dr. Johnson that Bekele survived two major operations, one after the other, within a period of two weeks. He left the hospital two weeks after the second operation, and lived eight more years. That was the first time he had been confined to bed.

When Addis Ababa was founded, Bekele's father Zewdu had been allocated a plot at Arat-Killo, where both father and son had residences which they used when they were on duty. When the property was expropriated in 1931 to build the nation's parliament, an alternative plot was offered to Zewdu in exchange at Filwoha. This was not entirely to Zewdu's satisfaction, but before the question could be settled the Ethiopian-Italian war broke out and the matter rested there. Fortunately for the family, Zewdu and his son Bekele had been allocated 15,000 square meters of land eight kilometers from Addis Ababa on the Bishoftu road for their mount and baggage animals.

Today, this is where the whole Bekele family group of 11 households has built its residence surrounding the family village. It is here that I built my own residence in 1954 and married in 1958, and where our first son, Tewdros, was born. After his retirement, Bekele and Assegedetch lived here among their children. Assegedetch passed away on 25 January 1983 and Bekele followed her 51 days later.

What a great pity my grandfather Biru did not live to see Fitawrari Bekele Zewdu, the son-in-law whom he despised because he was the son of an ordinary man, in the employment of the Imperial Court. He must have overlooked the facts of history and the many centuries of our cultures, systems, and traditions which ensure that titles and positions hardly matter for the purpose of family inheritance. Because of the traditional office competition, a man could be born the son of a peasant but born a leader and rise to wealth and power. It was only personal merit and ability that counted. What was the lineage of Habte-Georgis, the great statesman of Menilek's rule? What of Balcha and Alula? Practically all the great leaders of Ethiopia were the products of the great Ethiopian institutions.

1. Family Background

The traditional Ethiopian institutions which produced leaders, administrators, army generals, lawyers, public servants, and ordinary soldiers were the Imperial Court at the highest level, the Mekuanent household at the intermediate level, and church school and ordinary household at the primary level. At the household level training started at birth, a baby was only fed when he needed and asked for it by crying. The struggle to live started at birth. Although they were at first protected, the practice was to expose children gradually to the realities of life. Very little care was taken to protect babies from adverse climatic conditions and hazardous environmental conditions. Therefore only the strong ones survived by developing resistance and immunity. When one reached the age of four, one was considered to have reached the age to take part in the daily activities of the household. This was also the age considered appropriate (four years and four days to be exact) for a child to start the alphabet by going to church school. In the course of participating in the household activities, boys followed the footsteps of their fathers and girls their mothers.

It used to be an accepted cultural belief that to succeed in life, children should be exposed to its rigors and hardships at a tender age. The institutions through which one could pass these trials and tests of life started with the family household which was moderate and the church school and the Mekuanent household, and Imperial Court which were very thorough. The child was expected to attend in church school both day and night; therefore one had to sleep there with only a little straw over the earth floor and few covers. One went home for breakfast and midday meals, and to bring back something for supper if one's family lived near the school. Otherwise one was expected to live on food brought to church every Sunday and occasionally on other days by the parishioners to feed the clergy who conducted memorial services and the needy who were usually around the compound of the church. Failing this, the student would go around the neighborhood and declare himself a student living far from home. He was identified by his ragged dress or sheepskin (Debelo) and the Aqufada (the bag made of palm leaves) that he carried as a container for the food. Every household donated food to such a student. The belief was that a successful student would sustain these hardships; otherwise one would drop out early.

Besides reading and writing Amharic, a church school education consisted of oral recitation of various religious scriptures, collecting the raw material and preparing ink for one's own use, the shaping of pens out of reed for writing, preparing parchment, carving wood into crosses and other useful articles, book binding, cutting and stitching one's own clothing, doing housework for the teachers, collecting firewood and water, and serving in the church.

The next level in the traditional institution through which one who aspired to public office or soldiering had to pass was the household of a Mekuanent. A boy at the age of eight or ten from any class or occupation, presented himself to serve in the family of a Mekuanent. He could be recommended by a relative who knew the Mekuanent or one of his followers. It was here or in the Imperial Court that one's natural potential could be cultivated and one could rise from an obscure family background to a position of great consequence. To mention but two, there were Ras Alula, son of a simple farmer and Fitawrari Habte-Georgis, a man of unknown family background who had been taken as a prisoner in one of the expeditions.

Just as it was in the Imperial Court, in the Mekuanent household one began at the bottom of the hierarchy, with many others who came from all walks of life including the children of the master who must take orders from anyone senior in the hierarchy and carry out all sorts of jobs. Failure to carry out duties properly would be punished with rough treatment including pushing around and beating. In this way one's endurance, capability, and character were tried and tested. One was also exposed to the workings of the political, social, judicial, and administrative systems and processes which created the hierarchy in which one was participating, aiming to attain the level appropriate to one's capability. At the Imperial Court, which was the highest level of the institutions, the main center for political and social activities where every structure of society and social class was represented, the pyramid of the hierarchy physically exhibited, interaction of government politics, administrative, political, and social activities took place daily and the future leaders of the nation met together at the base of the pyramid to compete freely and to be completely exposed to the system. Opportunity was given to all. This was in keeping with the Ethiopian religious and cultural ideology that all people are basically the same but differ in abilities. There is an adage in Amharic: "Tefetron temekro aylewootewoom," which means advice or training cannot change inborn character. This was the system and culture our forefathers followed to produce and identify leaders and public servants until the end of the Menilek era.

Haggai Erlich in his book "Ethiopia and the Challenge of Independence" described it like this: "Long entrenched customs of land inheritance and title enactment, as well as the country's topography were factors in the creation of political culture which offered even the ambitious son of an anonymous peasant a good chance at climbing to both legitimacy and power. This flexibility enabled persons of strong character to join the system rather than revolt against it, born leaders of deprived background could well make their way without necessarily resorting to new ideology, ethnic, religious or social."[1]

The lineage Biru was so proud of could not have gone back beyond two or three generations and it did not continue after him. In a way he was lucky he died before he saw the Italian conquest of his country which took place only six months after his death. Biru was a very stubborn, conservative, and contemptuous man. In order to avoid subordination, he distanced himself from the court circle and lived on his estate in Qinbebit among his subordinates as a lord. After he divorced Yimegnushal, my grandmother, he married Kuribatchew Beshah, the half-sister of Dejazmatch Mekonnen Wossene. It was Dejazmatch Mekonnen who awarded him the title Fitawrari. Because of this, at the time of the Italian invasion, he reported to Dejazmatch Mekonnen and not to Haile Selassie. In 1935, he left his home for the first time in his life and went to Wolayta to join Dejazmatch Mekonnen to go to war against the invading colonial force. He was there for only a month when he became ill and died at the age of 50. He was buried at Wolayta/Sodo Arada Georgis. Only two of his eight children were present at the funeral, my mother and his only son Mulugeta who had come to Wolayta as one of the followers of the governor. Of course there were hundreds of other relatives and friends who attended the funeral including his brother-in-law, the governor of Wolayta, Dejazmatch Mekonnen Wossene. His untimely death was a great blow to all his children, followers, and friends. He was genuinely respected and loved by all those who were closely associated with him since he was very generous, sincere, and of strong character. When he went to Wolayta, he visited his daughter Assegedetch and his grandchildren and was welcomed with great rejoicing by his son-in-law Bekele and his daughter. Biru stayed with them one week. He must have changed his mind about Bekele at the time and regretted his earlier reaction to the marriage. This visit took place only three weeks before his death.

My grandmother Yimegnushal was a completely different sort of person, genuinely kind, who did not care about her lineage or status. She only cared about what could be done for those who were poor and homeless. Whatever she had, she gladly shared. As a child, I was so fascinated to hear her talk about her childhood and her marriages. She was given in marriage twice. The first time, on the night of the wedding, before the marriage was consummated she sneaked out of the bridal chamber and walked to the house of her uncle who gave her refuge. The marriage was automatically dissolved and then she went back to live with her parents. After her second marriage, she had no chance to sneak out, so she was determined to fight hard so as not to let anybody approach her. The next morning, the news reached her family that the marriage was not consummated. Her uncle came and found her in a state of emotion but resolute. She insisted that he take her back to his house. So the second marriage ended.

After that her parents gave up hope of giving Yimegnushal in marriage and she lived with them. Yimegnushal was the fifth of eight children, six girls and two boys. Her sisters were happily married and well-established. She told her parents she was not interested in getting married. She was happy living with them, doing housework, spinning and sewing. Biru, who was young and unmarried, lived with his father Asferatchew. This was a well-established and prominent family in the area. Biru heard about Yimegnushal and what had happened with her previous marriages and that her parents had given up all thought of her marrying again. All five daughters of Ayele were beautiful but Yimegnushal surpassed them all. Biru regarded the situation as a challenge. He started spying on her movements and discovered that she only left her parents' house to go and visit her uncle who lived 15 minutes away or to the nearby field to collect akirma, the straw which was used for making baskets. Biru started to frequent the neighborhood where Yimegnushal lived and the field where she collected akirma.

One day he found Yimegnushal picking akirma nearby her parents' house. He took her by surprise, galloping up behind her and sweeping her into the saddle in front of him. Before she knew what had happened, she found herself in a high-walled compound with three enclosures and only one gate which was always guarded. This was how Yimegnushal came to be married by Biru and they lived as husband and wife for 15 years and were blessed with six children, two boys and four girls. One of the boys died young; the others lived happily to marry and have children, except Mulugeta who died without offspring at the age of 31 in 1941. He died in Addis Ababa and was buried in Selassie Church.

Yimegnushal lived a happy and healthy life with never a day's sickness until she died at more than a 100 years of age in 1964 in the house of my parents in Addis Ababa, having seen so many great grandchildren. One evening after dinner she went to bed as usual and in the morning when my mother walked into her bedroom she found her wonderful mother sleeping peacefully forever. And the surprising thing about her was that she did not lose a single tooth; all were intact and snow white. She died in the month of August, the heavy rainy season in Ethiopia, and her will was that she should be buried in Qinbebit, 112 kilometers from Addis Ababa. Only 90 kilometers of this is all-weather road, the remaining 30 kilometers only negotiable by walking or on mule back provided that there was no rain on that day so as to cross the rivers.

My father was determined to fulfill her wishes in spite of opposition from the other family members who argued that the weather conditions would not allow it. A miracle happened! For five days following her death there was not a drop of rain. My father proclaimed that Yimegnushal was a saint. Her burial took place according to her wish by the grave site of her mother Etalemahu at Wootamayes Medhane Alem Church; Yimegnushal finally rested where she wanted to be. Her house in Sekoru\Qinbebit, where I was brought up, was burnt down by the Italians. Today on the same spot where it stood, there is a school and clinic serving the local people and it is connected by an all-weather road.

The Birth and Survival of the Third Child

Neither Bekele nor his wife Assegedetch could remember much about their birthplace or their relatives there, since they had left when they were young and gone to Wolayta, each with one of their parents. They grew up among the local people, spoke the language like any other Wolayta, participated in cultural activities, cultivated closer relationships and friendly ties, happily married and settled, and led a happy life within the community in which they grew up. The physical distance between Wolayta and Shewa, 325 kilometers, and the lack of modern means of transportation were the major factors which virtually separated the settlers in the south from their families in the north. The journey took ten days by mule and required advance planning to arrange transportation needs for riding as well as baggage, with tents for camping at night, supplies and provisions, and presents for relatives and friends. So home visits were expensive and tiring undertakings. Therefore, during and after the Italian invasion, a great number of the second generation of the settlers' families had completely lost their northern connections and became completely identified with the south.

Although, normally, Assegedetch could not have imagined that she would face any problem which could not be overcome with help from the community with whom she lived or that she would be obliged to ask for assistance from her relatives in the north, her memories of her life with her mother were fresh. Therefore, when she became pregnant after losing her first two babies, she felt the need to be with her mother to ensure the survival of her child. Her mother had left Wolayta and gone back to Shewa/Qinbebit to live with her relatives on the land which she had inherited from her father. That happened soon after Assegedetch got married when her mother lost her second husband.

So it was decided by everyone concerned that Assegedetch should go to her mother in Shewa/Qinbebit to have her third child. It took time to arrange the journey, which was expected to take 10 or 12 days. Bekele and Assegedetch set out on a journey which was both tiring and adventurous, especially for Assegedetch. Bekele was used to the yearly trip to Addis Ababa for duty. For Assegedetch, it was her first trip home in ten years. She looked forward to seeing her father, even though he had been opposed to her marriage, her brother Mulugeta, her mother, and her sisters who were married and living in Shewa.

Ten days after they left Wolayta, they arrived in Menjigso, at the house of her elder sister, Tsedale Biru, who was married to Kenyazmatch Bogale. Menjigso is close to and east of Addis Ababa, a day's journey short of Qinbebit. Since there was no way of communicating to announce their arrival in advance, they turned up out of the blue. It made a pleasant surprise for Tsedale to see her sister and both gave way to emotion when they met.

Tsedale, who wanted to see as much as possible of her sister, insisted that she should stop her journey there for at least three weeks. Only a week after arriving in Menjigso, Assegedetch gave birth to her third child, a boy, and a messenger was sent immediately for her mother to come to Menjigso. They agreed to name the child "Kassa," which means compensation. God had compensated them for the two lost infants. Although Kassa was the name I was given at birth, my grandmother later changed it when she realized all the children who followed me survived. She substituted the name Gaitachew, which means "master to those born after."

At first I found it difficult to say where my birthplace was because I was born when my mother was on a journey with the intention of giving birth in Bulga. I later decided for myself to take Bulga as my birthplace because it was the place my mother intended for me to be born, it was the place where I grew up, and also the home of my ancestors. Despite that, I have so many pleasant and unforgettable memories of Menjigso, my real birthplace. I remember the kindness of my aunt, Tsedale Biru, and her wonderful children Abozenetch, Tenagne, and Admasu Bogale, who died of natural causes during the Italian campaign. I remember as if it were yesterday the first time I went there, at the age of three or four, for the wedding of Abozenetch, the elder daughter of Tsedale and Bogale. I was with my grandmother and it was the first wedding I had ever seen. It was then that something happened which was to affect me for the first years of my childhood. My father picked me up and put me on the saddle of his mule, trying to take me away. I yelled for help and the wedding guests persuaded him to leave me alone. However, the incident left a feeling of shyness toward my father which took me some time to overcome. My grandmother and I must have stayed there for two or three weeks after the wedding before we returned to Qinbebit in September or October.

After nursing me for five months at the home of her sister, my mother left me in the care of her mother and returned to Wolayta. I went to Qinbebit with my grandmother and a nursemaid whose name was Shankilit, but whom I called Abaye, an Amharic term of endearment. So I was brought up by my grandmother until I was five years old and during this time my parents in Wolayta were blessed with three more children; my sisters Aleme-Worq and Ayelech, and brother Melaku. My mother had five children after me at yearly intervals and then there was a gap of six years, coinciding with the Italian war, between the eighth and ninth.

My father, who went away soon after the christening of Simon, the eighth born, joined the resistance movement and did not see his family for nearly five years. Altogether my mother and father had 12 children, including the first two and the last who did not live. I am the third born of six boys and three girls who are living. They adopted Habte-Michael Bekele making a round figure of ten of the Bekeles. Habte-Mikael joined Bekele's household at the age of 12. He was from a humble Wolayta family but had the character of a saint. A man of principle and a true Christian, he was a very devoted and loyal servant to my father throughout the difficult days of the Italian occupation. So Bekele declared him his eldest son and we all gladly accepted him as our eldest brother. At the end of the Italian occupation, at the age of 20, he joined Menilek School and managed to reach the third grade. He was then employed by the Ministry of Education as a physical training instructor and later on as a classroom teacher for the first and second grades. He built his residence on the same plot with the rest of Bekele's family living in Addis Ababa. He is married to Tsedale, a girl from Menz, and they have three lovely children, two young men called Mulugeta and Wondwossen and a young woman, Yirgedu.

Life with Grandmother

The daily life in Sekoru/Qinbebit and the loving care of my grandmother, Woizero Yimegnushal Ayele, has left a vivid impression on me of the pleasant and humane aspects of communal life in rural society. From the moment of my birth until I was five, my grandmother was responsible for my upbringing and I had no knowledge of the existence of my father and mother until I reached that age. I was breastfed for five months only and then my mother left me in the care of her mother and went back to the home in Wolayta where, after nine months, she gave birth to my sister, Aleme-Worq. I was told that she came back to Shewa, accompanying my father who had come back for duty, when she was expecting my brother Melaku, but I was too young at the time to remember seeing her then. So my first encounter with my mother was when I was brought to Wolayta by my father after forceful separation from the care of my grandmother.

My grandmother had come back to Shewa from Wolayta to live at Sekoru\Qinbebit with her relatives on her share of the family property. So I was brought up among the children of uncles and aunts of peasant households, cereal-growing agriculturalists with small-scale animal husbandry to supplement their diet and provide traction power for cultivation, unlike my brothers and sisters who were brought up in the more vibrant frontier society of Wolayta. Therefore I have a strong attachment to Qinbebit and the people among whom I grew up until I was five. During the Italian invasion of 1936, I was the first to leave Wolayta and go back to Sekoru\Qinbebit to live with my grandmother and later joined the resistance movement against the Italians.

Sekoru is a hamlet within the district of Qinbebit in the region of Bulga, consisting of a number of widely scattered clusters of homesteads established on individual family landholdings. Each cluster of homesteads is made up, on average, of five households. One of these clusters of homesteads in Sekoru belonged to the family of my grandmother and when she returned from Wolayta she moved into the house of her parents, both of them having died. The house was kept to be used as temporary accommodation for the family members who came to establish themselves on their share of the family property. She found that five households of the family members had already been established there, among whom were her elder sisters, Feleqech, Atkelesh, Achaye, and the younger brother and only male, Woldeyes, who were all pleased to welcome her and assisted in settling. Her own household members, including myself and my nursemaid, consisted of four adult females and five little boys. The two female members, Desta and Sewmamene, were maid servants she brought with her from Wolayta, and the four boys, Tettafe, Tameru, Settotawoo, and Zimamu, were their children born in Shewa out of wedlock.

This composition for a farming household was not ideal for organizing labor for agricultural production. Normally there would have been a male-headed nuclear family. In this case, with the adolescent and elderly members of the family being the primary production and consumption unit, this female-headed household managed to function long enough for the boys to mature and provide male labor essential for those tasks which are exclusively men's work.

The community helped in tasks such as ploughing, seedbed preparation, threshing, and winnowing. My grandmother would provide ploughing bullocks and seeds, and her brothers and nephews would pitch in to help. Women members of the household shared the collecting of firewood and drawing of water, the spinning of cotton, and preparation of food. Once a week there would be a trip to the market to barter the produce of the highlands which is barley, wheat, peas, beans, and lentils with the lowlanders who produced cotton, berbere (red pepper), oil seeds, citrus fruits, bananas, and sugarcane. The house was warmed by a fire which was kept going all day for cooking and the preparation of the ingredients of Tela (barley beer). In the living area along the wall was a raised seat of mounded earth and stone covered with sheepskin, called medeb and a Dink-Alga. The Dink-Alga is like a divan large enough to accommodate two or three people, but is the preserve of the master of the house or an honored guest.

Members of the family sat by the fireside on a circular, raised earth and stone mound. Once a week, the earth floor and raised seats would be dressed to keep them well-compacted with a compound of cow dung and clay covered with fresh grass. Work continued from sunrise to sunset, with the grown men cultivating and the boys tending the livestock. During the cultivating season, they would carry with them a midday meal, but during harvesting they would prepare their own roasted wheat, peas, and beans fresh from the field.

1. Family Background

As the men went off to the fields, the women started their daily chores right after the preparation of breakfast. They would break off in midmorning for coffee which would be an opportunity for socializing and cooperative activities. It was customary for the whole neighborhood to cooperate in any activity which called for group effort, whether it was usually men's or women's work. Sunday was the day for religious worship and every member of the household was free to go to church. After the service, there might be a christening ceremony or a memorial service to attend and then the community would gather for the weekly get-together, the Senbete, which was a social function in the church precincts.

The main purpose was for the whole community to get together to help those in need. At the end of the Senbete, the elders would sit together to reconcile any differences between members of the community and to bring about and maintain a peaceful, harmonious life in the community.

When some of the relatives who lived in the lowlands (Gedera) came to visit us they would bring loads of presents, mainly agricultural produce. There would be bananas, sugarcane, oranges, trengoes (citrus fruits), fresh corn, millet, and walking sticks. The few days they would spend with us as guests of our household would be days of rejoicing and listening to tales of life in the lowland community. They would tell us of the different climate, the geography, the wildlife, and the various crops and fruit trees grown there. It sounded like such a totally different world that it brought about a longing to see it.

Lowland Bulga is indeed a different world and its visual effect is striking. The rugged mountains of Central Ethiopia spread away to the horizon, their colors varying with the distance, from bright green to blue-green then a hazy blue. They are slashed apart by a gorge with sheer walls which plunge down from the summits. From any point on the escarpment which separates the lowland from the highland, the view is breathtaking. I first experienced it at the age of ten when I walked with Tettafe from Sekoru to Mugere-Afaf on the edge of the escarpment and was suddenly confronted with the panorama. We slowly descended and I lived there for the next few years of my life. In the rural community of Sekoru in the care of my grandmother, life was natural, peaceful, constructive, productive, and exciting all at the same time.

It is a generally accepted notion that grandparents tend to spoil their grandchildren. If spoiling means to pay great attention, to care and to love, remain serene and explain errors when a child misbehaves, then my grandmother spoiled me. I cannot recall any occasion when she so much as lost her temper and shouted at me, let alone beat me. So my parents, especially my father, were worried that I would be hopelessly spoiled and after I reached the age of four my father was determined to end my attachment to my grandmother and bring me to Wolayta to join the rest of the family, who were complete strangers to me.

21

You will recall that he had once before tried to take me away from Men-jigso when he had gone to attend the wedding of my cousin Abozenetch, but I had been saved the anguish by the guests. After a great deal of persuasion he had left me alone and gone away. But he returned a year later, this time to Qinbebit, resolved that I should go with him. When the time came for me to leave with my father, my grandmother and the rest of the household were all in tears, begging my father to have pity on me and allow me to remain, but to no avail.

He bade them farewell and ordered his retainer to lead the mule along the path while he held me pinned to the saddle. It was one of the saddest days of my life and even when I remember it today I feel the pain. I cannot remember when I stopped crying that day but the heartache did not stop until I returned to Qinbebit four years later.

2

Italian Invasion (1936-1941)

The Traditional Army

When the Italian army invaded my country in 1936, I was nine years old, having just completed the first course of the church school. Unless one intended to go into the service of the church, there was no need to continue completing the reading of the whole of the psalms. In those last months of my church school, I had noticed that the women were very busy in the house. It was not quite clear to us children why they were busy, day in and day out, making Enjera (bread), drying it in the sun, and pounding it in a wooden mortar to produce a coarse powder called Dirqosh. Some women were also soaking barley in water then pounding it lightly to loosen the husk. After it was dried in the sun and baked, they would lightly pound it again to get the husk off. The barley was then winnowed and ground into a fine powder called Beso. Another group of women sat in the kitchen with a pile of meat in front of them with sharp knives in their hands, slicing the meat into strings to be dried into Quantta. These and all the other items being prepared were packed into goatskin bags.

The tradition was that every able-bodied man should be ready to arm and provision himself to follow his chosen leader to defend his country. Traditionally there was no standing army. This meant that when war was declared, the army which sprang up was a people's army in the true sense. Each man bore arms only to defend what was rightfully his and once the war was over he would return to his peacetime occupation. A standing army is an altogether different proposition. It is a mercenary army, committed only to fighting and can very easily turn against the people it is supposed to defend. Recent Ethiopian history proves the comparative worth of a regular army against a volunteer army. The regular Ethiopian army which consisted of 2,000,000 soldiers, has been unable to defeat a couple of thousand Eritrean volunteers. When the Tigrean People's Liberation Front recently killed two Ethiopian regular generals, nine Ethiopian brigades surrendered. Mengistu has responded to the situation by executing generals whose armies surrender, but the policy has failed. An example of the traditional spirit is the declaration of war against the invading forces of Italy in 1896 by Emperor Menilek:

"YEHAGERE SEW SIMAGNI! NETSANETEN YEMIGGEF HAYMAN-OTEN YEMIAREKES RESTEN YEMINNEQEL AHEZAB TELAT METE-TOBENALENA TENESA TEKETELEGN SENEQEHEN BEAHEYAH AMELKEN BEGUYAH YEZEH."

The literal translation is: "Men of my country come and follow me, with your provisions on the back of your donkeys and dressed in camouflage, follow me to fight the heathen enemy who is coming to violate our freedom, to disgrace our religion and to deprive us the right of our "Rist" (inalienable right of landholding)!" It was a system that promoted individual freedom and a great sense of responsibility toward guarding the common heritage of religion and political freedom. It was a system that allowed born leaders to emerge and lead the people united to achieve greatness, to defend freedom, to promote culture and, to some extent, economic development.

While hereditary succession in leadership often results in a great leader being followed by a weak man, the traditional Ethiopian way was that the most popular and able leader would seize power. Since a soldier provided his own gun, his own equipment and his own food in the traditional army, he was free to choose his own leader and to change his allegiance at any time.

Thus, the concept of desertion did not exist. There was no oath of loyalty since it would have had no meaning within the traditional system. Only if there were a plot against a ruler would plotters swear an oath of loyalty to each other in their cause. It was Haile Selassie who introduced an oath of loyalty to the emperor by incorporating it into the role of his officials when he became emperor. However such an oath had little meaning in the event of his unprecedented and disgraced downfall, it did him little good. If a leader was defeated in a fight against a rival in an Ethiopian power struggle, his followers would submit themselves to the winning leader. Often such an event would be unnecessary because a leader, seeing himself heavily outnumbered, would submit to his superior without a fight. During the reign of Emperor Yohannes, Menilek was King of Shewa and Tekle Haymanot was King of Gojam. The two kings quarreled and although Menilek wanted to negotiate, Tekle Haymanot insisted on a fight, which he lost. Menilek took Tekle Haymanot prisoner and this disturbed the emperor, who reasoned that if Menilek had defeated Tekle Haymanot so easily he would surely be able to defeat Yohannes also. Yohannes began to arm, but at this juncture Menilek went to the emperor, submitted himself to him, and asked that the emperor reinstate Tekle-Haymanot as King of Gojam. It needs to be kept in mind that such chivalrous arrangements and switching of sides applied only in the case of disputes between Ethiopians. Foreign invaders were always fought to the death.

Only if the hereditary successor were able to rally support would he be able to follow his father. If he was not popular, he would not be able to do so. Unfortunately, the system held within it factors which militated against sustained economic development. It was inevitable that another born leader would come to power by force whenever the incumbent had become weak and vulnerable. This constant warring meant the interruption of development. Had this succession to power been peaceful, with one born leader following another, all would have been well. But there was no continuity and in the long intervals between the emergence of a great leader everything stagnated. After Amde Tsion (1314-44), the following great leaders were Zera Yaqob (1434-68) Galawdews (1540-59), Fasiledes (1632-67, the builder of Gondar), Iyasu the great (1682-1706), and then Menilek II (1804-1913). All too often the hereditary successor to a great leader turns out to be lacking in the necessary qualities of his predecessor—self-confidence, altruism, magnanimity, compassion, and courage. A leader who is lacking in these qualities immediately loses the respect of those born leaders at the lower level who refuse to accept such a mediocre leader. Stability is thus disturbed and the development process discontinued. The belief in the qualities of a leader is very strong in Ethiopian society. Even when natural disaster occurs, it is held to be the fault and bad luck of a leader. It is said a leader who is not born to lead brings with him bad luck and destruction while a born leader carries with him God's blessing and sows the seeds of happiness, unity, prosperity, and social justice. When Mengistu seized power, he was extremely popular at first because he had overthrown an emperor who was hated. Everybody expected that he would develop as a great leader because he promised peaceful change. During the 1974 revolution the motto of the Derg was: "Yaleminm Dem Ethiopia Tqedem," which means "Let Ethiopia advance without any bloodshed." Mengistu gained popularity with every section of the population as a great born leader. It was not until the massacre of 23 November that the reaction of the public became: "Aye Yebaria Negger!" which means "Just what you would expect of a slave." It was only the massacre which led people to refer to Mengistu as the descendent of a slave. In Ethiopian culture, slavery is not associated with color or features, but with character.

Here is another example of how the Ethiopian people associate the qualities of a leader with the fortunes of the nation. When Emperor Haile Selassie came to power there was a shortage of food due to drought. The popular song in the country was: "Beteferi Ttefa Frfari! Be Eyasu Dabo New Trasu!" which means "During the time of Eyasu bread was so abundant that one could even use it as a pillow but under Teferi (Haile Selassie's name before he became emperor) there is not even a crumb." The success or failure and dignity or disgrace of any nation depends on the leader. If the leader is endowed with all the qualities which make up a great leader, he can achieve whatever he wants because his aims, desires, and determination are not self-centered, but national. Therefore he carries with him, in a single mind, the whole power of his nation.

But a leader who is self-centered will find himself alone. None of the born leaders will associate with him. Therefore, he gathers round him opportunists, who are just as devoid of self-confidence. Whatever is achieved under such leadership is a baseless superstructure to satisfy the egotistic nature of the leader and will crumble disgracefully with the passing of that leader. That is what happened to Ethiopia after 32 years of supposed modernization by Emperor Haile Selassie. This only served to produce a generation confused in cultural values and lacking in self-confidence. The result of which was the surrender of Ethiopia's political independence and subordination of its glorious history, tradition, and culture to alien values.

I hear people say Emperor Haile Selassie was a great leader, that he introduced modern education and abolished slavery. But did the end result jutify the means? Did it promote greater happiness and unity among his people? Did it produce leaders ready to sacrifice their lives, like their forefathers did, in defense of their heritage? The answer, obviously, is no!

The emperor realized when he returned from exile that by running away from the country he had lost the support of the older generation and leaders. This was the real reason he advanced the younger generation to fill the positions of power around him. All of his modernization was merely his way of expressing contempt for the values of the older generation that rejected him for his opportunism and weakness. The sons of former leaders were pushed aside with their fathers. That all the officials of His Majesty's government were the sons of unknown men was neither a bad thing in itself nor would it have been in conflict with Ethiopian tradition had they just been chosen for their integrity and ability.

A meritocracy without regard for a man's antecedents was very much part of the old tradition and would have been accepted by the Ethiopian people. However, His Majesty deliberately surrounded himself with weaklings and opportunists who had no other source of influence and wealth, and were therefore slaves to his will. Modernization could have been possible by building on the traditional values without undermining the individual's freedom and sense of responsibility and dignity. For example, when introducing modern education, the existing institutions could have been expanded and all the subject matter could have been translated into the national vernacular. The educational curriculum could have been worked out in every subject including military training, thus strengthening instead of undermining the traditional values.

Some old practices were cast aside without a thought. Traditionally, wearing shoes was considered a shameful habit which debilitated physical fitness. Only people who suffered from leprosy wore shoes in order to hide physical defects. For a healthy person to wear shoes was unthinkable, especially men who were required to stand all sorts of physical hardship to be worthy of being called a man. Children were exposed to hardship to develop physical fitness: walking barefoot, being exposed to cold, sleeping on the bare floor, and eating and drinking sparingly. Our forefathers were successful in defending their independence because they looked down on their adversaries whose cultural values were decadent. With the abolition of this spartan spirit, the nation became weaker.

Let us examine the battle of Adwa where all these values were demonstrated. I have not come across any other example in history where a unit of the enemy, after surrendering, was allowed to rejoin its main army because the tactics involved in the capture of the unit were considered unworthy of a great leader. Yet that was just what Menilek did with the Italian troops who were besieged in Meqelle in the fort of Enda Eyesus for 15 days. When their leader, Major Galliano, had to surrender on 20 January 1896, Menilek received him honorably. Galliano was given mules for transporting his wounded men and allowed to fall back to Addigrat with arms and baggage. They were escorted by the soldiers of Ras Mekonnen and were permitted to take their rifles, cannons and loaded machine guns so they would not be attacked by other soldiers. Such was the strength of the traditional value of self-confidence and magnanimity of a leader.

The underlying principle of the traditional army was self-defense. In peace time, everyone was a civilian and pursued a peaceful and constructive occupation to earn a living. But a standing army, where soldiering is taken as a profession and the destructive element in human nature is developed by training, can foster and promote only aggression and destruction. The Ethiopian experience is good proof of this. While the traditional army proved its effectiveness in self-defense by maintaining its independence by repelling all aggressors, the modern standing army has been successful only in achieving complete destruction and spreading conflicts throughout the country.

When war was declared in 1935 my father, a member of the traditional army, left Wolayta for Addis Ababa to join his unit of 'Yenjera Assalafiwoch Denb.' With provisions having been prepared as described earlier, he had only to pack and load his mules and fill his bandolier with ammunition for his rifle. As his father in 1896 went to Adwa with Menilek's army, the son went to Maicho with Haile Selassie's army to fight the same enemy. While his father returned victorious, he was shamefully beaten. My father left Wolayta with six

27

followers, four baggage mules, and two riding mules. One of his followers, Asha, was killed with one of the riding mules by a bomb; the four baggage mules met the same fate. My father, with the remaining five followers and one riding mule, managed to survive the massacre of Maichew and returned to Bulga (his birthplace), not Wolayta where he had left his family because the enemy had already overtaken and occupied the country. When his followers realized he was not going back, all but one deserted him and returned to Wolayta. He remained in Bulga and joined the resistance movement, with his family in Wolayta 325 kilometers away. Fortunately for my mother, who was worried to death about the fate of her husband, the deserters brought news. She had her father-in-law close by to give her some comfort.

The community which was established in 1898 came close to collapse in 1936. The men of the community of Bollosso, following the tradition, all went to the front and did not return. Most of them were killed and those few who survived went to their birthplace to organize or join a resistance movement instead of returning to their families at Bollosso. Their wives and children were abandoned and remained at Bollosso. The very few who had maintained ties with their northern relatives managed to be repatriated.

Our family, if it had not been for our strong-willed aunt Weizero Askale Biru, would have had difficulties because my mother would never have managed to go to Shewa on her own. She did not have the courage and the determination. After all, she was among loyal childhood friends, including the household, and had her father-in-law close by. The only worry she had was what steps the Italians might take against the family of a man who was an enemy when they came to know about it. On the other hand, her sister Askale, who was married to the ruler of Kulo (a district in Kefa province bordering Wolayta in the West) Kenyazmatch Mekuria, was a woman with strong will power, determination, and courage. She was the de facto ruler of the district; her husband was docile and only a nominal ruler. When the Italians occupied Kulo, the first thing they did was collect all former officials of the district including Mekuria. They took them to the edge of a cliff (to save them from digging graves) where they machine-gunned the whole lot. This courageous woman Askale, under cover of night, took a couple of men from the household with her to the spot where the bodies had been thrown and miraculously she found her husband among the bodies, quite alive with only the loss of one of his middle fingers. She rescued him without the Italians suspecting and took him to the house of the local chief and asked him to arrange for her husband to leave Kulo the same night to cross the Omo river which separates Kulo from Wolayta to reach her younger sister (my mother). When Mekuria arrived at my mother's, she dispatched a messenger to her younger brother Mulugeta in Sodo (who was also preparing to leave) urging him to come to her without losing a day. When Mulugeta arrived, he found his brother-in-law had miraculously survived the Italian machine-gun bullets and took him back with him to Sodo where he arranged for him to travel with caravan traders to Shewa disguised as one of them. His resourceful wife Askale, who remained in Kulo until she heard of the safe arrival of her husband among his relatives in Shewa, planned and organized the departure of her family including that of her younger sister from Wolayta. She went to the office of the Italian governor in Kulo, first accusing the Italian government of killing her husband thus depriving the family of God-given support and then demanding a written pass for her, her family (five children), and her younger sister's family (six children) in Wolayta so they could go to Shewa. She secured this pass and left Kulo for Wolayta to collect her sister and the family and they traveled together to Shewa. Askale joined her husband who was living in Ada (35 kilometers from Addis) on his land under Italian occupation. She died two years later but he lived until 1945 after he had seen the enemy being driven out.

My mother and the family, after they arrived in Shewa, lived in Menjigso with her other elder sister Tsedale Biru for nearly six months before she could dare to join my father in 1939 in Bulga. After nearly four years of separation, she was to be taken prisoner only one year after being reunited.

After the Italian force occupied the capital Addis Ababa, the bombers turned their attention to the capital of Wolayta because the governor of Wolayta, Dejazmatch Mekonnen Wossene, who had a big force of traditional army, first thought of resisting the invaders. But his wife Weizero Tideneqialesh, who was in Addis Ababa at that time, intervened saying: "The emperor has left the country and gone into exile, who are you to fight a powerful enemy and compromise your family?" So he submitted to the Italians without fighting. But some of his followers such as Grazmatch Tekle and his own sons, Tedla and Gebre Kristos, refused to submit and joined the resistance movement.

My uncle, Mulugeta Biru, was the younger brother of my mother and one of the followers of Dejazmatch Mekonnen who left and came to Bollosso to stay with his sister when the Italian army moved into the capital, Sodo, and ordered all Dejazmatch's followers to surrender their arms. He exhausted all of the ammunition in target shooting and then returned to Sodo to surrender his rifle. I left my mother and went back to Sodo with him. I was so excited by the idea of going back to my home in Qinbebit and reuniting with my grandmother that I was counting the days of our departure from Sodo. My uncle was busy preparing for the journey which takes a week to ten days. He had his wife, Emama Turunesh, the maid Metchal, and myself to think about. He sold one of the two riding mules he had in order to buy one baggage mule on which to load the tent for camping at night, the provisions for ten days to feed four people and some clothing. The two retainers of my uncle who had tended the riding mules and assisted him had left him after he surrendered his rifle, so he was now alone and I was the only one to help him in tending to the mules and harnessing and loading. So one day, very early in the morning we left Sodo. His wife mounted the riding mule while the tent, the provisions, some clothing in a bag, and some cooking utensils were properly packed and loaded on the baggage mule. We completed our journey to Shewa in ten days, but I arrived with a raging fever. Fortunately, I was back at the home of my aunt Weizero Tsedale where I had been born and soon recovered. I went with my aunt when she traveled to Ada to visit her Teff farm there.

While I was thus away with my aunt, my father came to Menjigso to see me under cover of night because Menjigso was under Italian occupation. He left the same night without finding me. So I stayed for nearly six months with my aunt before my uncle Mulugeta came and took me to Qinbebit to my grandmother. We walked from Menjigso to Qinbebit. Since Qinbebit was a stronghold of the resistance movement, we could not very well go there in daylight; therefore, from Menjigso we went to Segele, an Italian fortress, which we reached about 5 p.m. We went to the house of a relative for dinner and left Segele about 7 p.m. for Qinbebit, which was about 25 kilometers away. We reached Jarso-Amba (my grandfather Fitawrari Biru's house, which had been burnt down by the Italians) about midnight. The dogs of the village started to bark announcing the approach of strangers; otherwise, the village was dead silent.

When we approached a tukul [thatch-roofed and mud-plastered hut] isolated from other tukuls, my uncle called out "Betochi" and then knocked at the door. Tefera (my uncle's tenant, related by marriage to his niece) opened the door and welcomed us, somewhat excited. His wife Bizunesh got up, lit the kerosene lamp and greeted us. She was especially excited to see me. We knew each other when I was living with my grandmother and she with her grandparents, Feleqetch and Wolde-Yohannes. She wanted to make a fire and prepare something to eat for us, but since we were both dead-tired the only thing we wanted was a place where we could lie down. That was improvised and we went to lie down. I developed a very high temperature, could not sleep, and passed a miserable night. Very early in the morning when my uncle got up and asked me to get up and ready to go to my grandmother's house, I told him I was very sick. When he touched my forehead, he said my body felt like fire. He asked Bizunesh to run to the nearby spring and fetch a jug of water. He poured it over my head and body which gave me a little relief. I was not capable of walking to my grandmother's house, which was half an hour's walking distance, so I was provided with a riding mule. Riding from Jarso-Amba to my grandmother's house with Tefera walking ahead and my uncle following us, my thoughts went back to my childhood.

2. Italian Invasion (1936-1941)

When we reached the my grandmother's house, I was overwhelmed by excitement, pleasure, and happiness. I saw my grandmother at the door looking toward us. I was trying to jump down, but Tefera came and helped me dismount. I ran to hug her and she cried, holding me tight saying: "Oh my son!" That was the happiest day of my young life, the fulfillment of my four years' longing. Since I still had a very high temperature, I was put in bed and my grandmother became my nurse. All the relatives who had heard the news of my coming home came to visit me and congratulate my grandmother for the reunion. All the men and grown-up boys carried rifles and wore bandoliers of ammunition round their waists. All the Ethiopian resistance fighters equipped themselves with Italian rifles which had been captured during the Italian wars, plus a few Belgian Mausers. There was a shortage of ammunition for the Mausers so the Italian ammunition was taken apart to make rounds for the Mausers. The homemade rounds functioned, but with a lot of misfires and loss of range.

On the fourth day of my arrival in Sekoru at about midday, while I was still sick in bed, there was a rattle of machine-gun fire which went on for nearly 15 minutes and then single shots from various directions not very far from my grandmother's house. Since the area was a stronghold of the resistance movement, the shooting was obviously an Italian raid. The Italians followed a scorched earth policy, burning everything in sight and killing anybody they found. The Italians behaved badly which provoked the Ethiopians to retaliate. The sort of atrocities the Italians committed included cutting off heads and displaying them. They would burn down houses with civilians inside. The British expected that Ethiopians would massacre prisoners when the Italians were defeated, but it did not happen.

As the Italian raid began, everybody rushed out of the house, except my grandmother who was left with me. She dressed me up and gave me support to walk. Qinbebit was a hilly and open farm land, with no woodland or forest for cover. With my grandmother supporting me, we walked down the slope of the hill from her house down to the valley. When we reached the small river Legebar, we met a gentleman leading a horse across it. He picked me up and put me on the horse. We were on the run for about an hour and a half before we reached the escarpment looking down on the magnificent valley of Bulga and the Kesem river flowing across it. The rattle of machine-gun and individual rifle fire could still be heard when we reached the house of a relative, Aleme, a niece of my grandfather, and we were welcomed with kindness and excitement. After a nice warm bath, I felt quite restored and enjoyed my dinner of lamb stew with Teff Enjera and drank Tella (homemade beer).

The next morning we got up early and left the house to look for a hiding place down the escarpment. Our hostess remained behind to hide some of their belongings and livestock in a safe place, but my grandmother's main concern was my safety. We walked a few hundred meters from the house and started descending a steep slope. About half a kilometer from the edge of the escarpment we found a small cave among the boulders into which we squeezed ourselves to hide. At about 11, right above our heads, we heard machine-gun fire which went on the whole day, keeping us tense and making us forget the uncomfortable feeling of being squeezed to an unbearable state. At about four when the shooting had stopped, we came out from that tiny hole and were able to stretch our legs. We waited there till six before climbing back up the escarpment.

When we got to the top of the escarpment, it was already dusk. We found the house where we had spent the night had been burned down and was still smoldering. The people near the ruins of the house were busy making a fire to cook their dinner. Many of them were men carrying rifles and a few were with their wives. We found my grandmother's niece Tsigie and her husband Argaw there. The owners of the burnt down house were nowhere to be seen and my grandmother started to worry about them. However, the others speculated that they must have gone far to ensure the safety of their livestock and might have seen from a distance the smoke of burning houses and decided to stay there until everything was quiet and the enemy returned to their camp.

Tsigie barbecued lamb and we shared that for the first meal of the day. We spent the night in the open. The next morning, we started walking back toward home, but from a distance we saw that all that was left of my grandmother's house was the circular stone wall without its thatched roof. Every other homestead was the same sad spectacle. Everything my grandmother had owned from her childhood to that moment was burned down; she had left the house with only the clothes she was wearing. She was very thankful to God for saving my life and did not worry about what she had lost. I thought I was lucky to have been able to sleep for at least four days in my grandmother's house before it was burned down by the Italian soldiers. Fortunately all of my grandmother's household was safely reunited except, my uncle who, we came to learn, had left for Menjigso.

Since Qinbebit was a place long bare of any kind of wood for building material, putting up a temporary shelter was not an easy job, but the weather left us with no choice. Qinbibit, being 3,000 meters above sea level, is always cold and at night during the months of October through January, there is frost although it was harvest time. The wheat, barley, oats, peas, and beans were ready for harvesting and fortunately there was plenty to eat. There was grass and the straw from the barley and wheat for thatching, but until the job was done the cooking went on inside the roofless wall. Otherwise life resumed its daily routine as if nothing had happened; everybody was busy with the daily activities of rural life, men in the field harvesting and women collecting firewood, drawing water, and preparing food. My grandmother was always busy spinning cotton. Now that she had lost every piece of cloth she had, she had to work hard to replace it.

After I had stayed two months with my grandmother, she said I must go down to lowland Bulga (about six or seven hours' walking distance) to see my father and my aunt Woizero Beleyu (wife of the patriot leader Fitawrari Wolde-Tsadiq) and she asked her farmhand Tettafe to accompany me there.

Resistance Movement

I left Sekoru with Tettafe in January 1938 for lowland Bulga. When we reached the edge of the escarpment called Mugere Afaf, after about a two and a half hour walk, I was overwhelmed by the breathtaking view of the valley below us. It looked like a completely different world compared to Qinbebit which had just one color, either green or beige depending on the season. The pine forest of Mugere stretched deep green, then blue green and then hazy blue. Tettafe pointed out Cheffa to me, further down beyond the pine forest in the valley where my uncle and aunt lived, which was our destination. From the edge of the escarpment it looked very close, but descending the almost perpendicular slope of Mugere took us an hour. Once we were in the valley, the track to Cheffa ran across one forest-covered hill after the other so it took us another three hours to reach our destination.

Finally, we saw a big compound at the foot of a small hill, fenced with a lattice work of branches surrounding a big, thatch-roofed chiqa house and a number of small huts. The place looked almost deserted but we met two soldiers who told us my uncle the Fitawrari was out on inspection tour and would be back during the night. The lady of the house, my aunt, was inside the Elfegni (the big house).

The door of the Elfegni was open because it was the only source for daylight and fresh air inside the house. We walked in and saw my aunt sitting and doing Bazeto (cording cotton) on the right-hand side by the wall on a raised and carpeted seat. We both bowed as we saw her and then approached her to exchange kisses on both cheeks. She asked me to sit by her side while Tettafe took a seat close to the door. My aunt had just lost two of her daughters. Turuworq, who was married, died in childbirth. The other one, a twin, died a few months after birth, so my aunt was wearing her Coota upside down as a sign of mourning. Wearing black is not Ethiopian culture. The traditional wear appears to be the development of a wiser consideration which took into account the environmental condition as well as the suitability to the general complexion of the users.

My aunt called out to a maid to bring my two cousins, Amezenetch, about three, and Woodnesh, the surviving twin, about a year old, to greet me and we were served food and drink immediately. In the evening when the Fitawrari came back, the whole compound and the house became very crowded with people and mount animals. Everyone wore long hair and was dressed in khaki trousers and jackets. I was much impressed by the little boys of my age. Some were armed while others were just attendants to grown-ups. The eldest among them carried a fine Mauser. My father was living further down the valley near Kesem river at Tedla-Mariam (his family land) about two hours' walking distance from there. I was not keen to go there so my uncle told me my father would come to see me, which he did a week later. When my father went off again a few days later, I was happy to remain as one of my uncle's household. He began the task of equipping me for war. The first piece of equipment was a bandolier which was made to the size of my waist. It did not take a long time before I became popular with my uncle. My Amharic handwriting was good; therefore, he made me his private clerk. About the middle of 1939, my mother and the family came to Bulga. On their way to Tedla-Mariam where my father lived, they first visited with her sister Belyu and brother-in-law Wolde-Tsadiq. Since malaria was endemic in Tedla-Mariam, it was decided that my mother and the family should not go there. My father went to Mugere and settled there with the family so the two families could also live closer together. After nearly four years the rest of the family reunited, but I remained with my uncle and aunt. Although the two families had their own individual houses at a walking distance of ten minutes, for all practical purposes they lived together at the elder sister's house. Every day the whole family dined there.

Soon after the family reunited, there were peace negotiations between the Italians and the patriot leaders which lasted for nearly seven months before they came to a sudden end and caused great damage to the security of the resistance movement. During the negotiations, the patriots were allowed to move freely to visit relatives living in the Italian fortresses, including Addis Ababa. When the negotiations suddenly broke down, many patriots were caught unaware while they were visiting relatives in Italian-held territory. The Italian army, using these captured men as guides, succeeded in penetrating patriot-held areas and inflicted serious damage. The Italian raids on the patriot-held areas became weekly affairs and were quite effective. My mother and family were taken prisoners. She was nursing my brother Daniel, who was four months old, and staying at what was considered a safe place before the peace negotiations started, but was suddenly exposed to the enemy. Not long after, my aunt and her two daughters were also taken prisoners.

The breakdown of the peace negotiations and the subsequent raids brought about an end to the unity which had held the resistance movement together from the beginning. The man who played a leading role in organizing the resistance movement was my uncle Fitawrari Wolde-Tsadiq Zewde. He was

2. Italian Invasion (1936-1941)

the one who identified Melake Tsehay Eyasu, the great-grandson of Menilek in a monastery called Abeye Gedam in Gedera, under the care of a monk called Aba Yirdaw. It was my uncle who then got in touch with the various resistance leaders who were scattered in the area and organized the proclamation that announced Melake Tsehay Eyasu as the Emperor of Ethiopia. The proclamation took place in a big marketplace called Embur Gebeya, close to the Italian fortress of Gina Ager, following the traditional beating of drums. This news spread like wild fire and resistance leaders from every corner of the country flocked into Bulga. A government was organized and established and all the leaders who gathered there were given traditional titles and appointed governors of the area from where they came. The patriot leader Ras Abebe Aregai of Shewa came to the gathering with 30 followers which was more than anyone else. His title was Balamberas, the lowest rank in the hierarchy. He was given the highest rank, Ras, and made minister of war and regent to the young emperor.

My uncle Wolde-Tsadiq, who played a key role in bringing this about, had only two followers, Gebre-Mesqel and Idiris (carrier of the rifle). Since he had no title, he was referred to as Aleqa, a name he earned when he was serving in the church as a clergy,before he joined government service as follower of former Emperor Haile Selassie's Aide-de-Camp Shaqa Belehu. Now he was given the title Fitawrari and made governor of the area comprising Tedla-Mariam Metti, Mugere Zala, Fura, Akermit, Mekenisa, and Jalo-Ager. All the patriot leaders in these areas came under him with the title Kenyazmatch and many other leaders in that part of the country.

During these peace negotiations which lasted for seven months, I do not know what soured the good relationship between Wolde- Tsadiq and Kegnazmatch Worqneh and all of the leaders, including my father. Many of the other leaders like Grazmatch Tinqeshu, the brothers Grazmatch Dagne and Feqe, and Grazmatch Yifru all sided with Kegnazmatch Worqneh. That left my uncle Fitawrari Wolde- Tsadiq with only a few followers. My father moved down to Tedla-Mariam to be together with his colleagues. This put my relations with my uncle in a precarious situation. I had no doubt in my mind as to my loyalty to my uncle, but this feeling was not shared.

One day a quarrel ensued between me and one of my uncle's retainers named Gebre-Mariam, a huge fellow who could have crushed me with one hand. Usually a placid individual, for no reason whatsoever he got mad at me and threatened to beat me. So I went to complain to my uncle. My aunt, who was present, started crying saying she did not want something bad to happen to me in her house and I must leave and go to my father. So I handed over my rifle and the bandoliers and left the service of my uncle to live with my father in Tedla-Mariam. With my mother and the rest of the family taken prisoner, my father's household had been reduced to three: himself, Habte-Mikael, and a cook.

I soon found an old French model of rifle called Nasmasser, armed myself and became actively involved in raids on Italian camps and fortresses by joining ad hoc groups. My favorite leader for these purposes was Grazmatch Tinqeshu, a quiet, solid, and fearless burly man of medium height. He only had his younger brother Hailu as a follower, but the two of them could engage a whole brigade of the Italian army for the day and keep it pinned down in one place until the Italians exhausted their ammunition. After the peace negotiations broke down, life became hard, food became scarce, and we were forced to raid Italian fortresses for food. There were a lot of casualties.

In one such raid on the fortress of Sidisto, which took place in the morning when the cattle were let out for pasture, we drove away all the cattle in spite of the machine-gun fire from the fortress. Three of the cattle guards were shot dead. From our side no one was killed, but three were wounded, including the leader of the campaign Kenyazmatch Worqneh. The bullet cut his throat and my father stitched it together; he recovered all right but his voice was changed into a falsetto. Another one of these raids, which ended in disaster, was the one on Ginager and took place at dawn. Everything was carried out to plan and we were returning with our loot of cattle and grain sacks carried by peasants. When we reached the edge of the escarpment we were ambushed by enemy soldiers who were coming from the fortress of Sidisto to Ginager. We lost seven of our men and all the loot except one sack of barley flour which Habte-Mikael Bekele managed to get through under a shower of bullets. This sack of flour was to save us from starvation.

In that last critical year of the resistance movement the grain which was stored away in the underground grain silos helped to sustain the life of many people. In the backyard of every burnt-down house abandoned by the inhabitants, we spent days sounding with an iron rod to hear the click of the cover stone. We dug the top soil off and when we lifted the cover stone we would find millet as good as if it were fresh. We would leave it open for the whole day to let in fresh air, which removed the unpleasant gas, and then take the millet out and distribute it to everyone equally. It was washed, dried, and ground into flour to make Enjera. Wild tomatoes and all sorts of vegetables were abundant in the backyard of these houses to supplement our diet.

On one occasion my father, who was on a watch duty, asked me to take his place and keep watch with the field glasses while he rested for a while. We were living in a makeshift hut at the foot of a hill from the top of which we sat under the shade of a tree and kept watch. The hill was covered with bushes which bore edible sweet berries. After looking through the field glasses in every direction for any sign of enemy movement, I went to pick the berries. In

2. Italian Invasion (1936-1941)

less than ten minutes of my absence from watch, there came a sudden burst of rifle shots and a continuous exchange of fire. The enemy forces had managed to approach the vantage position for guarding our camp undercover and the exchange of fire was with the guard. My father got mad at me saying that I had failed in my duty; had I been concentrating on my watch with the field glasses, I could have detected the enemy before they approached the vantage point. He was so much enraged he tried to beat me with a heavy stick, which I managed to avoid by running away. From that day on, there was no peace between my father and me so I decided to leave. I could not join any of his groups so the only choice I had was to go back to my uncle.

My aunt and her two daughters having been taken prisoner, leaving my uncle without his family, I thought he would be happy to have me back, especially since I had my own rifle and two hand grenades. So I left my father after we been together for nearly seven months and went back to my uncle Fitawrari Wolde-Tsadiq. I found his camp almost deserted because he was left with only a dozen of his 30 or 40 closest followers. His favorite bodyguard commander, Miskay, had been killed in action and he had no successor to him. The few men he had were stationed at strategic points to keep watch on the enemy to avoid surprises. I found his reception to me was very cool and on the day after my arrival he called Balamberas Haile Darge, the commander of one of the strategic advance guard positions, and I was assigned to him. Balamberas Haile Darge was a tall, well-built, daring man of about 30 who had only two men under his command, Wolde-Tensay and Berhanu. He also had his wife with him and they lived in a cave located below the summit of the ridge where we kept watch from a vantage point which dominated the view in every direction. We could see through our field glasses every movement in the Italian fortresses surrounding us: Segele and Gina-Agger in the north, Gorfo in the south, Shola Gebeya and Sheno in the west, and all along the escarpment of Bulga except Segele and Gina-Agger which were on the plateau.

We had no problem getting our supplies of grain. The farmers who lived in the fortress farmed close to the fortress and during the threshing period they could not transport all that had been threshed. So we observed through field glasses where they put it and at night we carried it to our cave. Harvest time supplied us with enough grain. For meat we could hunt klipspringer which were in plenty. Haile's wife, down in the safety of the cave, prepared our one daily meal which we ate in the evening. During the day we carried Qolo (baked barley or wheat) in our pocket which we chewed when we felt hunger pangs. It was tedious. Life with my father's group had been more exciting; we had always been on the move conducting raiding and hunting expeditions in the Danakils desert. There had been no dull moment. Fortunately, before long the situation changed overnight. One morning in late March or early April

1941 we looked through our field glasses and all the Italian fortresses seemed abandoned. During the day the news came that all the fortresses had been deserted during the night and we relayed the good news to my uncle. He sent people to gather intelligence about the situation and they came back with the news that the emperor had returned with the British army and the advance force had already occupied Addis Ababa.

The emperor's representatives had met Ras Abebe, the leader of the resistance movement, at Cheffe Donsa (one of the Italian fortress 70 kilometers east of Addis Ababa). After having confirmed that the enemy had been driven out of the country by a superior force and that our leader, Ras Abebe, had met the emperor's representatives together with the British army commander, we left our own fortress of Bulga to join Ras Abebe who already moved north of Addis Ababa to Debre-Berhan.

Our itinerary was to move to Segele, the fortress furthest from us but nearest to Debre-Berhan. To get to Segele we had to pass through Qinbebit, where the whole country was turned to a barren wild heath and grassland with no sign of life except rats, and no footprints or tracks to follow. I could not even identify where my grandmother's house had once stood. At Segele we were met by the local community leader who gave us accommodation and food for two nights. We moved to Chacha about 20 kilometers from there on the main road to Debre-Berhan and stopped for two nights. On the fifth day of our departure from our five-year redoubt, we entered Debre-Berhan, the capital town of Bulga and Tegulet. We met Ras Abebe and my uncle, Fitawrari Wolde-Tsadiq, was allocated a big compound on the outskirts of the town. It must have been an Italian army headquarters, with stores of food and everything self-contained. We were told to travel to Fitche from Debre-Berhan to meet the emperor who would come by road from Debre-Marqos (the capital of Gojam) to Addis Ababa. When the British army commander and the emperor's representative met Ras Abebe at Cheffe Donsa, my father and his groups were present there. The British army commander requested that Ras Abebe attach a contingent of the patriots to the British troops, not for action but for observing, following the fleeing Italian army north. My father and his groups, under the command of Fitawrari Tesema Wolde-Georgis, were attached to the British troops and left for Dessie following the path of the fleeing Italian army. We were informed of this when we arrived at Debre-Berhan where all the patriots of Shewa were congregated, ready to follow Ras Abebe to Fiche to meet the Emperor. (Fiche is a small village 70 kilometers from Addis Ababa on the way to Debre-Marqos.)

The end of the Italian invasion came as a pleasant surprise to many of us. Within a few weeks of the news reaching us that Italy and Great Britain were at war, the Italians disappeared overnight and the British army under General

2. Italian Invasion (1936-1941)

Sir Alan Cunningham occupied Addis Ababa on April 1941 without firing a single shot! When this happened, the leader of the resistance movement Ras Abebe Aregai was at Dofa-Mikael (Bulga), very close to Addis Ababa. When the news of the Italians' disappearance reached Ras Abebe he left Dofa-Mikael with all the patriot leaders following him (except my uncle Fitawrari Wolde-Tsadiq who was at Fura at that time) heading for Addis Ababa. He stopped at Cheffe Donsa and dispatched security men to survey the situation and come back with information. They came back with the good news that the capital was occupied by the British army led by the emperor. The commanding officer of the army occupied the capital and the Emperor's Representative Dejazmatch Endalkatchew Mekonnen Endalkatchew accompanied by Major Mulugeta Bulli, Major Nega Haile Selassie, and Major Abiy Abebe would be coming to Cheffe Donsa to meet the patriots.

So Ras Abebe waited. When General Cunningham arrived at Cheffe Donsa accompanied by Dejazmatch Mekonnen, he met Ras Abebe and inspected the parade of about 4,000 patriots. He could not believe his own eyes that these patriots could fight and live so close to the capital, besieged by so many fortresses. He kept asking the leader of the resistance movement Ras Abebe repeatedly how often encounters had taken place between the patriots and the Italian forces and how all of these patriots were armed and provisioned. When he was informed that all the armaments he could see were taken from the enemy, he expressed his admiration for the courage and determination of the Ethiopian patriots fighting the enemy on the capital's threshold. It was agreed that the patriots would enter the capital accompanied by the emperor. Until that time they were to stay in Debre-Berhan.

In April, we left Debre-Berhan for Fiche to meet the emperor. We traversed the beautiful countryside; it was a great pleasure to see old country houses still standing and livestock covering the green meadows of Tegulet, the home of Afe Negus Aregai, the father of the patriots' leader Ras Abebe Aregai. The father was dead, but the mother Weizero Askale Goben, daughter of Menilek's General Gobena, was still alive. We stopped overnight at Abechu and then arrived at Fiche on the third day.

The woman patriot, Weizero Shewa Regged Gale, came to Fiche with a message from the emperor and distributed five Maria Theresa thalers to each of us. The Maria Theresa thaler is still used in the remote areas of Ethiopia, its attraction being that it is an ounce of fine silver. When the Ethiopian currency was introduced, there was a silver 50-cent coin and the dollar was paper. The 50-cent coin was hoarded because of its silver value and is still sought-after today. The next day we were told to leave Fiche and move toward Addis Ababa to wait for the Emperor at Sululta, which was half an hour's march from Addis Ababa at the foot of Entotto.

39

The Emperor's Clothes

We camped at Sululta for four days and on the fifth day the order came that we should set off toward Addis Ababa. From Sululta we climbed up Entotto from the northeast, climbed down into the capital and lined up along the street leading to Menilek's palace, right by the main gate. We were standing there for nearly two hours before the emperor's party arrived. He was driven by in an open car bowing to greet those of us lining the streets and we bowed until the butts of the rifles on our right shoulders were touching the ground. We remained standing for another two hours before we were told to return to camp at Entotto. From Entotto to Menilek's palace, about four kilometers, the street was lined by only patriots. The population of Addis Ababa was told to remain indoors by the occupying British army authorities, therefore giving the capital the impression of a deserted city. On one side of the street at about every 100 meters, khaki-uniformed Ethiopian police were lined up. Every house along the street had its doors and windows shut.

We only had a glimpse of the emperor being driven in an open car into the Menilek palace where he raised the Ethiopian flag. We could not even see, from where we were, the flag-raising ceremony and it was a great disappointment to many of the patriots that the return of the emperor and their entry into the capital accompanying him was not celebrated with a great traditional feast. A further disappointment was the decision that the Italian prisoners would not be made to reconstruct all the houses and churches they had destroyed. This was something which the patriots had come to expect. Instead, the British took the Italian prisoners to Kenya where they were forced to build a road from Nairobi to Nakuru.

After camping at Entotto for two weeks, I left my uncle Fitawrari Wolde-Sadiq and went to look for my grandmother who lived in Sendafa with her young son Mulugeta (who brought me from Wolayta). She had left Qinbebit after the Italians raided it for the third time and took away all the livestock and burnt down the harvest in the field. Sendafa was a small town 35 kilometers from Addis Ababa on the Dessie road. I also found my mother and the rest of the family there and we were joined by my father when he returned from Dessie.

A few months after the return of the emperor, all the patriot leaders who had been camping around Addis Ababa and their followers went back to where they were before. They were given appointments as rulers of provinces, subprovinces, district, subdistricts, or as judges, depending on the strength of their followers, They were scattered all over the country following the traditional system of administration. But none of them were appointed to the region where they had been during war. Soon a new system of central control was introduced and the leaders were called to Addis Ababa while their followers were recruited into the army and police, and the older ones were given land to farm and settle. The leaders who were called to Addis Ababa were kept there, hanging around the palace (the traditional way referred to as Dej-Ttenat) every day to be seen waiting in attendance on His Majesty, hoping to be remembered for an appointment. For some, like Fitawrari Wolde-Tsadiq because of his role in bringing about the short-lived reign of Melake Tsehay Eyasu, this lasted their lifetime.

When Emperor Haile Selassie ran away from the country, not one of the patriots thought he would ever have the gall to return since it was his obligation to defeat the invaders or die honorably trying. Traditionally, Ethiopia could not remain without an emperor and the concept of an emperor in exile was inconceivable. It was for this reason that the patriots chose Menilek's grandson, Melake Tsehay Eyasu, as a leader to replace Emperor Haile Selassie. The young emperor died six or seven months after he had been proclaimed under mysterious circumstances which suggested he could have been poisoned. Nobody has a clear account of how he died and he was buried in an unmarked grave somewhere in Menz. Since Ras Abebe and Emperor Haile Selassie were close, there was a strong suspicion that the emperor could have had a hand in his death.

After that, His Majesty was distrustful of some of the patriots because of their support of Melake Tsehay and the contempt they had for the runaway emperor. The British ran a propaganda campaign to rally support for Emperor Haile Selassie before he set foot back in Ethiopia. The first question General Cunningham asked Ras Abebe was whether Haile Selassie was wanted back as emperor. It is interesting to speculate what might have happened if the question had been asked of the patriots as a whole, rather than of their leader who had always been a Haile Selassie man. Many patriots languished their lives away in disfavor as the reward for the sacrifice they had made to defend the freedom of their country.

Ras Abebe was appointed governor of Sidamo province, and my father, as one of his followers, went with him and he was appointed as a district judge of Bollosso. He was back to what had been his home before the invasion after nearly six years of absence. He found his father Basha Zewdu had moved to his house and he was welcomed with great excitement and rejoicing by all the inhabitants of the area. He was popular in the community, especially with his Wolayta friends who accepted him because he grew up among them, mixed with them freely and participated in their social activities and developed close social ties.

Ras Abebe was soon called back to Addis Ababa and appointed minister of interior. This completely isolated him from his followers who were left behind in Sidamo province. It was hoped that by handling the followers individually, they could be brought under control into the new centralized system. Each leader who led any appreciable body of men was isolated in this same way from his followers, leaving his followers to turn to the central government for its support. If they found the process hopeless, they could go back to their rural homes and take up farming. In this way, the formidable organization of the resistance movement was disorganized and most of the leaders were demoralized and vanished. The emperor looked more favorably on those who had run away into exile and those who had cooperated with the Italians, rather than on those who put up resistance to the invader. In the presence of the patriots, he could not feel at ease and did his best to humiliate and demoralize them.

Note

1. Haggai Erlich, *Ethiopia And The Challenge Of Independence,* (Boulder, Col.: Lynne Rienner Publishers, 1986)

3

Studies

In 1942, Teferi Mekonnen School was the first government school to be reopened after the return of the emperor to his capital in May 1941. To be enrolled there, I obtained a letter from Ras Abebe testifying that I was in the resistance movement and therefore entitled to free education. With that letter, I left Wolayta for Addis Ababa with my adopted brother Habte Mikael Bekele. We went to see the Minister of Education, Ato Mekonnen Desta, in his office in the Imperial compound. We were with a friend, Haile Breqneh, who knew him, and we were warmly received by the minister who expressed admiration that such a small boy as myself should have fought in the resistance. Although I was now 14, I was small for my age.

The minister said the only school reopened was Teferi Mekonnen and no fees were charged. Therefore, we could go there directly without any note and would be admitted. I was given a test in reading Amharic to decide which grade I should join. Those with no education, the beginners, started in classroom 25. The last classroom was number 1. I was put in classroom 15 and my adopted brother Habte-Mikael was put in classroom 25. Those who were well-qualified in Amharic but beginners in foreign languages started in classroom 15, and upward advancement from class to class was not measured on a time scale, but on the individual's effort and brightness. For example, I copied the alphabet the teacher wrote on the blackboard both in small and capital letters and within three to four days I mastered it as well as the writing of figures. After learning the figures from 1-10 in less than a week, I was moved up not to fourteen, but to eleven where I stayed for about three months. From there I was moved to seven and four months later, I left Teferi Mekonnen School to go to Menilek School where I was admitted to the top class.

In fact, the Menilek School had been renamed Asfawossen School, after the Crown Prince. Everybody regarded the new name as a joke and nobody used it. Menilek was a real reformer and leader and it made little sense to try to erase his name from the school which had always been associated with him. Among his many achievements, Menilek introduced the postal service to Ethiopia. Years later, in the Pallais de Nations in Geneva, I was to see the letter which he wrote to the Postal Union requesting membership for Ethiopia.

At Menilek School I won second prize in my class the first year and received from the emperor a Psalter. The second year, I won the school's first prize and received a table clock from the emperor. The clock I later presented to the school, but the Psalter and the certificates I still have. During the fourth year the top three—Getahun Tafese (now deceased), Sebhat Hable-Selassie (now a director in UNIDO), and myself—from Menilek School were chosen to go to the newly opened Haile Selassie Secondary School at Kotebe.

While we were preparing to go to Kotebe, Director of the Menilek School Douglas Fisher called me to his office and talked me out of going to Haile Selassie Secondary School. Instead he urged me to join the chief architect of the Ministry of Education, Mr. Clewer, with the promise that after working with him for two years the ministry would give me a scholarship to England to study architecture. Mr. Fisher was an Englishman of about 30, a Quaker who had come to Ethiopia in 1943 with a Friends' Ambulance unit. The same was true of the chief architect, Mr. Selby J. Clewer. He told me it was the best proposition he had for me considering my character and that the secondary school headmaster might not be tolerant like himself. If I should be dismissed from that school, since there were no other secondary schools in the country, he said that would be the end of my career. I knew Mr. Fisher had been tolerant with me so I had to give some thought to his advice. When Mr. Fisher had taken over Menilek School and wanted to introduce some changes in the school curriculum, he wanted to collect all of the previous exercise books. He came to the classroom to explain the reasons why he was doing that. I stood up and told him that since he had taken up the direction of the school and the changes he had been introducing were not satisfying our urge to learn, we found his regime more oppressive.

This made Mr. Fisher angry, his face turned red and he left the classroom without saying much. Once I was disgusted with him and wanted to leave the school and join the Military Radio Signal School which was being run by the British Military Mission. I was more attracted by their green uniform than anything else. When I saw these young boys in that uniform, I said to myself: "Why fight with Fisher? Let me join these." So one morning I left the school and walked to the old airport and presented myself to the recruiting officer, an Englishman. He asked me which school I was coming from and I told him

3. Studies

Menilek School. He picked up his phone and talked to the director. Mr. Fisher arrived there within ten minutes and drove me back to the school. He asked me why I had done that and I told him I did not like the way he was running the school. He talked to me for nearly half an hour explaining the reasons why he had to take the measures he did.

One of the changes to which we students objected was that he gave strict order that lights must be switched off at 8 p.m. This prevented us from studying in the evening. There had been no time limit before and we used to study up until midnight. Our second objection was that Mr. Fisher increased the time spent in sports and physical training and reduced the time spent on academic subjects. Those of us who had spent a few years before as soldiers felt we were racing against time to catch up on our education and had little need of games. However, after the signal school incident I came to understand Mr. Fisher better and went on with my studies quietly.

So when he talked to me about joining his friend the chief architect Mr. Clewer, I thought it over and decided to take his advice provided he could get a guarantee that the Ministry of Education would give me the scholarship to go to England. Arrangements were made so that I would be accommodated at Menilek School and the Ministry of Education would pay me 100 shillings per month as pocket money while I worked with the chief architect as an apprentice. I started working with Mr. Clewer. He gave me books to read on architecture, a set square, a T-square, drawing board, a box of compasses, work to trace, and training in brick laying and building skills.

After a week I found all that somewhat boring and felt I was not getting enough education. I told Mr. Clewer I had changed my mind and would rather go to the secondary school. Since he was going there twice a week to give art lessons he said I could go with him and attend classes two days a week and see how that arrangement would suit me.

When Haile Selassie Secondary School was opened, students from the last class of every school in the country with high credit marks were selected to attend. There was an age limit and for those above the age limit a Teachers' Training College was opened in the Menilek School compound. It is necessary to understand the special problem the country was facing regarding education and the student body. Due to the five years of enemy occupation, every student was five years behind. In one class, there were groups ranging from age 10 to 20. The educational curriculum was drawn up so as to cover the lost five years which meant two years' coursework was to be covered in one year. We students in Menilek School opposed Mr. Fisher's change, but of course he had his way.

After the teachers' training school was opened under the direction of a very dynamic directoress Miss Booker, the first students for the two years' course were selected from the last class of Teferi Mekonnen School and Balabat School. There were 24. Mr. Clewer suggested that instead of two days a week at the secondary school it would be more advantageous for me to attend morning classes every day during the week and spend the afternoon hours with him. I agreed. At the end of the two years' course I came out third in the final examination out of the 24 and received my diploma with distinction from the emperor on 18 July 1946.

During my two years, there was quite a number of occasions that I missed lessons, because I had to accompany Mr. Clewer when he traveled to the provinces to design new schools, to repair the old ones, or to convert an existing building into a school. I had to assist him in taking measurements and in theodolite survey. I accompanied him to Lekemt, to Dessie and to Jimma.

On our way from Addis Ababa to Jimma, the front axle of the old Italian car (a convertible Aridita) snapped off when we were descending the escarpment to the Gibe River. There was no sign of any traffic on the road which passed through a dense thicket. The whole area was wild, we were miles away from any kind of human habitation, and neither of us had been that way before. An Italian contractor was with us because we were going to have Miazia Haya Sebat School repaired. I suggested that I continue on foot toward Jimma and look for help while Mr. Clewer and the Italian contractor waited there.

After walking for an hour I came to Gibe Bridge and found some soldiers guarding the bridge. I told them of our misfortune and asked if one of them could go to where the car had broken down and guard two of our foreign guests from any shifta [bandits] until I came back with some help. They informed me it would take two to three hours to reach the small village called Abelti on top of the escarpment. Fortunately I got a lift part of the way and reported to the governor. I had climbed halfway when I saw in front of me a big diesel truck moving very slowly on a heavy gear so I climbed on it. After about an hour we came to the top and Abelti was right there. I jumped down and surprised the driver when I thanked him for the free ride. I found the governor of the area, told him what had happened, and asked him to organize for immediate help. There was a pickup truck which belonged to the Ministry of Public Works so the governor and the driver of the truck and myself set off. We found Mr. Clewer in his underwear sitting on the hood of the broken-down car which he had jacked up and propped with stones to remove the broken axle. So we loaded the two front wheels and the broken axle onto the pickup truck and drove back to Abelti, leaving one guard from the bridge to guard the car. We got up early and went into a junkyard close by and found an Ardita axle.

The advice Mr. Fisher gave and the arrangements he made for me worked out well. I did not miss much in academic education and I benefitted by working with Mr. Clewer not only from the technical aspect of practical experience, but also from learning general administration and seeing various parts of the region. Above all I enjoyed working with Mr. Clewer who was, to me, the ideal human being dedicated to serving others.

One afternoon while I was busy on the drawing board, the American Adviser to the Ministry of Education, Mr. Hambrouck, walked in and asked me if I could help him draw out the organization chart he had drafted. I did what he asked me to do. He invited me to his house for tea and offered me a scholarship to go to the American University in Beirut. I thanked him for his kind consideration and told him I would let him know my decision within the next two days. Immediately I went to Selby Clewer and told him Mr. Hambrouck had offered me a scholarship. Selby's response was "Oh, that is good!" The next day Mr. Littler of the British Council walked into the office and offered me a scholarship to go to England. I accepted and walked upstairs to Mr. Hambrouck's office to inform him of my decision to decline his offer.

Within a month, all the necessary preparations were carried out and the date for my departure was fixed. However, one day before I was due to go, Mr. Littler came to see me with a telegram which said all of the places were full for architecture, and there was only one place for education at Exeter College. I declined the place. Since I had resigned my position with the chief architect's office to go to England and that had failed to materialize, I was employed in the British Council library.

The Clewers were due to go on home leave in 1946 and suggested that I accompany them so that Selby could try to find a place for me in one of the colleges where he had studied. He put the proposal to the Director General of the Ministry of Education Ato Emanuel Abraham who agreed, since I had been promised a scholarship two years earlier. So in early October 1946 I left Addis Ababa together with Selby and Dorrie Clewer and their three-month-old son Sandy and their adopted daughter Hillary.

We took a Swedish airline flight which stopped over in Amsterdam - at the Victoria Hotel, I saw the waiters wearing tail coats, which I always regarded afterward as waiters' uniform. When palace protocol required the wearing of a tail coat, I refused to obey not only because of that but also because I felt it was ridiculous to put on borrowed finery for special occasion. As a result I declined every palace invitation. I always remember what my mother once said about dress. Before the Italian invasion, silk used to be a very expensive and exclusively high-class dress. During the Italian invasion, however, artificial silk flooded the market and it become an ordinary dress. My mother had a silk dress which was given to her as a wedding present. She used to treasure it and only put it on for special occasions. One day she saw a servant wearing a silk dress. She took out hers and said it should now go to whom it belonged and gave it to Desta, her servant.

The Emperor's Clothes

When we arrived, Selby took me around London. One of the things that impressed me was the waxworks at Baker Street, Madame Tussaud's. When I saw my emperor standing among the heads of state dressed in his national costume looking so unique and dignified, I felt happy and proud. But in 1955 when I returned to visit Madame Tussaud's, I found to my great disappointment and humiliation the emperor was wearing a British military uniform standing among heads of state with imposing stature. His tiny figure made him look like an aide-de-camp. I felt ashamed to say he was the leader of my country.

When I arrived in England in October 1946, the number of Ethiopian students would not have exceeded ten. But by 1949, it grew to 130. Excluding the royal family, the first students to England in 1945 were Zewdie Gebre-Selassie, Mikael Imru, Endalkatchew Mekonnen, and Amha Abera.They were studying at Oxford and in the summer of 1948, they organized a meeting of all Ethiopian students in Great Britain. At that meeting, the Ethiopian Students Association in Great Britain was formed. The main purpose of the Association was to bring together the Ethiopian students once or twice a year by organizing social activities, political discussions concerning their country, visits to historical places and manufacturing establishments, and opportunities to share experiences of their life in England. The officers who served as president, vice president, treasurer, secretary, vice secretary, editor, and assistant editor were elected by majority vote to serve for one year. The periodical publication called the Lion Cub came out once a year. It contained newsworthy stories concerning Ethiopian students abroad and also news from home.

The 1950 officers of the Association were Mikael Imru, president; Mary Tadesse, vice president; Mengestu Lema, secretary; Beyene Wolde-Gabriel, assistant secretary; and Gaitachew Bekele, treasurer. The Association's general meeting for that year took place in July at Leicester University. Beyene and I were responsible for the arrangements and it turned out to be one of the most organized and well-attended meetings, since it coincided with the emperor's birthday, July 23. A special thanksgiving service was organized to celebrate the occasion with a birthday cake. The Ethiopian Ambassador H. E. Ato Abebe Retta; the Director General of the Ministry of Education Ato Kebede Mikael, who was on a visit to England; Professor Tamrat, who was also on a visit; and the Ethiopian staff from the embassy; and Prince Sahele Selassie, who was a student in England, all attended the Leicester meeting. It was one of the most successful meetings the Association had held so far.

The last meeting for 1950, at which the election for new officers took place, was held in Torque during the Christmas holidays. One incident between two students, Dereje Haile-Mariam (married to a granddaughter of the Emperor Sofia Desta and killed fighting the rebels of the 1960 coup attempt) and Afeworq Tekle (the artist) was a very interesting episode which revealed the characteristics of the individual students, those who were opportunists and those who were conscious of their national responsibilities of history and culture. The incident took place at a vote to the health of the emperor when everybody got up except Afeworq, who remained seated. Dereje was so enraged by this demonstration of contempt toward His Majesty that he pounced on Afeworq, took him by his throat and said: "How dare you, stupid mutilated bastard, remain seated when the name of our beloved sovereign was mentioned and everyone in the room got up and raised their glass!" He was going to beat him to death if it had not been for those present who managed to intervene and save Afeworq.

Dereje's abuse of Afeworq was a reference to the fact that Afeworq had been a victim of an Italian inspired atrocity during the invasion. Menz and Bulga were the strongholds of the resistance movement and while the men were away fighting the invaders, the Italians brought a primitive tribe from the hinterland and turned them loose on the freedom fighters' women and children. Even small boys were castrated.

Those meetings of the Association were useful in many respects, especially to study and know one another's political views and inclinations. I used to argue against those who criticized the emperor's regime; my argument was that we were students away from home, we did not know how things worked in the real world, and it would not be fair to criticize until we ourselves had tried to become involved in the system at a practical level. For expressing these views I was labeled as an imperialist. To my later disappointment, those who used to preach socialism and criticize the emperor's regime completely forgot their criticism of the regime when they returned home. They adapted to the system to promote their self-interest. Mikael never criticized the government in his student days. However, once he became part of it, he worked assiduously to improve it.

During my first year in Leicester College, I had some problems with the Ministry of Education regarding the payment of my scholarship. I used to receive it in quarterly installments. The last quarter, they completely forgot my existence. Fortunately I was living in the college hostel, so I was safe from being thrown out or starved. But when the time came for the summer holiday, the students must leave the hostel. Since I had no money to leave the hostel and seek accommodations outside, I wrote a letter to our ambassador, Ato Abebe Retta, explaining my situation. He sent me five pounds and asked me to go to London. I bought a third-class Leicester/London return train ticket and went to London to report to the ambassador. He advised me to write a letter to His Majesty explaining the problem and he would put it in the diplomatic pouch. In the meantime, with the balance of the money he had sent, I was to live in a hotel in London.

The Emperor's Clothes

The next morning I went back to the embassy with my first letter to His Majesty. I had not put it in an envelope so the ambassador read it and said: "This is very critical. Can you soften it a bit?" I said: "No sir, I want it to go as it is because it represents the truth." He looked at me and then he asked: "From which part of Ethiopia do you come?" I remained silent. The gist of the letter was running down the administration of the government: If one took as an example what happened to me, I wondered what would be the fate of the 20 or so million people who came under such a government.

In less than a week I received 100 pounds and there followed a letter from the private secretary of the emperor saying the letter which I had written to the emperor had been received and the Ministry of Education had been questioned on the matter, but denied failing to send the scholarship. Two weeks later I received a letter signed by the Vice Minister of Education Ato Akaleworq Habte-Wold in which he said I was a thankless person to write such a letter forgetting everything the ministry had done for me. I responded to that letter saying I was surprised the ministry considered itself as doing some favor in fulfilling its public obligation and that I felt I was right in pointing out its failure to carry out its public service responsibility. There was no more correspondence after this and no further problem. When I returned home I was anticipating some confrontation with the vice minister, but I found him cooperative and his reception was extremely warm and kind.

4

Early Career

After completing my studies in Leicester in July 1951, I went straight to London to arrange for the return journey. The education attache at the Ethiopian embassy in London, Mrs. Holland, was able to arrange for me to receive a cash payment equivalent to the airfare which enabled me to travel home overland via Geneva, Lugano, Milan, Venice, Florence, Rome, Athens, Cairo, and finally Addis Ababa. When I arrived in Addis Ababa and compared it with Cairo, which I had left a few hours before, I was shocked by the contrast. Addis Ababa in comparison seemed like a burnt-out town with not a single building that appealed to the eye.

I was met by many of my relatives; they all seemed to me as though they had just got up from their sickbeds after a long illness. I mentioned this to my brother, Melaku, who told me with a smile: "Nobody has been sick and there has been no change in Addis Ababa since you left." Among the people at the airport to welcome me was a representative of the Ministry of Education, whose function it was to greet returning students and take them to the Itegge Hotel where the ministry had arranged full-board accommodation for them. Returning students were based there and paid monthly pocket money of Eth$30 until they were assigned jobs.

The emperor held the portfolio of education and the practice was that every returning student should be presented to him. He wished in this way to create direct loyalty to himself and to emphasis that he was personally responsible for the education from which the student had just benefitted. He hoped to create a personality cult for himself. The overseas study program in some cases took its toll on the students. Assefa Gebre-Georgis, a brilliant science student at Leicester University College, found it difficult to adjust during his first year and suffered a nervous breakdown. He was put into a nursing home and recovered in just four months. Although he would have been able to continue with his studies, the Ministry insisted he return home. When he did, he was put into Shewa Hotel and forgotten. There was no job and no pocket money. In a note he left when he hanged himself with his necktie, he said that since he was left without anything even to replace his shoelaces, his death should be a lesson to the authorities of their responsibility toward returning students.

The morning after my return I walked to the Ministry of Education where I was first directed to the office of Chief Architect Mr. Clewer and then to the office of the Vice Minister Ato Akaleworq Habte-Wold, who told me I had the choice of two assignments. One was in the technical school in Addis Ababa where I could take up the post of deputy director for one year and then assume the post of director, replacing an expatriate whose contract would be expiring. The other was that of assistant engineer in the port of Massawa. I chose Massawa. This seemed to delight the vice minister, who was aware of the need for young trained people to go to Eritrea to provide services which would strengthen the reunion of the province to its motherland.

Since I had no experience in port engineering, I asked the viceminister if I could serve a brief period of attachment with the Aden Port Trust until I took up my post in September. It was agreed that the ministry would sponsor my training and through the British embassy it was arranged that I should leave for Aden two weeks later. At the end of the discussion, the vice minister said: "Come here tomorrow morning at nine and we shall go together to the palace where I shall present you to the emperor. I advise you to have something to say and to have it prepared in writing."

The emperor liked to project the image of having a keen interest in the development and modernization of education. Ostensibly the budget of the Ministry of Education was one-quarter of the national budget, but in reality much of the money was wasted in grandiose buildings which were for the purpose of prestige, leaving little for the payment of teachers or for the purchase of books. The other motive for the supposed modernization of education was to break links with the past, particularly with the resistance movement in whose company the emperor felt overshadowed and ashamed. The emperor tried to impress on the younger generation that he had a strong personal hand in their education, with the aim of creating a new elite beholden only to him with no loyalty to the old establishment. However, this apparent close interest served only to raise the expectations of the younger generation and the emperor became increasingly dependent upon his security men for a power base. Once they realized he had become their hostage, they revolted against him.

I was presented to the emperor by the vice minister on the third day of my arrival in Addis Ababa, but it was not the first time I had met him. Twice at

4. Early Career

Menilek School I had received prizes from his hands and on two or three other occasions I had accompanied other students to be given Christmas presents. It was the custom that we would be given pullovers or cakes by the emperor on Christmas Day. The vice minister took me to the Genete Leul Palace where the emperor had a small office on the first floor. One had to climb a flight of stairs to get into the office and as one approached the top the emperor could be seen seated directly facing the stairs at a writing desk.

It was necessary to bow before proceeding up the last few stairs. The vice minister was ahead of me as we entered the office and I remained standing as he explained what I had been studying and the choice of assignments I had been offered. When the emperor was informed that I had chosen Massawa, he asked whether I had any previous experience of the place. When I said I had not, he said it would be better for me to go to the place before confirming my acceptance. Massawa was regarded as a hardship assignment, while any appointment in Addis Ababa was cushy in comparison. Although the emperor was trying to impress upon me his personal concern for my well-being and comfort. I felt he doubted my commitment to put the national interest before my personal comfort.

I took pride in the vice minister's congratulations that I should have chosen the tougher assignment. I was given the signal to read out the few lines which I had prepared, having chosen the subject of the need to show that we could make a success of our freedom. If we were seen to fail, it would be an impediment to the freedom of other African nations. The emperor responded: "That is why we are educating you."

I traveled to Aden in the last week of November to be met at the airport by an official of the Aden Port Trust who drove me to a Turkish Hotel in the Crater District. The representative told me there were only two hotels in the whole country. One was the first-class hotel run by the Shell company at the steamer point and the second, Turkish Hotel, was 20 kilometers away from the steamer point, which of course was where the Port Trust office was. So every day I had to commute 40 kilometers between the steamer point and the Crater. I went to see the chief engineer, Mr. Grey, to discuss what I was going to do in the next eight to ten months so that it would be possible for me to cover all the main activities on the engineering aspects of port operations. His office had already worked out the schedule and my first day was spent going around with one of Mr. Grey's assistants to be introduced to the staff of the organization. The schedule included the following:
- Marine survey with Sir Bruce White, consulting engineer, on Little Aden Port Development Project.
- Port Engineer's office: administration, planning, and maintenance scheduling.
- Marine equipment maintenance workshop, including slipway.

- Harbor master's office: pilotage.
- Port Administrator's office.

I had to spend one to three months in each department, depending on the importance of the aspect to the activities of the port engineer. The field activity of the marine survey department, especially the flow recording from the echo sounder, which had to be done continuously for 12 hours beginning at 6 a.m. was tedious. I had to do this for nearly two weeks and not only was I bored to death, but I was also annoyed that I was wasting my valuable time. When I discussed this with Mr. Grey, he told me that I did not have to go on doing anything which I found boring and I could drop it and continue with the rest of the schedule.

Another problem I faced was transportation from Crater to the steamer point to arrive at work every day at 6 a.m. and then the return journey. Public transportation was deplorable and taxis were prohibitively expensive. The only solution was to have a private car and I found a tiny Fiat Topolino which cost 200 pounds, which I calculated would be half the money I would spend on taxis during my stay. The Ministry of Education provided me with the money within two weeks. At the end of my stay I shipped the car to Djibouti and from there to Addis Ababa by train where it was handed over to the Ministry of Education.

While I was in Aden, 12 Ethiopian students of port administration arrived at the port with their Belgian professor for a few days visual training on port operations so I was assigned the task of taking them around and showing them various aspects of the operation. I was pleased to know them because they were destined to be my colleagues in Massawa. Since the Ethiopian government had no experience in dealing with maritime affairs, after the federation with Eritrea had been decided by the United Nations, the need for educated personnel to fill the positions which were going to be vacated by the British became apparent and the Ministry of Education took the initiative to do something about it.

Twelve volunteers from the University College were selected: Abebe Wolde-Selassie, Admasu Tessema, Demisse Abebe, Negash Garedew, Wolde Aregai, Teke Gebre-Yesus, Meharei Tewalde-Medhin, Bereket Mehretab, Afework Yisehaq, Tesfa-Igze Woldehawarya, Melaku, and Yohannes Kidane-mariam. But the irony of it all was that when the federation took place, they were forgotten completely. Nobody thought of them and they therefore took employment elsewhere with private organizations in Addis Ababa. A year after the federation, when the emperor came to Massawa, I took up the matter with him and they were chased up from where they were. Eight were traced, four of whom were posted to Massawa. The other four were distributed among other government departments dealing with maritime services.

4. Early Career

The other Ethiopian whom I found working in Aden as chief mechanic of the maintenance workshop of the Aden Port Trust was Berhanu Tesfay, a man of about 28. I managed to persuade him to return to his country and join Massawa Port Office by offering him better pay. So started the Ethiopian maritime services, the development of which was to be completed in less than ten years.

While I was serving my apprenticeship at Aden, I started having health problems. Since the British doctors were not able to diagnose the cause of my sickness, I was advised to go on climatic leave to Asmara. So I left Aden in the last week of May 1952 for an hour's flight to Assab. It was a desolate place with no proper runway and every building was roofless with bare trusses. With no doors or windows, they were a depressing sight. We drove with a Land Rover belonging to the airline from the airport along the beach to Assab town, another depressing place, which looked deserted.

When we reached the center of the town we entered a small U-shaped courtyard with a veranda all along the front of the building. It consisted of about six rooms in a row which also looked deserted and I was told it was the only hotel accommodation in town. I had no difficulty in getting a room for five shillings a night, no meals. There were two eating places run by Italians which were quite good. The room was clean, the only furniture being a simple spring bed with a light mattress, pillow, and two sheets. There was a common shower and toilet in the middle of the building.

At sunset the town seemed to come a little more alive with people crowding into the town's only cafe-bar, run by an Italian married to a local woman. Others streamed into the only cinema. In the hotel I met Salah Gullaye, the chief accountant of Massawa port who was there with an Englishman, the legal adviser to the British military administration of Eritrea in Asmara. Apparently, they were investigating some financial case involving the Assab port administration. I had met Salah Gullaye before when I visited Massawa before going to Aden so he introduced me to the legal adviser. They planned to go by boat the next day to Caleb Island and they invited me to join them. The British District Officer there invited us to lunch and I took the opportunity to ask him about the astonishing state of dereliction in which I had found Assab Airport.

He told me: "Well, in the first place we had no use for the buildings and to maintain them at the taxpayers' expense seemed a waste. On the other hand there seemed no point in letting everything go to rack and ruin and we therefore decided to sell off what we could of the materials and use the proceeds for development. We are entitled to do this under the agreement between the partners in the war effort. Besides, what we have done is a blessing in disguise for the Ethiopian government for we shall avoid a repetition of what happened in Gondar, Addis Ababa and Jimma, where all the beautiful buildings which were left behind by the Italians, with all the fine wood, were allowed to fall into ruin." I felt embarrassed for having asked the question, since everything he said was the truth.

The next day I left Assab for Asmara and found it a wonderful change. First, there was the climate, similar to the Mediterranean. Then there was the good fortune of meeting Ato Amde-Mikael Desalegni at the airport who was there to meet another passenger. We renewed a friendship which was to end only with his death in the 1960 attempted coup. He took me to lunch at his home where I met his wife Zewditu Ambatchew, then on to my hotel, the Albergo Italia. Asmara impressed me with its cleanliness, its modern buildings and shops, the beautifully paved roads, the cinemas, the hotels, and the small pensions. There were several Italian restaurants and cafes.

While in Asmara, I met Blata Kidane-Mariam, who had attained the rank of vice minister in the government. He had been responsible for the construction of the bridge across the Blue Nile linking Shewa to Gojam. He had returned to Eritrea four or five years earlier because he could not get along with the emperor. I found him sincere, open-minded, kind, helpful, and very democratic in his outlook, which perhaps explains why he could not get along with the emperor. It was he who arranged for my medical treatment which led to a full recovery.

The federation was due to take place on 11 September 1952, so it was necessary for me to return to Aden and then to go back to Addis Ababa in the middle of August to prepare to take up my assignment in Massawa. When I reported back to the Ministry of Education, Vice Minister Ato Akalework immediately instructed his secretary to prepare letters announcing my appointment to the various ministries concerned, which were the Ministry of Finance and His Majesty's Viceroy-designate Ras Andargatchew Mesai. The vice minister also briefed me on how I should go about taking up my appointment and advised me to see Ras Andarge so I could plan to travel on the same aircraft as him to Asmara.

I was told Ras Andarge had a temporary office in one of the buildings in the compound of the Genete Leul Palace. I had met him twice before. When he and his wife, Princess Tenaqne-Worq, had been staying in the Kensington Palace Hotel, I had been in London for my summer holidays. Another Ethiopian student, Gebre-Kirstos Mersehazen, took me to be introduced to the them. I found them both to be unpretentious.

The second occasion I met them was when I arrived back in Addis Ababa from my studies in England and was invited to lunch at their home by their son, Eskinder Desta, who was on home leave from studies in England where we had gotten to know each other well. So as I went to see the viceroy in his office I was anticipating he would be pleased to see me and would be happy to have me as one of his followers to go to Eritrea and serve our brothers and sisters there in a political union after 70 years of separation.

To my utter amazement, the first words he spoke when I entered his office were: "I hear that you have been complaining that I was the one who had you assigned to Massawa." I replied forcefully that I had been offered two posts and that Massawa had been my first choice. The reply seemed to mollify him a little although he muttered: "Well, that is what I have been told by your close associates." I replied that I had no close associates who went around talking rubbish. He changed the subject and asked the purpose of my visit. When I explained that I wished to travel with him to Asmara, the arrangements were made. Later I discovered he had been told the story by another recently returned student who had been offered a position of chief engineer in the capital, but wished to go to Asmara for his own reasons.

On 10 September 1952, I left with the viceroy, his wife, his deputy Bitwoded Asfaha, and others on an air force transport Dakota and for the first week I stayed with some of the federal government officials in the Albergo Chiao Hotel, which gave me the opportunity to get to know them all. It was disappointing that all their discussions centered on their salaries, their houses, cars, and other benefits and they gave not a thought to how they were going to foster political unity. The Eritreans were excited by the prospect of unity after such a long time, but those from Addis just took it for granted as another opportunity for self-aggrandizement and a chance for riches.

The day before I left Asmara for Massawa, I went to the office of the representative of the Ministry of Finance, Seyfu Gebre-Yohannes, to ask him about the arrangements for my pay. He informed me that it had been decided by the viceroy that federal officials would receive a pay increase of 30 percent during their service in Eritrea and that I would be entitled to it. There were other officials sitting there but I could not contain my contempt for the arrangement. I pointed out there was already too great a difference between the salaries of the federal officials and Eritrean officials and the proposed arrangement would only widen the gap. I remember telling him: "You as the director already earn Eth$500 while an Eritrean minister earns only Eth$200 and now you want to increase your pay by 30 percent. It makes no political sense and is not justified economically since the cost of living here in Eritrea is less than half that of Addis Ababa."

Those living in the Albergo Chiao Hotel were paying less than half their salaries for full-board accommodation with all the services provided, while those who chose to rent their own accommodation could get a three-bedroom villa for Eth$30 or less a month which would have cost Eth$300 in Addis Ababa. He said simply: "Since you take such great exception to the increment, I shall inform the viceroy and you will not be paid it." I retorted that even if they tried to pay me I would not accept.

The Emperor's Clothes

He left the room and came back a few minutes later to announce bombastically that he had informed the viceroy of my opposition to federal government policies and that my attitude had been noted. I would not be paid the increment nor would I receive a service car. With a clear conscience I left the room and the next day I left for Massawa with the chief engineer, Mr. Bartley, who had driven to Asmara to collect me.

I had been keen to go to Massawa because although there was already a customs department in existence, there was no maritime service. It was clear to me that until the federal government could train Ethiopians, we would be dependent on expatriates. I wished to play whatever role I could in setting up a wholly Ethiopian maritime service.

On the first day of my assignment as assistant port engineer, I was formally presented to the port manager, Captain F.S. Barron. He impressed me as a man who lacked self-confidence and tried to make up for it with an authoritarian air. That was the attitude he used when he told me there was no office accommodation for me and I would have to spend my time in the workshop area. It was with even greater surprise that I discovered the port engineer had no office and was based outside a bar near the workshop where he would sit all day sipping cold melote beer and signing overtime chits.

Neither the port manager nor the port engineer had any academic background and I realized it was my opportunity to put into practice what I had learned about port administration at the Aden Port Trust. In making a tour the first day to meet the port staff, I found a large empty office and organized basic furniture for it. Four days later, I had established offices for the port engineer and myself as well as working out job descriptions for both of us. Apart from the local messengers and cleaners, the port manager, his deputy, the port engineer and the captain of the port police were English and the rest were Italians except for a Sudanese storekeeper.

Realizing he would not last long and wishing to save face, the port engineer gave the administration an ultimatum that unless they would provide a house in Asmara for his wife, who found the climate of Massawa unsuitable, he would be obliged to retire. So within six months of my arrival I succeeded him.

The other piece of deadwood was the port police captain, whom I was able to have replaced by his Ethiopian deputy. By the time I left Massawa in March 1954, the only Englishman remaining was Captain Barron and Ethiopians had replaced all but a handful of the other expatriates. That there previously had been no Department of Marine meant that initially we had no parent organization in the capital and the viceroy took advantage of the fact to form his own department of marine in Asmara, which he tried to make autonomous. He employed a Greek Captain Mellisinos as marine adviser and from that moment on, everything which required any financial outlay, however small, had to be

58

channeled through the Asmara marine office. Mellisinos aspired to omniscience and prepared projects on shipping, port development, and dredging, and the viceroy blithely signed everything Mellisinos prepared.

One morning a young Frenchman walked into my office and handed me a document signed by the viceroy which turned out to be a contract between Batignol of Djibouti and the viceroy of Eritrea for Batignol to use the quayside cranes to dredge the quayside for a fee of Eth$100,000. The whole scheme was an obvious sham and quite absurd. There was no drawing showing the original depth of the quayside and the depth at that time, and according to pilots there had never been evidence of silting up of the quayside. Therefore, there was no need to dredge and certainly not with the quayside cranes.

I told the Frenchman any dredging that might be required, if ever, would be the responsibility of the port engineer and he should therefore go back to whomever had sent him to inform him that the port engineer would not allow any dredging. The next day the viceroy telephoned me in a rage and expressed his anger that I had refused to accept the signed contract. I politely informed him that I was the port engineer, not him, and that so long as I remained the port engineer I would not brook any interference in my responsibilities from him. He threatened to have me dismissed and I told him that in that eventuality he would be free to do whatever he liked, but not so long as I remained in office.

So the contract was scrapped and the viceroy set out to make as big a case of the affair as he could with the emperor, trying to portray me as opposed to any kind of development at the port and holding me personally responsible for any silting up which might take place. This was precisely what I wanted, an opportunity to confront the viceroy in front of the emperor, for in my naivete I thought at that time the emperor was not aware of what was going on and when he knew he would take remedial action. My idealized picture of the emperor was molded by what I had been told by my grandfather Zewdu as a child about the way in which Menilek conducted the affairs of the empire.

In December 1953, the emperor made his second visit to Eritrea since the federation, flying direct from Addis Ababa to Massawa. A week before his expected arrival the viceroy, Princess Tenagne-Worq, and all the high-ranking federal and local government officials had travelled to Massawa, so the place was bustling with political activity.

The Imperial entourage from Addis Ababa included Crown Prince Asfawossen, the Duke of Harar, Leul Ras Kassa and the minister of pen, Tsehafi Tezaz Wolde-Georgis. The exchanges between myself and the viceroy had reached the ears of some of the palace officials and not all of them were displeased that I had the guts to take him on. I took the opportunity of conducting the emperor around the port area to explain to him at the quayside that the depth of water was more than enough to take the draught of the ships calling at the port and if any silting up were to take place, we would use a mobile crane to dredge. I had rigged a mobile crane with a grab and was able to demonstrate dredging operations to the emperor. I emphasized that the dredging contract had been an absurdity and a waste of public money. At the end of the tour the Crown Prince called me and said: "Well done. I am pleased with what you have achieved here."

The next morning at seven, I was called to the palace and ushered into the reception hall where the emperor was sitting alone. I bowed and he said: "Come closer." I stood close to him on his left side. Then he said: "You have been here now over a year. Tell us what you have accomplished and what problems you have encountered." I was excited and thought that my moment to confront the viceroy had come. I told the emperor: "Your Majesty, I would like your permission to make my report in the presence of Ras Andarge." As we were discussing the point, the Duke of Harar appeared, bowing low, and he was dispatched to fetch Ras Andarge.

Once the three of us were together, I reported about the 30 percent salary increase for federal government officials and how unwise the policy was, both politically and economically. I cited the case of the dredging contract as a good example of the corruption of the administration. When I had finished my report, there was no response from Ras Andarge or comment from the emperor, who simply told me: "It is all right, you can go back to your work." A week after this incident, at about nine in the morning, I was called to the palace and found the courtyard filled with the emperor's people. The emperor was standing on the first-floor veranda of the Turkish-built palace, surrounded by all the dignitaries. I was told to climb up the steps to join the emperor and the others. Everybody was dressed in white suits and ties, except for myself in a short-sleeved shirt. I always dressed that way because I hate formal dress. The emperor started dictating an order to the viceroy who was standing in front of him. He began by indicating me and said: "He should be given a furnished house, an official car and a 30 percent salary increase like the rest of the federal officials."

The viceroy bowed and I stood in a state of shock until I blurted out: "Your Majesty, I did not ask for any of this." The aide-de-camp signaled me to leave at once and, forgetting to bow, I walked down the steps. At the landing the secretary of the viceroy, Girma Sebhat, handed me a sealed envelope which I did not open until I was back in my office. My confidence in the emperor was shattered, but I was determined to renew my fight against corruption and abuse of authority. The letter proved to be an instruction to the Seferian Company, the Volkswagen dealers, to give me a VW car. I decided I was entitled to the car because of my official duties, but the salary increase and the furnished government house I would never accept.

4. Early Career

In January 1954, Dejazmatch Zewde Gebre-Selassie was appointed director general of the Department of Marine. By that time, the government in Addis Ababa had finally come to realize the viceroy had established a government of his own, especially as far as marine affairs were concerned, and was conducting government business without anyone in Addis Ababa being able to control him. So the appointment of Dejazmatch Zewde was intended to reduce his interference in marine affairs. In reality there were two departments of marine and for the next three years there was an ongoing fight to close the Department of Marine in Asmara which the viceroy had set up. There was not the same problem in other areas of administration because all the other departments had parent ministries in Addis Ababa to which they had always been reporting.

Dejazmatch Zewde Gebre-Selassie came to visit the port of Massawa in the first week of February 1954 and, since we were close friends, we discussed openly the problem which he was going to face with the viceroy in his attempt to control and administer the affairs of the maritime department. He expressed his desire to have me transferred to head office in Addis Ababa and I told him I had no objection. He must have discussed the matter with the viceroy because two weeks after the discussion I received a copy of a letter dated 4 March 1954 addressed to the Massawa port administrator, and signed by the administrator of the Asmara Department of Marine, Abebe Bitew. It referred to the letter of the viceroy dated 27 February 1954, which stated that my application for transfer to Addis Ababa on health grounds, which had been presented to the emperor, had been duly approved. According to the letter, I was now transferred to the Ministry of Marine in Addis Ababa effective 10 March and the port administration was instructed to provide me with a one-way ticket from Asmara to Addis Ababa and to ensure I handed over any government property in my possession. It left me with only two days to pack and leave Massawa for Asmara. I was more than a little put-out since I had neither requested a transfer in the first place nor was there a copy of this transfer under Imperial order to the imaginary ministry. It was a ploy to deprive me of the formal letter of transfer which they must have been aware was under process. It also attempted to ensure that on return to Addis Ababa I would be subjected to the frustration of the long and sometimes interminable process of presenting myself daily at the palace as a supplicant for a new position. The procedure was well-established and clear. Any transfer was always effected through the Ministry of Pen and this unorthodox letter was clearly a concoction of the viceroy's office in Asmara. The practice of haunting the palace in the hope of getting the attention of the emperor in pursuit of a new position was known as Dej-Tinat and they were determined that I would feel the full frustration of the system.

I was equally determined that they should be disappointed. Within a week of receiving the letter, I handed over all of the government property I had, except for the car which I had been given by Imperial decree. What the emperor had given, I decided, only the emperor was going to take away. In Addis Ababa I would have more need of the car than before and I was not going to be denied it. It was also clear that because the car was new, several selfish officials would be clamoring for it if I were to go without it. I loaded my few personal possessions into the car and left for Asmara on 15 March. Early next morning I left for Addis Ababa, intending to spend nights at Koiha and Dessie and to arrive in Addis Ababa on 18 March.

About 100 kilometers out from Asmara at Adhi Ugri, I met a retired policeman hitching a lift to Addis Ababa, so I had good company on the road. We reached Maichew, which in 1936 had been the battlefield where the emperor's army had been routed by the Italians. The retired policeman told me he had fought in the battle on the Italian side. He explained it had not been a battle but a massacre and showed me the strategic position from which the Italian army had poured concentrated fire into the Ethiopian mass attacks. At the end of the day, the field had been strewn with Ethiopian dead, but there was hardly a scratch on the Italian side.

While I was on the road, my departure was discovered by the officials in Asmara, who contacted the viceroy's office which sent telegrams to the police stations at Mekele and Dessie to have me detained. Despite their scurrying to the post office, the telegrams arrived only after I had reached Addis Ababa. Ras Andarge took the trouble to compile a four-page report on the affair, accusing me of not having formally taken leave of him, which he portrayed as an expression of contempt for the emperor, as personified in the viceroy. He said going with the car was an unpardonable offense and I should be reprimanded and the car returned to Asmara.

The day after my arrival in Addis Ababa I went not to the palace, as the authorities in Asmara had assumed that I would, but instead to the office of the newly formed Department of Marine, which was housed in a seven-room, two-floor residential building behind Dejach Balcha Hospital. When I appeared out of the blue, my friend Zewde, the director general, was pleasantly surprised. When I told him about the manner of my departure from Massawa, he agreed I should start work immediately as chief of technical services in the department. In order to avoid the complications of a formal transfer, he would pay me the same salary which I had received when I started work in Massawa. I was back in business without having wasted a day.

In its infancy, the department was comprised of only the director general, Administrative Officer Wolde Endeshaw, a chief of registry, two or three secretaries, drivers, messengers, and now myself. A week later, the emperor received Ras Andarge's report on me. After reading it, the emperor passed the report to the Minister of Pen, who passed it to Zewde, who passed it to me. The charge of contempt for Imperial authority was cunning and potentially dangerous so I decided to compile my written response carefully. It was important that I should shift the emphasis to the second charge, that of taking the car without authority. I reminded His Majesty that he was well-aware of the bad blood between myself and the viceroy. I went on to say that as far as I was concerned the car, which was the substance of the viceroy's complaint, did not belong to the Asmara Department of Marine because when he was dishing out cars to all and he chose to leave me out. I emphasized that everything else in the report was a malicious fabrication caused by the viceroy's frustration over losing the car. I handed my response to Zewde so that it would return to the emperor through the same channels it had come to me. Some time later I was called to the palace to be told by the emperor: "As regards this matter of yourself and Ras Andarge, just ignore it." I bowed and left his presence and kept the infamous VW for another three years, to part with it only when new government regulations abolished service cars and introduced an allowance system instead. Every official was expected to buy his own car with a two-year government loan and receive a fuel allowance.

Zewde was promoted to vice minister and transferred to the Ministry of Public Works late in 1956. Mikael Imru, who was director general in the Ministry of Defense, was promoted to assistant minister and transferred to head the Department of Marine. The surprising thing was that all the time from March 1954 when I presented myself at the department and started work on an oral understanding with the director general, there was no official written confirmation of my status. Since no one chose to question my position in the department, I gave it little thought, preferring to get on with what I saw as my duty to the nation.

5

Department of Marine, Addis Ababa (March 1954-1957)

You will remember that I had arrived in Addis Ababa on the night of 18 March 1954 by road. I had no close relatives well-established in Addis Ababa, except my younger sister Ayelech who was newly married and my younger brother Melaku, an officer in the Imperial Body Guard living in camp. My parents lived in Wolliso, 120 kilometers southwest of Addis Ababa, so I took a room and board in the Shewa Hotel for Eth$150 per month. After a week, I moved out into a rented two-bedroom house. I soon worked out that for what it cost me to stay in the hotel alone I could rent a modern house which I could share with Melaku and employ a houseboy and cook. The main staple food, teff, cost Eth$15 to$20 per 100 kilograms which could feed a family of 10 for one month and the other ingredients such as meat, butter, and so on came to about Eth$20 to $30 per month. My monthly expenses, supporting four to five people and entertaining visiting relatives and friends, amounted to Eth$200 per month and my monthly salary after tax was Eth$400. This meant a savings of Eth$200 per month.

It took me one week to move out of the hotel and six months to move out of the rented house to one of my own. I found the house I was renting was simply constructed from cheap material, so I conducted research on the cost of material and labor. With my architectural training, I designed a two-bedroom house with sitting-cum-dining room, kitchen, and bathroom and calculated the cost at Eth$4,000.

I knew the government had a scheme to accommodate graduates returning from abroad by giving two-year, interest-free house building loans. So I could put in a request for such a loan and my monthly savings of Eth$200 would be sufficient to pay for it, but what about the site for the building? I knew both my father and grandfather owned a plot on what were then the outskirts of

Addis Ababa (now the center). Both of them had told me about the plot and although I did not know where it was, my adopted brother Habte-Mikael did. It was 200 meters off the main road to Bishoftu and 8 kilometers from the center of Addis Ababa, an open field with cattle grazing on it, a large plot measuring 15,000 square meters. I selected one corner as the site for my house. It took me about four weekends to organize everything and start the construction work (during working days I was busy with my new assignment). Three months after the construction began, one of the two bedrooms, the bathroom, and the kitchen were completed with running water, but there was no electricity so we were using a pressure lamp for lighting. I moved in to save the rent money to finish the remaining part of the house. Little by little it was completed. A year later, my brother Melaku came and built next to me and the 15,000 square meters of land was divided between 10 of us. Today everyone has built on his share.

This was what I felt I had to do in order to free myself from the worries of house rent, in case I was suspended from my job due to my independent mind. I would likely be thrown out of the rented house and that was what my political enemies would like to have seen. For food I would not have to worry—I could get support from my relatives—but cash to pay for house rent would have been a problem without a monthly income.

The Assab Port Development Project

My main occupation was to assist in the organization of the Department of Marine and a particular priority was the Assab Port Project. It was a constant spur that my boss and I worked well together. We hardly differed in our views and so we constituted a good team. In a short time we managed to progress in all the activities of the department. In the process, the staff of the department increased by more than 100 percent. The preliminary study for the Assab Port Project had been completed in less than a year by a Dutch consulting firm, NEDECO. The technical section of the department was well-organized with two German port engineering experts and one Ethiopian apprentice, Demisse Abebe [he was later given scholarship to study engineering in the U.S. and on his return he became port engineer of Assa], to prepare preliminary plans, supervise, and review the work of consulting firms. Once the appropriate site had been determined and the survey results proved favorable for the construction of the port, NEDECO's contract was extended to prepare a master plan for a phased development.

The first phase was to accommodate the traffic and shipping requirements of Ethiopian international trade for the next 10 years. The investigation to determine the appropriate site confirmed the existing location where the Italians had built a small jetty at Assab was the only one suitable. The deep water coastline along this site, which was available for port construction, was only one kilometer. The problem facing the planners was how to make optimum use of this deep water frontage to meet the long-term port facility needs of the country. All previous Italian plans were reviewed and the Department of Marine engineers and NEDECO devised a four-phase development plan to accommodate up to 32 modern commercial liners passing through the Suez Canal.

The first phase provided berthing facilities for six Victory-type ships, which were expected to meet the needs of the next ten years while the second phase was an additional six ships for another ten years. The third phase would accommodate twelve and the fourth, eight Victory-type ships. In the 40-year development period, the available deep water coastline of one kilometer would be completely built up to provide 32 berths for larger liners. NEDECO's first phase project proposal, costing Eth$64 million was submitted to the World Bank for a review which recommended scaling it down considerably to reflect the real economic conditions prevailing before it would consider financing the project.

In the meantime, interested governments started sending economic and technical missions to Ethiopia, with the intent of finding out the economic and technical possibilities for international participation in the project. The economic and technical mission of the Federal Republic of West Germany headed by the economic adviser of the economic ministry, Dr. Hans Kuntze, arrived in Addis Ababa in May 1956. He left at the end of June after submitting a detailed report of their findings and technical recommendations for modification on the NEDECO project proposal which scaled down the cost to Eth$34 million. A Yugoslavian government mission proposal followed practically the same formula as the German one, but cost Eth$26 million. The aim was to build a port which would ultimately be able to accommodate all the liners passing through the Suez Canal.

The final estimate for the first phase, 2 half-jetties with berthing capacity for 3 liners each, 12 quayside cranes, 6 warehouses, and a breakwater of 700 meters amounted to Eth$26 million. The tender offers varied between this and 50 million. The closest offers to the final estimate were from Pomgrad of Split, Yugoslavia, and a West German construction firm. Pomgrad was selected because, not only was their offer attractive, but they also were going to finance 50 percent of the construction cost at only 3 percent per annum interest, with a 10-year grace period and payments being made in kind through commodity exports.

The German Economic Mission

I was attached to the West German Federal government mission during the one month of economic and technical study. One of the mission's recommen-

67

dations in its final report on the Assab Port development was the offer of a scholarship for me for practical training with the Hamburg Port Authority for six months.

At that time, the head of the Department of Marine was Lij Mikael Imru and we discussed how best to utilize this training offer in relation to the Assab project. Since the short listing for the construction consisted of a Yugoslavian and a West German firm, it was necessary to evaluate the technical performance and the organizational setup of Pomgrad in Yugoslavia and the West German firm. So on my way to Germany, I first went to visit the port construction that was being undertaken by Pomgrad in Latakia, Syria, and from there to visit the head office in Split, the ongoing port construction in Bar, and the port of Rejeka, all in Yugoslavia. From there I proceeded to Hamburg.

In Hamburg with Strome and Hafenbau, I followed a practical training course covering all aspects of port development and management activities for six months, from May to October 1957. One of my assignments in Germany was to interview the candidates for the position of a port engineering expert in the Department of Marine. The candidate whose credentials were submitted through the German embassy in Addis Ababa was Dr. Ferster, a staff member of Strome and Hafenbau. Dr. Ferster was head of a small, unimportant section in the organization of the Port Authority, so I thought the best option would be to take my first assignment with his section. I rapidly formed the conclusion that he was not the man for us.

I communicated my finding to my department and declared my intention to identify another candidate during the course of my stay in Germany and to ignore Ferster. I identified a young engineer who was heading the planning section of the Strome and Hafenbau organization and talked to him about the position in Addis Ababa. He was already aware that the organization had submitted Ferster's name. He indicated his willingness, but only with the blessing of the organization. So I went to see the director of Strome and Hafenbau, Dr. Muehlradt, and raised the question of the candidate for the position in Addis and informed him the choice of our department rested not in the high qualifications of Dr. Ferster but in a more junior engineer, Mr. Hoeft. He nearly got up from his chair with anger and he said: "Hoeft! No! But we can put up a notice about the position and you can choose from those who will apply." I knew the best ones would not apply and he also knew it, but to comply with his wish and to come back to the question of Hoeft, I agreed about the notice.

I went back to the director and informed him that none of those who had applied were acceptable and I would like him to reconsider my request for Mr. Hoeft. He said: "Sorry, we cannot help you in this matter anymore. Look somewhere else and do not raise the question of Hoeft anymore, he is indispensable." On my return to Addis Ababa I took up this matter with the German

5. Department of Marine, Addis Ababa (March 1954-1957)

embassy. I got Mr. Hoeft and the success of the Assab project was mainly due to his expert advice. His contribution during three years of service with the department was invaluable.

During my stay in Germany, I went to Bonn and attended a meeting at the Ministry of Economic Affairs on the Assab Port Project, reviewing the report of Dr. Hans Kuntze's mission and the port construction firm in Bremerhaven. I compiled a report covering my mission to Latakia, Yugoslavia, Bonn and Bremerhaven and posted it to my department. While I was in Germany in October 1957, the contract for the construction of the Assab Port Project on the based offer submitted by Pomgrad was signed.

Ras and Arge and the Assab Port Project

Despite the establishment of the Department of Marine under the Constitution, Ras Andarge was still using his powers of viceroy to run his own illegal Department of Marine in Eritrea. The initiative for the Assab Port development was taken by the head office in Addis Ababa and the viceroy's office in Asmara, which concentrated its activities in Massawa and must have felt bitter for missing this opportunity, was laying in wait for an opportunity to get its hands on the project. The viceroy's Asmara office was following the development and preparing secret counterproposals to present at the opportune time.

After the consulting engineers had finalized their studies and investigation and a final project document with cost estimates had been submitted to the department, its head official, Dejazmatch Zewde, had to go overseas to look for financing. That was when the viceroy chose to give his counterproposals to the emperor with the hope of getting approval on the spot to take over the Assab project. His partner and the expert in preparing the counterproposal was Batignol, the owner of the port of Djibouti.

Ras Andarge had been the Ethiopian consul in Djibouti before the Italian invasion; he had been educated in French in Addis Ababa which fitted him for the post. A relative of one of the important families of Shewa, he had remained in exile in Djibouti throughout the war of occupation. Ras Desta, husband of the emperor's eldest daughter, was killed by the Italians and she went into exile with her father. When they returned, Andarge was under suspicion of collaboration with the Italian prisoners and although he was able to use high government connections to escape court martial, he was really in disgrace. Despite all this, the emperor agreed to give his daughter to Andarge in marriage and to elevate him to the rank of Ras. He was appointed governor of Begemdir, where he engaged himself in business with his erstwhile Italian friends. When Andarge was further promoted to viceroy of Eritrea, he rapidly alienated the Eritrean population with his rapacious business methods, while ignoring their political aspirations.

Ras Andarge was working in cooperation with Batignol and Captain Mellisinos. As soon as the director general of the department was out of the country, all three of them presented themselves to the emperor with their counterproposal, the main attraction of which was an apparent savings of 50 percent. They had no doubt that the counterproposal would be accepted at once. To their disappointment, the emperor decided instead to set up a committee to look into the matter. To make their chances worse, the chairman of the committee was none other than the minister of defense, Ras Abebe Aregai, known for his strong character and good judgment, and among the members was another strong nationalist, Ato Mekonnen, the minister of commerce and industry. The committee was ordered to meet immediately and present its findings to the emperor without delay. As soon as it was convened, the chairman asked the key question: "Do we not already have a department responsible for such matters?" The viceroy explained: "Yes, we do, but its head is out of the country at present." the chairman answered: "Maybe so, but he must have left somebody in charge of his department." He had indeed. Me. So I was called to the palace where the committee was sitting. I entered to find Ras Abebe at the head of the table with Ras Andarge, Batignol, and Mellisinos sitting on one side and Ato Mekonnen Habte-Wold, Ato Minasse Lema, and Ato Tefara-Worq on the other.

I was told to explain what I knew of the plans laid on the table. It was the old Italian scheme drawn up to establish Assab as a naval base during the war. The available deep water coastline was to be used for the construction of just two jetties to provide berthing for only six ships drawing only five to six meters of water. This old Italian plan had already been reviewed by NEDECO and its disadvantages clearly noted in their report. So my response was to reiterate the consultants' findings and to shock the opposition a little by adding my own opinion that any attempt to resurrect the Italian plan was a blatant attempt at sabotaging the whole project. The whole of the deep water frontage of the port was to be used for only 6 berths instead of 32.

When I had finished my report, the chairman told me to call by telephone to bring the German advisers from the Department of Marine to the meeting. I used the committee room telephone and called Mr. Boetcher to the meeting, where I acted as his interpreter. When he confirmed everything I had said, nobody present asked questions or tried to refute a word. The chairman summed up brusquely by saying that since none of the members of the committee were experts, he could not see the point in listening to some outsider's opinion which flew in the face of the advice they were paying their experts to give. The matter was therefore closed. I was instructed to prepare the minutes of the meeting and circulate them to the offices of all concerned to be signed.

Had I been less blunt the matter might have dragged on, but once I spoke of sabotage everybody had to play safe by rejecting the counterproposal. The affair ended so embarrassingly for Ras Andarge that he made no further attempt. I had reinforced his political hatred of me but gained a political friend in the process. Ato Mekonnen Habte-Wold was an upright man who was exploited by the emperor because of his national outlook. After the meeting he called me aside and congratulated me on the stand which I had taken. He remained forever after my staunch supporter within the government.

Training of Tugboat Operators

As soon as I had left Massawa, the viceroy's Department of Marine in Asmara had become free to act as port engineers and come up with any project which would bring benefit in the form of commission to the giver of the contract.

In less than a month a project proposal to purchase four tugboats for service at the two ports, Massawa and Assab, was prepared and a contract was signed between the viceroy and a Dutch shipbuilding firm for a cost of Eth$2.5 million. Massawa had a tugboat and the traffic in both ports did not justify the purchase of two for each port, without consulting or informing the Department of Marine in Addis Ababa. I got the information through my contact in Massawa after the contract had been signed and the Greek marine adviser had already drafted another contract to employ eight Greek tugboat operators.

I immediately informed the director general of this, although there was nothing to be done about the unnecessary purchase of the tugboats. We could at least take steps to stop the unnecessary employment of the eight Greek tugboat operators and the director general agreed I should act immediately. I went to see the director of the technical school and asked him to give me the names and addresses of his school's graduates the previous year whom he considered best in their technical capability and sense of responsibility. I told him I needed eight of the previous year's best graduates. He gave me their names and where they worked: Tessema Gizaw, Alemayehu Betru, Tsige Abrha, Kebede Tilahun, Sultan Hayilu, Berhanu Woldesemayat, Manbegroh Adera, and Kebede. I saw each of them in their workplace and informed them of the scheme. The Department of Marine would send them immediately to Holland for training in their future occupation as tugboat engineers. They would have the training at the shipbuilding yard and would take part in the building of the tugboats and diesel engines, which they would operate when they were completed.

The graduates would be responsible for bringing them from the shipyard to the port of Massawa. They all agreed to take the offer and resign their present posts. The department provided them with winter clothing and some pocket money during their training period. The scheme was communicated to

71

the contractor, who agreed, and within three weeks the eight Addis Ababa technical school graduates flew to Amsterdam. On the next day after they left Addis Ababa, the viceroy in Asmara was notified of the plan and reminded to stop his scheme of employing Greek nationals. On receiving this telegram he got mad and flew the next day to Addis Ababa to inform the emperor that the Department of Marine in Addis Ababa was going to send the Eth$2.5 million tugboats down the drain by sending Ethiopians, who had never seen marine craft let alone operated them, to sail from Holland to Massawa. Moreover, these boys had neither been to sea nor seen it. This was simple madness on the part of the Department of Marine.

The emperor immediately sent for the Director General Dejazmatch Zewde to respond to the accusation. He responded to the accusation by pointing out the principle the department was following to be self-sufficient; others were not born with the knowledge but acquired it through training. Therefore, this was the best opportunity for these eight boys to get the training they would need to operate those tugboats. He explained in detail what the operation of tugboats entailed, and where the safety of the boat depended on the captain provided by the contractor who had the responsibility of bringing the boats to our berths and handing them over. After six months, the eight Ethiopians entered Massawa harbor with their four tugboats triumphantly.

Fisheries Administration Course

Within a year of its establishment the Department of Marine was gaining recognition for its administrative efficiency and effectiveness. The FAO representative in the Ministry of Agriculture, Mr. Innes, called on the director general of the Department of Marine to discuss the transfer of Fishery Administration from the Ministry of Agriculture to the Department of Marine. The jurisdiction over fisheries was transferred under the Federal Act because there had been only inland water fisheries in Ethiopia before the federation of Eritrea.

Mr. Innes pointed out that it only existed on paper as far as the Ministry of Agriculture was concerned since not a single person was assigned the responsibility for fishery questions. He requested that the director general assign one officer who would participate in a three-month FAO fishery administration course in Denmark from June to the end of August 1955.

I was chosen for this course which covered all aspects of fishery development in seminars and site visits. There were participants from 24 developing countries. All the participants, except those from Ethiopia and Somalia, were working in the fishery administration in their countries. The participant from Sudan, Eliasa Khalifa, became a good friend of mine and due to our close association, the participants started to call us 'father and son.' He was about

50, and I was about 30. He was an old hand in fishery administration and his present post was as inspector of fisheries.

As soon as I returned from Denmark I started to organize the Ethiopian marine and freshwater fisheries. I recruited fishery administrators to be stationed in Massawa and Assab and sent them for training in Sudan and Israel. A fishery administration section at the head office under a director, Wolde-Aregai, was established. A fishery training boat was built and a plan to train the fishermen in all methods of fishing techniques and fishery regulations were introduced. An agreement was concluded with Israel to carry out a marine fishery survey. Whereas fish had been in short supply before, the new measures created an abundance which served to further stimulate demand. The fish price in Addis came down from one Eth$1 to 50 cents, but the fishermen were still better off. Only high-priced lake fish were previously available, but now fish merchants were encouraged to truck fresh fish under refrigeration to Addis Ababa.

Naval Training Establishment

During the Italian occupation of Eritrea, Massawa was a naval base accommodating 10,000 naval personnel. Since the British had no use for maintaining all of those facilities, during their 10 years of military administration, it put the material of the base to better use. When the federation took place, the former Italian naval base had nothing to show for its former importance except a couple of doorless, windowless, roofless, bare brick walls. The viceroy immediately took the initiative to rehabilitate the naval base to train the nucleus of an Ethiopian navy.

The Italian architect Mesedimi was commissioned for the architectural drawings and the construction contract was given to Commandatore Buschi who had been a partner in business with the viceroy since the days when he was governor of Begemdir, way back in 1946. So the facilities to start the naval training had been put in place within a short time and by late 1954 recruitment of instructors had started.

Now, because the head office for marine affairs had been established in the capital, the viceroy's powers were being limited. His plan for instructors was to recruit Greek Naval officers. But the head of the Department of Marine, Dejazmatch Zewde, who accompanied the emperor when he went to Norway on a state visit, negotiated with the Norwegian authorities on this matter and got the Imperial blessing to recruit Norwegian naval officers. The head of the naval school, Captain Harlofson, arrived in Massawa in early 1955 and started the organization. By the middle of 1955, the recruitment of trainees started with the head office in the capital fully participating.

Admiral Hoarve was a retired Norwegian naval admiral. He was employed as naval adviser to the Department of Marine not because at that stage of development an adviser of his rank was of real necessity, but for political reasons to boost the prestige of the department by pressuring the close the of Department of Marine in Asmara and bringing about a final decision to have a single Department of Marine in Addis Ababa.

Much of the department's energy and time were being dissipated in the fight against the interference of the department in Asmara, so when the admiral came into the picture as a result of the two monarchs meeting during the emperor's visit to Norway, the head of the department thought having the admiral could be the route to a single authority. After his contract had been signed and his monthly salary commenced with the excuse that he was drawing up the future development plan for the naval school, he stayed for six months in Norway. He came with his wife and moved to Ghion Hotel at the Department of Marine's expense. He insisted on a Colonel Strander as his assistant, a naval commander, and a lady secretary, all Norwegian nationals. The secretary only came to the office to collect her salary while the others came to the office daily, but only to warm their chairs.

I watched this situation until I could not stand it any longer. I started to discuss my observations with the head of the department, who expressed his hesitation to do anything about it because of the emperor's involvement in the admiral's employment. I said that as an Ethiopian my conscience would not let me overlook such a thankless abuse of public funds. At the end of it all, these people would put the blame on our administration for our lack of initiative, competence, and creativity.

I wrote down my views and submitted a copy to the director general of the department, Dejazmatch Zewde, and another to the Ministry of Defense. Before long the director general left the capital on a mission abroad and as usual I became the acting head. The director general left the same day. I called Admiral Hoarve to my office and asked him if he could provide me with copies of plans or reports of whatever work he had accomplished since he had been employed, which was more than a year by then. I asked him what the duties were of the two staff members, the army colonel, the navy officer, and the secretary who only came to the office once a month. I pointed out to him that he was living off the taxes collected from poor peasants who dressed in rags and felt themselves lucky if they saw a daily meal.

His response to my request for a copy of his work was negative and rude, which was proof of my observation. I said to the admiral: "I am quite aware of the fact that you have nothing to show and that is exactly what I wanted you to understand. Think of an honorable way to quietly leave this expensive post. Otherwise I will be obliged to issue you with notice, which I am going to do to the other three." At this point the admiral walked out of my office angrily and in less than half an hour I received his resignation and responded

74

with acceptance. For the other three, in accordance to their contracts, I gave two months' notice.

The admiral, after receiving my acceptance note, went to the Ministry of Defense to report what had transpired between us to result in his resignation. At the ministry he came up against the chief of staff, General Mulugeta Bulli. He was the most capable general and a great administrator for whom I had great respect. He was quite aware the admiral and his staff were complete deadwood so he was delighted with the steps I had taken. From there the admiral went to see the private secretary of the emperor, Ato Tefera-Worq. There he got a symphasizer and the news reached the emperor's ears. In order to avoid confrontation with the emperor when the situation was volatile, I flew to Massawa the next morning. In Massawa I received a telegram from the palace asking me to report there without delay, so I reported the next day.

Fortunately there was no confrontation, but the director general, Lij Mikael Imru, from the Ministry of Defense was ordered by the emperor to be the acting head of the Department of Marine and I was assigned a temporary job with H.E. Ato Mekonnen Habte-Wold, the minister of finance, to be the liaison officer of the German economic mission. Mikael was instructed by the emperor to offer Admiral Hoarve an apology and ask him to withdraw his resignation. Fortunately for me, Mikael was not a yes-man. He was quite aware of the case and submitted a short note justifying the steps I had taken.

At this juncture, the emperor thought I was behind the writing of that note. He became furious and I was called to the palace for him to shout at me. What had I done regarding the admiral and now influencing Mikael not to carry out his orders? I was forced to speak in defense of my action, stating all the arguments and recalling my report to the director general on the matter which reached the emperor through the chief of staff. When he had heard me out, the emperor shouted at me to leave, so I bowed and went, but I won the fight thanks to Mikael. Hoarve and his colleagues left after two months.

I thought Hoarve had left the country and the case was closed forever but that was not quite so. When Hoarve arrived in Oslo, the press interview he gave, as I expected, put all the blame on the administration, especially mentioning my name as creating difficulties for their work. Three months after Hoarve left, the Norwegian commander of the naval school, Captain Harlofson, came up with a request for additional instructors to be recruited. The Norwegian naval commander, Admiral Jacobson, was a close friend of Hoarve but because of what had happened, relations between the Norwegian navy and the Department of Marine in particular, and Ethiopia in general, were now strained and the possibility of recruiting Norwegian naval officers was very unlikely.

When the suggestion was made to the emperor about sending a mission to Norway to negotiate this matter with the Norwegian naval officials and the

Ministry of Defense, the emperor decided the person responsible for creating the problem should go. The reason behind this decision was quite clear. When the mission failed, which the emperor believed it must, that would give him the golden opportunity to put all the blame on and take appropriate measures against such a person. So in September 1956, I was instructed to go to Oslo to negotiate the recruitment of additional instructors for the naval school.

The assistant minister (the status of the head of the Department of Marine was raised from director general to assistant minister) Lij Mikael Imru, and the chief of staff, General Mulugeta, gave me all the encouragement that I needed. I left Addis Ababa for Oslo the last week of September 1956 equipped with two letters from the Minister of Defense H.E. Ras Abebe Aregai to the Norwegian Minister of Defense the Honorable Nibs Handal, and from General Mulugeta Bulli to the C-in-C Royal Norwegian Navy Vice Admiral Johns E. Jacobsen. The first day of my arrival in Oslo I telephoned from my hotel our honorary consul, Mr. Magnus Udjus, whom I had known for some time, and informed him of the reason for my being in Oslo. His immediate reaction was: "Why you of all people, after the bad publicity that has been spread by Admiral Hoarve and his group?" He was pessimistic about the chances of my mission but willing to assist me in every way he could.

I informed him that I had two letters, one for Vice Admiral Jacobsen and the other for the minister of defense and asked him to make an appointment for me with the admiral first. He reminded me that the admiral was a good friend of Hoarve's and my meeting with him was not going to be a pleasant one. At 6 p.m. he came to my hotel and gave me the appointment schedules for the next two days. The day after my arrival in Oslo I met Admiral Jacobsen and his second-in-command, Rear Admiral R.K. Andersen. As expected, Jacobsen's attitude was completely negative; he said the navy had not enough manpower even to meet its NATO obligations so we would have to look elsewhere for instructors.

I did not try to hide my irritation and told the admiral frankly that Hoarve and his group were deadwood and that they knew it themselves. I stated that if they had been decent people they would have resigned in an honorable manner instead of forcing me to have them removed. The meeting with the second-in-command went smoothly and I briefed him about the Hoarve case. Since everybody's mind had been poisoned I had to do what I could to retrieve the situation.

The second day I met the minister, together with his defense counselor, Mr. Modalsli. The discussion lasted an hour. I briefed them in detail about Hoarve and my unpleasant meeting with Admiral Jacobsen. It was a wonderful meeting. Both the minister and Mr. Modalsli were very positive and understanding. They felt sorry for the bad example of the Hoarve affair and assured me of their goodwill for a successful conclusion to my mission and the responsibility of the Norwegian government to stand by their commitment to the Massawa project.

The minister assigned Mr. Modalsli to follow up this matter and see that my mission was accomplished to my satisfaction. I stayed two weeks in Oslo, by the end of which I had recruited all the instructors required. The Norwegian government, considering how to make up for the bad example of Hoarve and his group, decided to send one high-ranking naval officer, a commodore, at their own expense to serve as adviser to the Department of Marine for one year. After that, if the Department of Marine found his services useful, he would be given a contract. Standby instructions to the Norwegian navy to consider the Massawa project one of its responsibilities were given by the Ministry of Defense.

To prove how seriously the government of Norway took this matter, the defense counselor, Mr. Modalsli, came to Ethiopia on an official visit soon after my return and had discussions with the Ministry of Defense and other officials concerned, and visited the naval school at Massawa. On his return, he wrote me a nice letter expressing his satisfaction at what he had seen. General Mulugeta Bulli told me later he had never doubted from the beginning that I would succeed. The emperor never referred to the incident again.

6

Assistant Minister (November 1957 - December 1960)

I had left Addis Ababa in May 1957 via Yugoslavia for Germany for six months of practical training in the administration, development, and operation of port services. When I returned to Addis Ababa at the end of October 1957, the assistant minister in the Department of Marine, Lij Mikael Imru, had been transferred to the Ministry of Agriculture as vice minister and the contract for the construction of Assab Port had been signed with the Yugoslavian firm Pomgrad of Split. I returned to find the Department of Marine without a head, which was not a very pleasant feeling, and started to wonder who was going to succeed Mikael. I had been lucky so far because when Zewde left he had been succeeded by Mikael and they were both my good friends going back to the days when we had been students in England.

Mikael and I had served together as officers in the Ethiopian Student Association - he as the president and I as the treasurer. So I had been lucky to have as my immediate superiors these two selfless, dedicated leaders and genuine friends. What was worrying me even more was the fate of the Assab project, for the contract had already been signed and the successful implementation would entirely depend upon who was heading the Department of Marine. In the implementation process of a large project, there are so many obstacles which are not foreseen that require a courageous person to undertake responsibility for them. Otherwise such projects become bogged down in a bureaucratic, costly mess.

On the second day of my return I had a telephone call from the chief of staff, General Mulugeta, who said he was writing me a letter of appointment as the acting head of the department until somebody was officially appointed. The letter came the next day. The staff were informed by circular letter and the two port managers were informed by telephone.

The Emperor's Clothes

Four days after my appointment as acting head, at about 4 p.m., I was summoned by telephone to go immediately to the palace. When I arrived I was directed to join the line which was formed in the doorway to one of the office buildings. The line started to move in, with nobody returning out. I wondered what was happening, since this was a new experience for me and I was last in line. When my turn came to go in I came face to face with Prime Minister, Ras Endalkachew Mekonnen, Tsehafi Tezaz Tefera-Worq, and Kassa Woldemariam.

I bowed and stood facing the three. The prime minister said: "By the grace of His Imperial Majesty you are appointed assistant minister of the Department of Marine." I said: "Who? Me? How could it be possible? The prime minister said smiling: "Yes you. It is possible." When I went into the adjoining room, it was full of people. I found Endalkachew there. He approached me and asked what appointment I had been given. I replied: "I did not get quite clearly what your father said, whether assistant minister of the Department of Marine." He told me he had been appointed vice minister of education. Before we came to the end of our conversation the prime minister and his two colleagues entered the room and led us into the main building where the emperor lived, in the inner enclosure of the palace. The three dignitaries were ahead of us and we followed them in a line in order of protocol according to rank. We entered the main door of the Green Salon, a large hall where the emperor and the empress were seated. I watched what those ahead of me were doing, kissing the feet of the emperor first and then the empress, moving to their left side and taking their seats on chairs which had been placed along the wall. I followed suit and heard the empress asking the emperor: "Who is this one?" The emperor responded: "Can't you remember seeing him in Massawa?" I moved away and could not hear the rest of the exchange. I think the empress must have singled me out because of the way I was dressed.

Everybody was in a dark suit except me. I was wearing a light-colored sports jacket and flannel trousers. It is probable that I also performed the formalities in an unorthodox way since it was my first time. We sat there for a while and were served a glass of red vermouth. As we got up we bowed, left the room and went off to our places of work; at least that is what I did. I went from there directly to my office. I did not mention to any of the staff what had taken place. I was still doubtful about the words of the prime minister. It was impossible. How could it be without following the progression through director general and then assistant minister?

I had stayed late in the office when the telephone rang. It was my sister Ayelech calling from my house. She asked me what I was doing there and why I had not told them about my appointment: "The house is full of people who have come to congratulate you and we were taken by surprise when we saw people streaming to your house. We wondered what happened and came over to ask. We were informed by the guests about your appointment. Please come at once. The first person who arrived was the Minister for Commerce Ato Mekonnen who waited for you for about 15 minutes and left; the rest are waiting." How the news spread, I do not know. The evening news of Radio Addis had not yet been broadcast. Since I never went to congratulate people on their appointments and this being my first occasion, I had mixed feelings about the whole thing. Should you wonder why, I have to go back to examine the meaning of the word appointment in Amharic. The word appointment in Amharic is "SHUMET," a corruption of the word "SHIMOT" which means a thousand times death. In the monastries even today, after identifying the administrator to be, the rest of the members [monkes] stand in front of the one and beg him to die for them.

A person appointed to a public position has the responsibility not only for one life which is his own but also for 1000 other lives. If this is the ideology of our ancestors behind the appointment to a public position, then they had a good reason to rejoice and congratulate such an appointee who was going to serve them selflessly. But when this ideology lost its value with the modern generation and an appointment was taken as a personal honor and benefit, I could not see any reason for the public to rejoice congratulate an appointee. This being the reason for not going to congratulate people when they were appointed, I had a mixed opinion of my guests. Those who knew me well genuinely rejoiced while the others did so to fulfill their social obligation. I was pleased with the appointment because it would give me a free hand to deal with the administrative problems the department was facing and also to see through the proper implementation of the Assab Port Project.

On the other hand, I knew very well that I had not done a single act to merit this favor; on the contrary, every single action I had taken since I joined the system was against the convention for meriting such an honor. I never went to show my face at the palace. I never executed orders first to please my superiors against my principles; therefore I never expected any upward change to my status. Downward, yes. So I started to wonder who and what was behind it, who could have influenced the emperor? The only government official who could have was Ato Mekonnen Habte-Wold, the minister of commerce who had become my strong supporter after that incident with the viceroy in connection with the Assab Port Project. My only other possible supporter was General Mulugeta Bulli, the chief of staff whom I had come to know after he moved to the Ministry of Defense. In connection with my work at the Department of Marine, whatever problem I discussed with him, he encouraged me to go ahead and do it the way I suggested. He was a great administrator. He knew how to get the best out of his staff. Very punctual and decisive, he also became a victim of the 1960 attempted coup d'etat.

The Emperor's Clothes

Whatever other reasons the emperor might have had for this unprecedented appointment from nowhere to assistant minister, I was very happy especially considering the timing. If someone else had succeeded Mikael, my position in the department would have been very difficult and the fate of the Assab project and the administrative problems of the department could have proved insoluble. I felt the opportunity might not last long. It might be a trial to see if advancement could change my difficult personality. When the emperor found out the trial did not work, I would be thrown out. I had to move fast.

On the fourth day of my appointment, I was called to the palace. Outside the office of the emperor were a great number of people, some seated, the rest standing. Those who had not come to the house to congratulate me came to where I was standing and to offer their congratulations on my four-day-old appointment. The Chief ADC General Mekonnen Deneqe remarked that I had not gone back to the palace after my appointment which I should have done the next day. I did not respond to that remark. He knew very well I never frequented the palace before and that I only came when I was called. That habit would continue whatever my political status might be. I did not stay long outside before I was ushered into the office. This was the first time I had been to this wing of the main Imperial palace (Genete Leul). It was a large carpeted room and in the left-hand corner of the entrance was a mahogany writing table behind which the emperor was seated alone with his cape on.

I bowed at the entrance to which the emperor responded with "Indet aderk" which is "good morning." Then I moved closer to the desk and stood facing him. He talked to me with the smile he always used when he wanted to put someone at ease, asking me whether I was pleased with my appointment. I said that I was and he told me: "If you serve us well there is no reason why you should not reach the top with the others around here who are all people whom we have raised up from nowhere." I replied: "Your Majesty, I always feel that dedicated service rendered to one's country is always service rendered to its leader and I assure Your Majesty that I will serve my country with dedication." At that, our conversation ended and I went back to my office with the understanding that my appointment was a trial to see if I could change my ways and become part of the system. I decided that if my tenure was to be under constant review I would make the most of it while I could.

This seems a suitable moment to discuss Mekonnen Habte-wold. I agree with John Spencer's contention in his book "Ethiopia at Bay" that Mekonnen Habte-wold was a remnant of the old school who was exploited wrongly by corrupt leadership. His traditional upbringing blinded him to the stealthy corruption; he steadfastly believed in the emperor and was incapable of questioning his wisdom or dedication to the glory of Ethiopia, qualities which had been inherent in previous Ethiopian leaders. So he became a dedicated servant of the emperor and because of this he wrongly acquired a reputation for being a corrupt hatchet man.

"Ato Mekonnen Habte-wold then (1936) director general of commerce and communication... came almost daily to the house to discuss the hopeless situation with me. He came also to use one of the few telephones in operating condition from which he could communicate with both the Northern and Southern fronts. The telephone was to become a central passion with him.....His frail body, the bony planes of his skull, bald except for a grizzled fringe of close-cropped hair, his shabby clothing all bespoke Mekonnen's traditional upbringing in the church. A total ascetic, he slept little, ate sparingly and drank not at all. His detractors have long accused him of corruption. From years of intimate knowledge of the man I can state emphatically that this very asceticism effectively preserved him from such temptation. His tired clothes and, after the liberation, his ancient Volkswagen, were no pretense. They were the skin on the flesh of the inner man. He was a dedicated patriot and Haile Selassie, realizing this, reposed in him his total confidence." "Mekonnen's death (in the 1960 attempted coup) afflicted me the most severely. His friendship was completely uncalculating, totally altruistic and totally affecting."

You will remember I had left a virtually autonomous Department of Marine in Asmara. I will quote here what Mr. T. Diesen, marine adviser to the Department of Marine, Addis Ababa, said in one of his 240 notes to the head of the department on 9 January 1957: "No final decision has been taken on the single authority to deal with maritime affairs. This has resulted in little action having as yet been taken by the Department of Marine on the implementation of our plans or practical steps to utilize the budget which it should control. No government can expect successfully to run its maritime affairs the way the Imperial government is doing today." From the day the head office for the Department of Marine was established in Addis Ababa with Dejazmatch Zewde Gebre Selassie as its director general in January 1954, all the steps to close the Asmara Department of Marine under Director General Abebe Bitew, appointed by Ras Andarge in the middle of 1952 and the Marine Adviser Mellisinos had failed. The shelves of the registry of the Department of Marine were half-filled with documents concerning this matter.

The first step I took after receiving my letter of appointment in November 1957 was to write a letter to the director general, Abebe Bitew, instructing him to close the department and to report to the head office in Addis Ababa. The marine adviser Mellisinos was posted as deputy port manager to Assab and the rest of the staff, furniture, vehicles, etc. were to be handed over to the port manager in Massawa. I copied the letter to the viceroy. When they received this instruction, they simply laughed and asked: "Who does he think he is?

Can't he learn from his predecessors? All their efforts got them nowhere." They did not care even to respond to my instruction letter. But the viceroy's office responded for him on the basis of the copy they received. The response was that the letter had been received but that the department was established by the viceroy's office and I had no authority to close it.

A week after I received this response the emperor was leaving for his annual visit to Massawa and I left Addis one day ahead of him to wait for him there. The same day he arrived, I requested an audience. I was told to go to the palace the same afternoon at 4 p.m. I was the first to see him. He was sitting on the veranda with the viceroy, who stood.

"Your Majesty," I said. "You graciously appointed me only three weeks ago to this high office. I am now doubting whether I will be able to carry its heavy burden of responsibility. If I am not allowed to run the department the way I feel is right, I will not be prepared to take the responsibility upon myself. The way the department has been run for five years with two authorities fighting one another, is not what I am prepared to do. When I attempted to use the authority that was conferred upon me by you as the head of the department, I was laughed at and this is the letter I received. Read the letter. In this case, your Majesty, I prefer to be relieved of my responsibility. If something will go wrong in a setup like this, the actor is someone else but the blame received is the one officially appointed, who is known both by your Majesty and the public and l will not be a party to such an arrangement."

Then the emperor turned to the viceroy to respond. He replied saying he established the Asmara Department of Marine just as one of the federal government's offices, like the representatives of commerce, finance, etc., which he found necessary. In the case of maritime services, I said, that was a different matter. Those government agencies took their directives and orders from their head office, if what he said was correct. I had written to Abebe Bitew about closing the Asmara Department of Marine, but he did not respond.

The emperor interrupted me and said: "We would go back to the matter the following morning with other officials present. For now do you have other matters to raise?" I said: "Your Majesty, until this matter is settled, who am I to bring up other matters?" The emperor replied: "All right, you go now. We will see tomorrow."

I walked down the steps to the lower veranda of the ground floor where all the federal government's officials from Asmara, local officials, and those from Addis crowded and mingled. I was down there for only five minutes when the viceroy came down, looking gloomy, and called to his director general, Abebe Bitew. With a sad voice he told him to comply with the letter he had received from me because it had been decided that the department should be closed. Abebe Bitew could not control his emotions and broke into tears.

6. Assistant Minister (November 1957-December 1960)

So ended the drama of the Asmara Department of Marine. Abebe Bitew begged the viceroy to approach Eskinder Desta, the navy commander, so he could be transferred to the naval department in Addis Ababa. Mellisinos went to the viceroy's office as his personal adviser. I appointed as liaison officer an ex-police major Bemnet Gebre-Amlak, an independent-minded individual who managed to frustrate all further efforts on the part of the viceroy to interfere in the activities of the department. What was surprising was that the budget voted for the Asmara department was in the range of Eth$3 million while that of the head office was only half a million. Where all that money had been allocated was a mystery because there was no development plan or project related to the budget.

So I was faced with the problem of utilizing the money before the end of the budget year. I had no idea how all that money could be spent, and I had only eight months left. So I had my support staff work out a viable project which would utilize the money. A coastal shipping project was identified as a priority. A consulting firm, Sir J. H. Biles and Company of London, was commissioned to prepare the details of drawings and specifications and contract documents, and to issue tenders. A German shipbuilding firm, D. W. Kremer and Sohne, won the tender and the contract was signed in April 1960 for a 1,000 ton coaster to be delivered on 31 May 1961.

Mr. Diesen, the marine adviser, was asked to prepare office organization for the headquarters with directions for staff work and a complete distribution of duties for the staff: preparation and introduction of a new filing system and training of staff; drafting and finalization of new port regulations for Assab, Massawa and Lake Tana, and fishery regulations; regulations on steering and navigation; preparation of drafts for the basic regulations of conditions of service for seamen; control of seaworthiness of ships; manning and registration of ships; a five-year plan to cover the development of the civilian maritime service, including the establishment of the infrastructure for merchant shipping; and a fishery development plan to cover both marine and inland fisheries.

Mr. Hoeft, the expert in port engineering and planning, was asked to review the Assab Port Project and recommend modifications. To assist him in this and also to supervise the construction, a Norwegian consulting firm, Norconsult, was engaged to complete the review work before the arrival of the contractor. It was decided that if the review resulted in major modifications it would be necessary to negotiate with the contractor without hampering the progress of the construction. For all of this we had only three months. However, the review identified the areas where modification was required in the breakwater, the transit sheds, and the quayside cranes which would result in a cost-saving of about Eth$6 million. We started negotiating with the contractor on a way to reinvest the savings on necessary additions to the port facilities, major items which would include provision of a fresh water supply, a security fence, cold storage facilities, fire protection, an access road, and port and customs buildings.

The contractor agreed to the project's modifications prepared jointly with the consulting engineers and the port engineering expert. These changes in the specifications had to be endorsed by the original authority who had signed the contract document. At first I thought this would not present a problem since the modifications reduced the cost by Eth$6 million which would result in additional facilities vital to the whole project of providing port facilities. With this justification in mind, I presented the modified project document for signature to Ras Abebe Aregai, the minister of defense. The contractors were already on site doing preparation work at this tme. To my great disappointment, the minister refused to endorse the changes. His reason was that he never signed any document written in a foreign language. He had signed the original document because he had been ordered to do so by the emperor.

So it meant I had to present the new document to the emperor and have him ordered to sign it. This process was going to take a long time and I had to think of a time-saving device. I called the contractor and asked him to prepare for the laying of the foundation stone and to arrange for the director of Pomgrad to be present. Within a matter of two weeks, every preparation had been made. I requested His Majesty to lay the foundation stone. He readily agreed. I informed the minister of defense and gave him a prepared speech to read at the ceremony. He declined and asked me to deliver the speech myself. The consulting engineers were asked to prepare a briefing explanation of the advantages of the additional facilities incorporated in the modified project document. On 25 March 1958, His Imperial Majesty laid the foundation stone for the port facilities at Assab, comprising two half-jetties to provide six berths for Victory-type commercial ships, a 700-meter-long breakwater, four transit sheds, administration buildings for the port office and customs, a security fence for the port area, water supply for Assab town as well as the port, an access road, cold storage facilities, and berthing facilities for a small coasters.

After the ceremony, the emperor was briefed on the modification to the original project and I requested that he instruct the minister of defense who signed the original document to endorse the document containing the modification. The minister of defense was present. The emperor responded with approval but did not give the instruction to sign on the spot. I repeatedly reminded the emperor that it was important to give the instruction then and there but his response was : "Yes, we shall do it." My strategy failed. The emperor returned to the capital the next day without instructing the minister of defense to sign. This was going to delay the contractors who were ready to start. We were going to have to pay penalties of Eth$100,000 per day. I had to

6. Assistant Minister (November 1957-December 1960)

find a way out. Perhaps it was the emperor's way of making me go to the palace every day, but I am allergic to waiting for things to happen.

There was an Assab Port Construction Implementing Committee which the emperor had established. I was the chairman. Assistant Minister for Public Works Ato Kebede Abozen and two director generals from the Ministry of Commerce and Industry, Ato Araya Equba-Igzi and Ato Assefa Defaye, were members. The former was a man of action and I had no probem working with him, but the latter two were obstacles to any progress. They placed more importance on formalities than practical steps; they would be wasting time. So Kebede and I got together and drew up the procedure for the committee so as to have a quorum without the two with the chairman having two votes. Whenever the committee met, a notice was sent to the two which was so late as to exclude them from attending; therefore, Kebede and I met to decide on the agenda's matters.

On returning to Addis Ababa, I called an extraordinary committee meeting in which only Kebede was present. We discussed the problem facing the implementation of the project because of the delay in endorsing the modified documents and its consequences which resulted in unnecessary penalties. We decided that I should endorse the modified project document in order for the contractors to proceed with their work. I called the chief engineer of the contractor and told him I had been instructed to endorse the document. We both endorsed it and the construction work was completed six months ahead of schedule without any problem.

Another incident that resulted from the modifications was the extra funds required for the laboratory tests for the breakwater alignment. The usual procedure to get an extra budget was to prepare a memorandum to present to the emperor and appear in the palace once a week with it. If that fixed day was missed because the emperor was busy with other government problems, one had to wait for another week. This would go on for a month. So I went down to Assab and sent an urgent telegram to the emperor stating that unless these funds were immediately authorized, the progress of the construction work was going to be hampered and one day of delay in the activities of the contractors would make the government liable for payment of penalties of Eth$100,000. I begged a response to enable me to take immediate action on the matter. I got the approval immediately and the laboratory test was carried out by Hanover Institute of Hydro-technology.

While the construction of the Assab Port was in progress, the Department of Marine embarked on an inland water development program for both waterways and fisheries. On Lake Tana, inland waterway transportation had been operating since 1948 by a private company called Navigatana. This company had been established by refloating for motorboats the Italians had sunk when they were thrown out of the country. When Ras Andarge was governor of Begemdir, he had given permission to an Italian entrepreneur, formerly an official of the Italian regime called Commandatore Buschi, to refloat these boats. Ras Andarge and Buschi went into partnership to operate inland water transportation on Lake Tana between Gorgora on the Begemdir side and Bahr-Dar, a distance of 90 nautical miles.

Although this company was providing a useful service to the area, its charges were exorbitant, taking full advantage of a monopoly free of any government control. Safety was ignored with boats operating from makeshift landings without any navigational aids whatsoever. To carry 100 kg of farm product from Bahr-Dar to Gorgora the charge was Eth$6. This could have been transported for 100 percent profit at only 50 cents.

In order to bring this company under the control of the Department of Marine and lay the foundation for proper development of the inland water transportation system, we needed to provide landing facilities, navigational aids, port regulations, and a port authority in Bahr-Dar. Another German engineer, Mr. Spengler, was employed for the inland waterway project. The project consisted of landing facilities at Bahr-Dar, Zege and Gorgora, a warehouse, navigational aids, port office and residential house for the port manager, an electricity generator and fresh water at Bahr-Dar, and a motorboat. All was prepared and financed by the U.S. Technical Assistance Fund. A tariff was then set for transporting farm produce and other items, based on a calculation that would give the operating company a 75 percent profit. The new rate per 100 kg was 50 cents.

Navigatana started threatening to stop services after the tariff was activated. We responded by threatening expropriation because they had been using government property without paying rent for so many years. So they continued operation under the new tariff, always grumbling. Since this company was still owned jointly by Ras Andarge and Buschi, and the former had now been transferred from Eritrea to Addis Ababa as minister of interior, both got together and planned a strategy to annul the tariff regulation and revert to the old tariff. They waited for the moment I was out of the country. Two months after the new tariff had been operational, I had to go to Yugoslavia in connection with the Assab project. The very day I left Addis Ababa a telegram of protest against the new tariff was received by the emperor, sent in the name of the people of Gojam, who complained that the introduction of the new tariff had stopped the lake transportation that had been serving the region for the last 10 years. The emperor called the man acting on my behalf, Girma Belew, to the palace and asked him what this was all about. Girma explained the situation very well and the emperor appointed a committee chaired by Prime Minister Aklilu Habte-Wold. Girma sent me a telegram informing me of what had taken place and the date the committee was going to meet, urging me to be present.

I managed to finish my work in Yugoslavia and returned to Addis Ababa the very day the committee was going to meet. I arrived in the morning and the committee met in the evening at seven in the prime minister's office. I arrived there on time and found the prime minister with Ras Andarge and Mamo Tadesse, vice minister in the office of the prime minister. I think they were surprised to see me; they were expecting Girma. Before the meeting started, I requested the chairman to clarify in which capacity Ras Andarge was present, whether in his capacity as the minister of interior or as the president of Navigatana? The main issue was left and the prime minister adjourned the meeting, never to reconvene. Ras Andarge could not afford to press the issue further because he knew I was aware Navigatana paid no taxes and was not properly registered. The salvaged boats had been government property and no payment had never made to acquire them legally. He decided it would be wise to drop the matter because if he did not. I would raise all of these issues.

Another incident related to the same thing. In the Department of Marine, I had inherited a staff member who was related to Ras Andarge. A young man in his mid-twenties who had not been recruited into the department in the normal way, but imposed on us by a letter from the Ministry of Pen, which means by Imperial order. He was an incompetent and irresponsible young man. I put him in charge of the shipping section and found him hopeless. As the head of the shipping section, he was scheduled to fly to Bahr-Dar in company of the marine adviser, Mr. Diesen, to inspect the grounding of one of the motorboats of Navigatana. When he arrived at the airport, the flight had already left.

Instead of coming to the office and reporting that he had missed his flight, he went back to his house. He took the next day's flight to Bahr-Dar. In the meantime the marine adviser, who took the scheduled flight, arrived at Bahr-Dar and finished his work, returning to Addis Ababa on the aircraft the young man took to Bahr-Dar. All the expenses incurred by him for that mission were recovered by deducting from his monthly salary. He had an uncle in the Ministry of Defense who was personnel manager; he went there and complained. His uncle called me on the phone and asked why I did this. I replied: "Ask me in writing and I will send you the complete report." I heard no more.

Anyhow, I thought I might make better use of this hopelessly incompetent and lazy young man if I sent him to Bahr-Dar as the deputy port manager when I introduced the new tariff so he could fight it out with his uncle's company. When he received the letter of appointment, he went to the Ministry of Defense and complained that I was sending him out of Addis Ababa while his position in the department there was confirmed by the letter from the Ministry of Pen. He brought a letter from the Ministry of Defense stating that the step I had taken to send him to Bahr-Dar was contrary to the letter that had secured him the position in the department so I was advised to withdraw my instruction. I responded, stating that the letter from the Ministry of Pen did not entitle the staff to be pensioned on the department. On the contrary, he was sent to work and it was the responsibility of the head of the department to asign the staff where they could be more productive. I had given him an assignment and if he did not report for duty as he had been instructed, he was immediately dismissed from the organization by copy of this letter. That was the last I saw of him.

Although one would have thought the case was closed, after 10 months' silence to my great surprise the minister of defense appointed a committee to look into that complaint against the Department of Marine.

In spite of the findings of the committee, which supported the action taken by the department, it recommended his reinstatement to his new position and payment of half of his salary for the time he did not report to work because he was waiting for a decision from the ministry. The department responded by refuting this decision.

I was told he came back to the department when he heard my name in the news as one of the ringleaders in the attempted coup of December 1960 and ordered the staff to take down from the notice board any paper with my signature on or any picture in which I appeared. I have been informed that my succesor, Ketema Abebe, paid him compensation on account of the action I had taken. The Lake Tana project was completed by 1959 and became fully operational. The construction work for landing facilities was in progress at Lake Abaya when the attempted coup took place. I was scheduled to go there on a field visit the following Thursday, but the coup took place on Tuesday night.

Lake Tana is a freshwater lake, 90 kilometers long and 60 kilometers wide in the northwest region and is shared by the large Amhara-dominated provinces of Begemdir and Gojam. It is the source of the Blue Nile and the Tissisat waterfall is 30 kilometers south from the mouth of the lake. The town of Bahr-Dar is located at the edge of the outlet on the western side of the river along the border of the lake. The altitude is 1700 meters above sea level. The climate is moderately hot and ideal for growing all kinds of tropical fruits and crops and raising livestock. The lake, full of Nile perch, has islands famous for their age-old monasteries. Traditional lake transportation is boats made from the reed which grows along the border of the lake and islands. It is amusing to see what can be transported with these fragile-looking boats, including sheep, goats and heavy loads of grain. One famous patriot, Fitawrari Ambaw, told me he used these reed boats to attack the Italian army at Bahr-Dar. The inhabitants along the border of the lake use the water freely for drinking and washing, but analysis shows the lake water is infested with bilharzia. The water supply for the town is taken from the lake, but chemically treated.

Lake Abaya is another freshwater lake in the southern region and like Lake Tana, it is shared by the two large southern provinces of Gamu-Gofa and Sidamo, both inhabited by different ethnic groups. Both provinces are potentially rich with fertile soil, natural forest, and minerals such as gold which was being exploited from Sidamo. The lake is rich in Nile perch and is the easiest, cheapest means of linking the two provinces to exchange their agricultural products and develop social contacts.

Baro River, which rises in the western region of Ethiopia in Illubabor Province, is a tributary of the White Nile in Sudan. Baro River is navigable during the rainy season when the water level rises for three months in a year. The British administration of the Sudan had a special agreement with Ethiopia in the time of Menilek to establish a trading enclave inside Ethiopian territory 50 kilometers from the border along the Baro River by creating a river port there. The enclave was an enclosure of about 80 hectares of land bordering the Baro River. Very fertile, red flat land, suitable for growing all tropical fruits like mangoes, bananas, and oranges was cultivated in the enclave which served as a free port for merchandise imported from Sudan. A large percentage of the trading community of the country established themselves in the enclave and it became a prosperous village of about 600 inhabitants.

When the British administration of the Sudan came to an end in 1954, the enclave returned to Ethiopia. The administration of the river port became the responsibility of the Department of Marine. One of the inland water development projects of the Department of Marine concerned Baro River transportation. On the basis of this project, in 1958 the Department of Marine got the U.S. Technical Assistance Fund to provide a 25-passenger motorboat. The boat was built at Massawa shipyard by Brunnelo, transported to Gambela via Port Sudan through Khartoum and reached Gambela after a three-month journey.

Mr. Diesen, the marine adviser of the department, and I had been sent to Gambela in June 1954 to make a survey to assess the development needs and administrative requirements. We recruited two members of the local tribe (Yambo) and sent them to Massawa to be trained in the marine maintenance workshop and in the operation of motorboats. The whole idea was that after they mastered the training they would be brought back to Gambela to man the operation. But they turned out to be outstanding in their field of training and became indispensable in Massawa, one as a port pilot and the second as chief engineer in one of the merchant ships. One of the priorities of the department was manpower development in all fields of its activities—marine engineering, pilotage, fishery, management, etc. As a result of the extensive training program within eight years every service was manned by Ethiopians. Tessema Gizaw, one of the eight trainees sent to Holland to be trained as tugboat operators noted in the preceding chapter, pursued his training further, eventually qualifying to be the only Lloyds Surveyor for that part of the Red Sea region.

The merchant shipping section of the department was set to study how to go about operating the coastal ship being built in Germany. The study resulted in two alternatives. To set up a shipping company with one small coaster would not be economical. Alternative one was to lease the ship on time charter basis to a company with good shipping experience. Alternative two was to organize the merchant shipping section to carry out the business operation, with the technical operation to be carried out by the port administration operating the coaster on a liner basis. F.I. Massawa, Jeddah, the Yemen ports, Assab, Djibouti, and Aden made an agreement with an existing shipping agent for the freight and passenger booking and cargo handling at these ports. The advantage of this was the opening of a good outlet for agricultural products and diversion of some of the trade from mother ports to our ports for transhipment, thus creating the nucleus for the development of national shipping. The Ethiopia shipping company of today grew from that single coaster and its present general manager is none other than Tessema Gizaw.

As the result of the reorganization of the Department of Marine undertaken soon after the closing of the department in Asmara in early 1958 which inevitably expanded the activities of the department, maritime legal questions had to be taken care of and the need for a legal adviser became evident. Mr. J. Vogt, a Norwegian, was employed with an Ethiopian assistant, Kibret, who was a student in the Faculty of Law at Addis Ababa University. There was always a tendency to employ foreign advisers throughout the Ethiopian government and they had their uses.

The emperor always wanted to please foreign advisers and so was deferential toward them. He was so keen to project himself as modern in his thinking that it became his Achilles' heel since anything at all which could be presented to him as having the support of foreign advisers won his easy acquiescence. It was comparatively easy to manipulate the emperor by dressing up any necessary changes as modernization, submitting one copy of them to the ministry and another copy to the emperor himself. He always went for projects which were grandiose rather than simpler projects which were practical in nature. His personal interests always came first.

The inland water development project required the employment of one expatriate engineer, Mr. Spengler, a German, with one Ethiopian assistant engineer, Mekonnen. Fishery development required one fishery expert and two Ethiopian officers, one each for Assab and Massawa. I should mention here the importance of fish in the Ethiopian diet because of our religion. Fish

6. Assistant Minister (November 1957-December 1960)

was eaten on Wednesdays, Fridays, and throughout Lent. Wednesday was the day of Christ's imprisonment and Friday the day of his crucifixion. On these days, no animal products—milk, eggs, or meat—were eaten. Pigs, of course, were not kept or eaten at all.

The Department of Marine was housed in a two-story, six-room building. With this expansion the need for larger office accommodation became evident, so I prepared a memorandum to the emperor explaining that need. On the basis of this request, the authority responsible for government property under the Ministry of Finance was instructed to provide the department with a government building with enough room for its needs. I was shown one of these buildings at Kasa-Inchis, a residential apartment of two stories, occupied by four families. I asked the Director General Ato Guessess what was to become of the occupants. "It is their problem!" he responded. I said: " But this building is constructed for residential use and now to convert it for office use requires modification and that will involve quite a lot of expense." "That is your problem," he responded. I went back to my office and called the department engineering staff, briefed them on the problem and asked them to go and see the building and work out an estimate to convert it for office accommodation. With this estimate in hand, I asked the engineers to prepare a plan for an office building to meet our needs adjoining the existing one occupied by the department.

A two-story building with 12 office rooms and one conference room with toilet facilities was prepared and estimated to cost Eth$60,000. The estimate to modify the residential house was Eth$40,000, so I prepared another memorandum to the emperor revealing these facts and requesting him to authorize the Eth$60,000 so we could build the office accommodation, instead of spending Eth$40,000 to demolish the residential building. He authorized this and construction work started immediately. It was completed in less than six months. When I went to Addis Ababa in September 1988, I went to visit the Department of Marine, now the "Marine Transport Authority," and I found only one staff member of the old group, Abebe Menasse, the registry clerk who is now chief of the registry. Abebe was so pleased to see me and excitedly introduced me to the others saying: "He was the one who established the department, he was our boss." He accompanied me to the office of the head of the Marine Transport Authority, Commander Zeleke Bogale, who was occupying the same office that was occupied by all predecessors. Zeleke was one of the first naval cadet recruits so we knew each other. He has been heading the organization since the changes of 1974. He has expanded the organization. I noted a third floor added to the office building, and consultants were working on the tender document for the construction of the second phase of the Assab Port. I was very pleased to see the progress made by the organization.

The Emperor's Clothes

Until late 1958, the Department of Marine was responsible for the administration of the naval training establishment in Massawa. Eskinder Desta, the grandson of the emperor, who had been undergoing naval training in England, got his first naval officer's commission in 1958 and returned home. So with the rank of commander, he was appointed to head the establishment under the Ministry of Defense.

The succession was simple; there were only files concerning the naval establishment. The only staff member specifically assigned to deal with naval question was Commodore Lund, so I handed over the responsibility of the Naval School to Eskinder with all of the files and transferred Commodore Lund. During this process a minor incident took place. Usually at lunch time I left the office half an hour earlier than the official time and returned half an hour earlier. One afternoon when I went back to the office I heard someone typing in Commodore Lund's office and I opened the door to see who it was at such an unusual hour. There was Commodore Lund startled at the sight of me and very apologetic saying he was doing something for Eskinder which he requested Lund not to reveal to me. I was embarrassed, I had not asked him what he was doing. As a matter of fact, I was going to express my appreciation for his conscientiousness in coming to the office half an hour earlier to do his work, but the fact that he was doing something behind my back made him feel guilty and he started to talk about it.

As I said, I was embarrassed that Eskinder should conspire with my subordinate, especially a foreigner. So I said to Lund: "No, do not worry. I know about it and I was the one who told Eskinder to tell you like that so that you yourself could take care of it." I put him at ease and left him to continue. Later in the afternoon I saw Eskinder entering the gate. When he came out from his car I called him from the window and asked him to come to my office before he went to see Lund. I told him of the incident and criticized him for his lack of confidence in himself. I asked him to amend his silly blunder by confirming to Lund what I had told him about the secrecy being my suggestion. Although I dismissed this matter from my mind after I talked to him, it seems that Eskinder was holding a grudge against me and trying to find an excuse to undermine my position by creating obstacles against the progress of the Department of Marine's activities.

About six months later, the emperor was in Massawa for his annual visit. I was awakened in Addis Ababa, and one night after midnight I was woken by a telephone call: "This is from Massawa palace. You are instructed by His Majesty to report here tomorrow. If there is no commercial flight, take the air force transport plane from Bishoftu scheduled to fly here." I knew at once some great disaster must have occurred at Massawa and after that, I could not sleep with worry. At five I called the Ethiopian Airlines office to find out if there is a flight to Asmara and was told there was one taking off at seven, so I went to my office to leave a note informing them I had left for Asmara and to tell the liaison officer to meet me at the Asmara airport.

When I checked in at the Chiao Hotel in Massawa at 1 p.m., I met the viceroy. Fortunately for me it was no longer Ras Andarge, but General Abiy Abebe. There in the lobby of the hotel he greeted me: "Oh, you have arrived. The situation is under control because I have intervened. Eskinder told the emperor that you were sabotaging his work by issuing uniforms similar to the Navy to the port office staff. The emperor was mad about it and ordered for you to report, but when I informed him that what I know about the uniform he calmed down. Most probably he may not even raise it. Anyhow you take your lunch and rest a bit and come to the palace at 4 p.m."

I was relieved to hear that, had a good appetite for my lunch, and rested two hours before going to the palace. As usual, there were many people standing and waiting outside so I mingled in the crowd. After about 20 minutes the emperor appeared on the veranda and walked down the flight of stairs, so I moved forward and bowed so that he could see me. I heard him say "Endet senebetk," which means "How have you been?" He entered his automobile and drove to the naval base. We all followed for a tea party given by Eskinder. He returned to the palace about 6:30 p.m. The next morning, I went to the palace at 8 a.m. to arrange to escort him around the port to see development activities. The real reason for my having been disturbed, Eskinder's complaint, was not mentioned.

From the palace I went to the port office and discussed with the port manager, Captain Mortimer, the emperor's program to visit the port. We drew up the program together so the emperor could be shown what development had taken place since his last visit two or three years before. We arranged for him to be well briefed on the significance of the port office staff is uniform in terms of efficient management and presentation in compliance with international shipping practices. The same afternoon I submitted the program and the next day from 11 a.m. to 1 a.m. the visit took place. He was pleased with what he saw so I took leave and returned to Addis Ababa.

I owed to General Abiy, the new viceroy, this turn of good fortune. Had this incident taken place during the time of Ras Andarge the story would have been told quite differently. On the whole, I was very lucky throughout my career. Whenever I found myself in a potentially tight corner, somebody would come to my aid quite out of the blue. General Abiy succeeded Ras Andarge in late 1958. He was a real gentleman, a man of principle and integrity. We had not known each other prior to his appointment to Eritrea. After he came to know me through my work with the ports of Massawa and Assab, he became one of my supporters and that is why he came to my aid when the emperor got enraged against me on account of his grandson, Eskinder. It had been suggested that I was usurping the prerogatives of the emperor by granting commissions to port office staff which were comparable to naval commissions.

I was to cross swords with Eskinder again over the matter of Mr. Diesen, the marine adviser. Mr. Diesen was an officer who served in the Norwegian Navy with the rank of commander. During the Second World War, he joined the British Royal Air Force and reached the rank of group captain. After the war, he served in various capacities with English maritime organizations. He applied through the Ethiopian embassy in London in 1954 for a maritime adviser's post in the Department of Marine and was employed.

Diesen was full of energy and initiative, quick in mind, well-informed, and always ready to assist. He served three heads of the department: Zewde, Mikael, and me. I liked his openness, drive, and positive attitude. Both of us served under my predecessors and our minds always met. We cooperated closely in trying to solve the problems the department was facing. When I became the head, that cooperation started to show more tangible results. The progress made within a short period of time after I took over startled people who saw themselves as my political enemies.

The progress made was due to the fact that I took over everything in preparation under previous heads of the department and implemented the plan. But those who were watching with jealousy and wished me doom, thought the progress was due to the advice of Mr. Diesen so they tried to find a pretext to get rid of him. They were particularly determined to see him gone because he had been critical of their incompetence. The commander of the navy, Eskinder Desta, was used for the purpose. He told his grandfather, the emperor, that as long as Mr. Diesen remained as the adviser of the Department of Marine, all his efforts were being frustrated. He submitted all sorts of fabricated evidence prepared by his adviser, Commodore Lund, who was an archenemy of Diesen and was afraid of me after that afternoon incident in the office.

So the emperor called the minister of defense, Ras Abebe Aregai, and instructed him to terminate the contract of Mr. Diesen. In May 1960, the minister called me to his office and asked me about the contractual status of Mr. Diesen. I informed him that I had renewed the contract recently for two years. He said: "It is the emperor's order that his contract should be terminated." I said: "All right, but what good reason do we have?" I already knew Eskinder was trying to bring this about. I informed the minister Eskinder was, feeding the emperor false information to come to this decision. I was not going to take any step to cancel Mr. Diesen's contract to satisfy Eskinder's destructive ideas. If I was to be presented with satisfactory evidence that Mr. Diesen had committed anything against the interests of Ethiopia, I would not hesitate to see that he was thrown out of the country within 24 hours.

6. Assistant Minister (November 1957-December 1960)

The minister said: "But this cannot be your answer to an order of the emperor." I said:" Yes sir. I beg you to inform the emperor exactly what I have said here and now." The morning after the incident at the minister's office I had a telephone call from the minister of states of the Ministry of Pen, Ato Gebre-Wold Engda. He said: "How is it that you refuse to execute the orders of your superior?" I responded that I was not in the habit of executing orders blindly; I was conscious of my responsibility to answer for my actions and therefore I only took orders from my superiors when my conscience was clear. That was the end of the conversation. Here again I was lucky.

The man in charge of the Ministry of Pen was a docile man, not powerful and decisive like his predecessor, Wolde-Georgis, who would never have attempted to deal with such a matter on the telephone but would have instead called me to his office and given me a tough time. The office of the minister of pen was the decisive arm of the emperor to appoint or to demote. Just a signal of dissatisfaction was sufficient for the minister to take any action against the person concerned. Fortunately for me, this minister was devoid of any initiative and only executed specific orders which, fortunately for me also, this emperor seldom gave.

On the second day after that telephone conversation, I had a telephone call in my house at 6 a.m. from Ato Mekonnen Habte-Wold, the minister of commerce, who wanted me to go to his office immediately. He started the conversation by stating that I have offended the emperor by refusing to take orders. Why should I do this? He went on telling me about the virtues of the emperor, how he was working day and night to overcome the many problems the country was facing and how it was our duty to serve him so that he succeeded in his endeavor. I started to wonder why I was hearing this from Ato Mekonnen, who had nothing to do with Department of Marine. I had heard stories about Ato Mekonnen being the secret arm of the emperor to punish those thought to oppose the government. I saw how concerned he was. It was the same man who had behaved so well over the matter of Assab Port and Ras Andarge, yet here he was ending his lecture with the admonition that to disobey the emperor was like disobeying God. I explained the background of the whole affair in detail and said if the emperor wanted to listen to his grandson and please him by taking such improper action, he could do it by removing me from the department. I was not going to be an instrument for such action. Fortunately, Ato Mekonnen knew Mr. Diesen also. After he heard the background of the case, he did not try to argue the matter.

Some weeks later I got another early morning call from Ato Mekonnen and found him looking happier. He said: "Since I spoke to you last, I have been thinking how to bring about a rapprochement between yourself and the emperor. Luckily the emperor has now asked me to recommend to him somebody of

The Emperor's Clothes

integrity who can carry out an important and sensitive assignment. I have given your name and you can expect a summons to the palace at any moment. I ask you please not to be stubborn but to carry out whatever the emperor assigns you to do to his satisfaction. I am doing everything I can for the emperor to know you better." It struck me at the time that Ato Mekonnen was naive if he thought the emperor did not know me, but it was not polite to say so. I thanked him for his kind concern and left.

The same day I was called to the palace and was ushered immediately into the study to see the emperor. He received me with the smile he always used when he wished to put somebody at his ease. He spoke gently to me and outlined the assignment which I was to carry out. It sounded to me like a matter for the security service, but in view of the work which Ato Mekonnen had done to try to bring about an understanding, it seemed better not to say so abruptly. I tried to avoid the assignment by making the excuse that I was the only official of the Department of Marine and that all of my efforts to have an assistant appointed together with heads of the various sections had failed.

When I pointed out to the emperor that I could not leave the department without an official head to act in my absence, he replied: "Call the staff members you want to appoint right now." Unfortunately, all but two were out of the capital on a mission and I lost a golden opportunity to have them appointed on the spot. However, the director of fisheries, Wold-Aregai Reda-Igzi, and the principal secretary of the department, Girma Belew, were called and appointed. Now I had no option but to carry out the wishes of the emperor.

It seemed a certain businessman from Asmara, Asfaw Mesfin, was the brother of a certain lady with connections to the palace as an informer. Asfaw had complained to the emperor, no doubt through his sister, that certain bank officials in Asmara were corrupt and were trying to block his purchase of the Fenili bottling company. I was to go to Asmara with Alemu Tessema, an official of the National Bank in Addis Ababa, to investigate the complaint.

We left the next day and it would appear that Asfaw was informed of our arrival in Asmara by the palace informer because the same evening we arrived, he looked us up at the hotel, introduced himself, and told us he had important information which would simplify our mission. He gave a document to Alemu which purported to be a letter of intent from Fenili for the sale of the company for Eth$1,500,000. He dropped crude hints that if the matter could be speedily concluded in his favor a suitable bribe would be forthcoming as soon as he secured the bank loan he was looking for. The deal stank.

The next morning we went to the criminal police and asked them to verify the signature on the letter of intent. It proved to be a forgery. We then took Asfaw with us to see Fenili, who repudiated the alleged signature. He told us

Asfaw had expressed an interest in buying his factory and that they had verbally agreed on a figure of Eth$700,000 but nothing had been reduced to writing. We took them both to a notary public, recorded statements from them and returned to Addis Ababa to report to the emperor. In reporting back to the emperor, I told him I was disgusted that such a swindler should have access to him and be given so much attention. The emperor dismissed my comments as childish. This all occurred in September 1960.

Three months later, Ato Mekonnen was one of the 13 people killed in the abortive coup. He died without ever understanding the true nature of the emperor whom he served with such loyalty and dedication. He could never understand the difference between the personal interests of the emperor and those of the nation. However, during his life I was able to appeal to the better side of his complex personality to promote the national interest.

7

Attempted Coup D'Etat

By 1960, every thinking man in Ethiopia was ready for the removal of the emperor. He had lost the confidence of the people when he fled the country during the Italian invasion. He had alienated the natural leaders of the various provinces and also those of the patriotic movement by ignoring them and appointing his own henchmen about him. He had lost the confidence of young progressive men in his administration because of the corruption he allowed to flourish. He was a weak leader kept in power only by the Imperial Guard. It would be thought that if the Imperial Guard turned against him, with the support of his chief of security, he would be finished. They did turn against him, yet the emperor survived.

He survived because of the incompetence of the two men responsible for the attempt against him and the fact that they did not take into their confidence at the outset men who would have willingly supported the coup if they could only have known it was to be attempted. One such man was myself. I was an assistant minister in the government, but felt my loyalty was to the best interests of Ethiopia, not to a leader who put self-interest above his duty. Events proved that there were many like me, but we were prevented from participating in the planning of the coup because we knew nothing about it in advance. To some extent this was a result of the Emperor's policy of ruling by dividing. Nobody knew for sure, in an atmosphere of opportunism, who could be trusted.

On 8 December 1960, Mr. Niasmic, the director of Pomgrad, the contractors for the Assab Port project, arrived in Addis Ababa from Split, Yugoslavia, and was joined by the chief engineer of the company, Mr. Tartalia, from Assab. On Monday, 11 December, we met at the Department of Marine to discuss the progress of the construction work. The agenda was so long we adjourned and continued the next day. On Tuesday night, the Department of Marine organized a dinner at the Ras Hotel which was attended by the minister of state in the Ministry of Defense, General Nega Haile Selassie, the two guests from Pomgrad, Mr. Diesen, Mr. Hoeft, myself and others. At the end of the dinner, the minister of state excused himself, saying he was not feeling well. The rest of us stayed for coffee and did not leave the hotel until after eleven. The next morning I got up early as usual and left the house at six, with the intention of returning for breakfast. My friend, Kebede Abebe, had entrusted me with the supervision of the construction of his house when he had been sent unexpectedly on an ambassadorial assignment to Nigeria and early morning was the most convenient time for me to meet the contractor.

Wrapped in a gabi, which is a homespun toga-like garment, I set off in my VW for the site. As I turned onto the main road to town, I passed a group of soldiers of the Imperial Bodyguard at the road junction. As I returned half an hour later I was stopped by one of the soldiers in the group, who by then had been joined by a crowd of civilians. The soldier ordered me out of the car, but I told him that I was only going as far as my house 200 meters away. When he became insistent, I lost my temper and demanded to know whether he had clearly understood whatever orders had been given to him or was merely harassing people to disturb the peace. Then my father stepped forward from the crowd and told me: "Why argue? You are not the only person who has been stopped and asked to leave their car. Park it there and walk to your house." I did, still not realizing there was a coup in progress. After all, who could have suspected the Imperial Bodyguard?

It was my intention to call the commander of the Imperial Bodyguard, General Mengistu Neway, at his house to complain, but I found my telephone was dead. My brother Melaku who lived next door had been a major in the Imperial Bodyguard until he was transferred to a staff appointment in Defense Headquarters. I called him from his house and, dressed in his uniform, he drove me to the road junction in his own VW which had a military registration. The soldiers saluted my brother and the officer commanding them whispered something in his ear. We drove on toward the headquarters of the First Army Division where we were stopped by Colonel Zewde who merely asked us where we were heading and allowed us to continue.

We arrived at the Bodyguard HQ, which was a modern, white, three-story office block with green windows. It faced the Imperial Palace named Genete Leul (The Paradise of the Prince). The car park was full, but there was no movement of people. My brother told me the Bodyguard officer at the road block had not told him specifically what was up, but that there was a serious problem and he should go to the office. Melaku added: "The other day, when the emperor was leaving for Brazil, the Bodyguard officers handed in a petition through their commanding officer which was critical of the government policy of discriminating between armed forces officers in pay scales." The substance of the petition was that the first graduate of the Harar academy, a lieutenant, was paid the same as a major, which was regarded as an insult by the rest of the armed forces who requested the anomaly be rectified.

The emperor's reaction to the petition was to throw a fit of rage and to promise the commanding officer of the Imperial Bodyguard that when he returned from Brazil he would teach them all a lesson. Once we reached the Imperial Bodyguard HQ, Melaku asked me to wait while he went inside. As I waited, I saw the arrival of the Addis Ababa police commander, Colonel Gashaw, and the minister of state in the Ministry of Foreign Affairs, Blata Dawit Iquba-Igzi (he is one of the thirteen killed). A young officer then came and called me into the office of Colonel Worqneh, the chief of security. Since he was the same age as my younger brother Melaku, Colonel Worqneh addressed me as gashe, or elder brother, and was pleased to see me. He had been the adjutant of the Ethiopian contingent to Korea in 1950 and was a sound administrator. He had been hand-picked by the emperor as chief of national security and when the emperor was told Worqneh was in the plot against him, he could not believe it at first.

In fact Worqneh was not in the plot, but found himself overtaken by a fait accompli. I asked him what was happening and he said, "Have you not heard? The crown prince has seized power." My immediate response was: "What stupidity, with the emperor in Brazil. The emperor will go straight to the United States to seek military assistance on the pretext that there has been a communist takeover. There will be unnecessary bloodshed. The better way would have been to detain the emperor and his supporters, replace them with your own men and then force the emperor to accept a constitutional monarchy. He would have accepted, but now you have given him a chance to destroy the country."

I feared American intervention because the Americans, like the British, always support the status quo in their foreign policy, believing that the devil they know is better than the angel they do not know. It is for this reason their foreign policy has largely failed in corners of the world where corrupt regimes have existed. They have supported these corrupt regimes until too late. Those running the corrupt regimes have been able to gain Western support by characterizing any opposition as communist. The opposition all too often has turned to the East not for ideological reasons but because it has posed as the only force willing to support the struggle against corrupt regimes.

Colonel Worqneh told me: "I know you are right, but I found out about the plot after the event. If I am seen to oppose change now, I will be killed by the plotters. I have decided that I would rather die fighting with them to bring about change." Worqneh had been out of touch at a critical stage of the instigation of the coup. Wishing to rest, he had given orders that he should not be disturbed. The insurgents repeatedly called him, only to be told by his servant that he was not around. It was only after most of the day was gone that he became aware of the coup. Colonel Worqneh fought bravely on the side of the plotters and died by his own hand when all was lost and he had only one round remaining.

Worqneh was telling me he had discovered the plot when two brothers, General Mengistu and Germame Neway walked in. They both saluted and said: "Well, the change is here. Let us cooperate." I replied, "You could have done much better than this, as commander of the Bodyguard." I broke off as Worqneh signaled me to hold my tongue but Germame, anticipating what I had been about to say, said: "Your way would not have been possible. The emperor was planning to scatter us to the four winds on his return from Brazil. My brother was to have been sent to Gojam and Tsige Dibu, the police commander, to Gamu Gofa. So this was the best opportunity we had to act while we still could."

I had been at the Teferi Mekonnen School with Germame, but since he was three or four classes ahead of me, we had no opportunity to become acquainted. He had been among the first group of pupils to be called to Haile Selassie Secondary School from Teferi Mekonnen School. I only got to know him after we had both returned from overseas studies. Germame had joined the Ministry of the Interior and after two or three years was appointed governor of Wolamo. He was a man with progressive ideas which, in Haile Selassie's regime, meant he was regarded as a leftist. Germame did nothing to play down his leftish image, choosing to parade around in combat fatigues with a red tie. He was a populist, alienating the landlords and endearing himself to the common people by dictating land reforms in Wolamo. He was then transferred from Wolamo to Ogaden, which was his official posting at the time of the coup. It is said that when the emperor was leaving for Brazil he demanded to know what Germame was doing in Addis Ababa and ordered him to return to his province immediately.

I found Germame to be a stubborn and headstrong man, unable to listen to reason. On the other hand, his elder brother, the commander of the Imperial Bodyguard, was docile and easily manipulated. That is the main reason why a golden opportunity for change was lost - a stubborn man at the helm with no proper plan and a pliant stooge following his every whim.

At nine in the morning following the discussion in Worqneh's office, Germame asked me to accompany him to the Ministry of Information four kilometers away to broadcast the crown prince's taped message of having taken over. We traveled in a chauffeur driven car, Germame with the tape in his left hand and a carbine slung over his right shoulder. We arrived at the Ministry of Information just as the staff was reporting for duty and were met by Beyene Desta, who later was to become general manager of telecommunications and is now with International Telecommunications Union (ITU) in Geneva. Germame demanded to know who could broadcast the tape and Beyene replied: "It is I, but I can only do so under instructions from my minister." Despite threats from Germame, he remained adamant that he would only broadcast the tape on orders from the minister, Amde-Mikael Dessalegni, whom Germame knew to be back at the Bodyguard HQ, so we drove back to fetch him. [Dessalegni was one of the 13 killed]

The brothers did not share the plot with certain key people until the die was cast. The command center for the coup was on the first floor of the Bodyguard HQ where I found the police commander, General Tsige Dibu, who looked thoroughly fed up. I asked him what was wrong and he told me: "I am disgusted because my association with these senseless, immature people has put me in an impossible situation. I was invited for dinner last night at Mengistu's house and it was only then that I realized what they were up to. I pleaded with them to let me go to Nazret to take command of the armored brigade, but they refused." General Tsige, although he had been transferred to command the police, was a career soldier well-respected by the army and if he had been allowed to go to the armored brigade, they would certainly have obeyed him and fallen in with the coup. He was cursing the day he had become involved with Mengistu. He was to die fighting on the third day of the coup.

On that first day of the coup I found Colonel Worqneh, as I left the conference room, with Mamo Tadesse, who was complaining about the rough treatment he had received at the hands of the soldiers at the airport, who had dragged him to the Bodyguard HQ by force. Mamo was a vice minister in the office of the prime minister and I remember that he warned me to stay out of the situation. Unlike some of us, he resisted the temptation to become opportunistically or emotionally involved. He remained in the Bodyguard HQ until evening when he asked Germame for permission to go home and was allowed to leave. He later became the minister of justice and then minister of finance, a post he retained until February 1974 when the Derg [the military junta] detained him for eight years. After his release I met him with his French wife in their Paris flat and found him grayed, but in good health. While I was with Mamo, Germame called us away to join the group of officers who were drafting a communique to foreign missions in the capital. In walked Ketema Yifru who was then a vice minister and private secretary to the emperor, but a good friend of Germame. Ketema was to become foreign minister a year later, but was also detained for eight years by the Derg. On his release he joined the World Food Programme in Rome and I met him in Lusaka in 1985. As he arrived at the HQ of the plot, he told Germame: "I heard you were looking for me so I drove here through the city. Everything is calm." We chose him as the man to draft the communique.

At 11 it became clear that there was opposition to the coup, led by the chief of staff, General Merid, and the commander of the ground forces, General Kebede Gebre. The support of these two had been taken for granted by the brothers, who had wasted their time and resources arresting harmless civilian ministers through the night while Merid and Kebede were taking over the First Division HQ, Worqneh advised General Mengistu to move against them, even if it meant fighting, but Mengistu believed he could capitalize on his friendship with Merid by persuading him to support the coup without bloodshed.

At the outset, the Imperial Bodyguard could have easily captured the two generals. The Bodyguard was a highly trained unit, complete with its own armored brigade, but the group opposed to the coup continued to grow in strength as it was joined by Ras Asrat Kassa, president of the Senate, Abuna Basileos, the Air Force Commander and all the army commanders. On the side of the coup, only the two brothers were carrying out the negotiations with the other side and nobody knows what they were thinking.

I spent most of the time with Worqneh and periodically Germame or the General would come in to tell us negotiations were going badly, although they would not say how they were going badly except that the other camp was growing in strength. They gave no information at all to the officers of the Bodyguard, except for five junior officers all of captain rank: Asrat Deferesu, Mamo Habte-Wold, Baye, Kifle, and Messel who were Mengistu's close friends. Baye was to die in the fighting and Kifle was sentenced to death and hanged. The rest had served prison terms and are still living, and even these men were told at the eleventh hour. If the brothers had only taken the trouble to brief the officers of the Bodyguard at the outset, the coup could have succeeded without bloodshed. The Bodyguard, which covered itself in glory in Korea, was the elite of the army.

Even now I find it incredible that Germame had no proper plan of the details needed to effect the coup. It was plain that it was no sudden impulse, but something he must have been planning from the time he returned from studies in the United States. With his brother placed as the only pillar on which the regime was supported, he should have succeeded, but managed to snatch defeat out of the jaws of victory because he took no one into his confidence. He could have learned from Ethiopian history what the simple peasants of Begemdir had done in 1774 when Emperor Tekle Georgis introduced a new tax which was contrary to the traditional system. The people of Begemdir sent a petition to the emperor which he refused to consider. They then called the regent, Ras Ali, to a big gathering and told him: "If you wish, you can be our representative and take over the administration of the country subject to our counsel. On the other hand, if you wish to remain loyal to the emperor, we are determined to settle the matter by force." Ras Ali accepted the offer of the people and became the governor. The emperor was informed that his power to govern had been taken from him and given to a representative of the people but that the emperor would remain in his palace since the Crown was a symbol of unity and tradition must be recognized.

So Germame and Mengistu had a precedent in Ethiopian history which they could have used to confront an unpopular and stubborn monarch face to face instead of trying to go behind his back. It is clear that they did not understand where the emperor's power base lay. They discounted the army completely in their assessment of potential opposition and concentrated on the civilian ministers. Their strategy seems to have been grounded in the belief that the emperor was so unpopular that just announcing his overthrow would lead to an upswell of support for the coup. They most probably thought that since they were the favored ones of the emperor and they were revolting against him everybody else would automatically follow suit. If they had only followed the advice of Worqneh and arrested the two generals, they would have succeeded. Instead, by nightfall on Wednesday, it became obvious a fight was imminent. At about 8 p.m. General Mengistu asked Worqneh to draw up a plan to attack the First Division HQ. The planning went on through the night, with everyone dozing off in their chairs.

The next day, Thursday 14 December, I went early in the morning to my house to find only the servants. My wife had taken the baby to her parents' home. I set off by an indirect route to avoid the First Division HQ. The road block where I had been stopped the day before had been abandoned by the Bodyguard and taken over by troops of the First Division. Since I had not been to the office the day before, I passed there to brief my staff on what was happening.

As I was talking, I was told there had been a radio announcement that General Mulugeta had been appointed chief of staff. I told my staff I would go to the Bodyguard HQ to verify the announcement and then return.

When I arrived at the Bodyguard HQ, I met General Mengistu in the corridor and asked him where General Mulugeta was. I said: "I have heard that he has been appointed as chief of staff. Where is he?" He turned to Major Addis-Alem, who was with him, and said: "Take Gaitachew to the general." I was taken to a small room on the second floor which was bare except for two small chairs and a canvas bed on which the general was laying. General Mulugeta had been detained by the plotters and thought I was being brought to join him in detention. He was not aware his name was being used to try to rally support for the coup and he asked me: "Why do they have to bring you?" I replied: "I came to see you when I heard that you had been appointed chief of staff." He sat up on the bed: "Who is appointed chief of staff?" I asked him: "Do you not know that since yesterday the crown prince has been in control of the country?"

He sat up in surprise and began to put on his shoes. As he did so one of the shoelaces snapped and Addis-Alem was sent to find another. It is quite probable that General Mulugeta, being very security-conscious, snapped the lace deliberately because once Addis-Alem left, he told me how he came to be in the HQ and asked me how the coup was proceeding. Mulugeta had been the popular founder of the Imperial Bodyguard until the emperor decided he was too popular and set out to isolate him. He was appointed chief of staff and succeeded by his deputy, Mengistu. The emperor succeeded in creating enmity between the two because Mulugeta had recommended that Mengistu be appointed acting commander of the Bodyguard. The emperor showed the recommendation to Mengistu and construed it to mean that Mulugeta wished to block his advancement. He then promoted Mengistu to the substantive rank of Bodyguard commander.

Mulugeta's appointment as chief of staff was meant to kick him upstairs, but Mulugeta chose to take his new duties seriously. He insisted that the chief of staff should have overall charge of all of the armed forces including the Bodyguard. The Bodyguard had never been part of the army, which was again a part of the emperor's divide-and-conquer tactics. The Bodyguard was trained by Swedish instructors in a college which was opened specially for the purpose and closed once their training had been completed. When Mulugeta made it plain that he was not willing to be a figurehead, he was removed and appointed as minister for social services. However, he still retained the popular support of the army at all ranks and the announcement that he had been reappointed chief of staff received great acclaim.

General Mulugeta knew he was out of favor. On the Tuesday night of the coup, Bodyguard officers and men went to his residence and told him he was required to go with them to Bodyguard HQ. General Mulugeta assumed the emperor, before his departure to Brazil, had ordered that he should be detained. His first reaction was to resist, but he was concerned for the safety of his small children with whom he was alone in the house, his wife being away to visit relatives in Lekemt. For the sake of the children, he went quietly, driving in his own car, followed by those who had been sent to pick him up. He had been placed in a room in the Bodyguard HQ and left wondering why nobody had come to interrogate him.

I asked the General how we could save the situation. "Well," he said, "Tell me first what strategic steps have been taken. Is the army cooperating? Have the provincial governors been asked to support the coup?" I interrupted him and told him nothing had been done. General Merid and Kebede Gebre had rallied the army at the First Division HQ and were ready for a showdown. The only step taken by Mengistu had been to detain the crown prince and force him to make a statement announcing that he was taking over power as a constitutional monarch. General Mulugeta said: "If that is the case, tell Mengistu to leave the country immediately any way he can and seek political asylum. Otherwise he will cause unnecessary bloodshed which can only result in the loss of his life and the country's degeneration into chaos like the Congo."

The General then asked me a favor which was to save my life. He asked me to go to his house and instruct the maid not to send his children to school. I left him and went to the house, but the Bodyguard soldiers guarding the house refused to admit me because the identity card which I had been issued by the coup makers the day before had to be renewed daily and mine had not. Instead of returning at once to the Bodyguard HQ to renew the card, I passed by the house of my in-laws to check on my wife and child whom I had not seen since the morning before. I took the chance of a hurried meal and while I was eating, machine gun and mortar fire broke out from the direction of the First Army HQ, with the thunder of jets overhead. I sprang up and made for the door, but was restrained by my father-in-law. By five the shooting became sporadic and we received the news that the Bodyguard soldiers were on the run. This did not surprise me because I knew nobody had informed them of what was going on nor, so far as I knew, had they been fed since Wednesday morning.

The sporadic firing continued all night Thursday, all day Friday and only on Saturday did it fall silent. I was sitting on the veranda with my father-in-law when my friend Negatu arrived, looking unusually grim. I asked him to pull up a chair, but he said he wished to speak to me privately. Once we were alone, he asked: "What are you doing sitting here outside? You have been listed as one of the three ringleaders of the coup and your life is in danger. Get away as soon as possible." He left right away at 10 in the morning. He was a tough character willing to defy all risks to assist his friends.

To deprive the insurgents of their propaganda arm, the first action of the army had been to bomb the broadcasting station, but of course this meant they had no means of announcing they had defeated the coup except by their low-power military radios. They used these sets to announce who had been killed, who was on the run and who the ringleaders were. This was how Negatu had heard my name. I ate lunch and gave the matter some thought. After the meal, I used my small transistor set to monitor the broadcasts and heard my name so I informed my wife that I must leave if my presence was not to endanger the rest of the family. My mother-in-law arranged for me to be smuggled out of the city dressed in a gabi and escorted by one of her tenants, Ato Gesso, heading for Akaki, about 25 kilometers from Addis. We were dropped by car just outside the city limits and walked the remaining 20 kilometers.

The Emperor's Clothes

After two days of thinking through the alternatives which faced me, I was listening to the radio when I heard the emperor's announcement that civilians should give themselves up to Dejazmatch Kebede Tessema and that soldiers should surrender to General Isayas. I decided to give myself up and dissociate myself from the embarrassing affair. I tore pages out of my pocket diary and wrote a note to Dejazmatch Kebede Tessema explaining the extent of my involvement and offered to give myself up if the facts of the matter were broadcast in the same way that I had been named as one of the ringleaders, on the radio and in the newspapers. I sent the note with Ato Gesso to my father-in-law for it to be passed on. In the afternoon of 20 December, my father [not my father-in-law] appeared at my hideout to hand me two letters and an oral message from Dejazmatch Kebede. The letter was brief, advising me what to do and telling me he had also discussed the matter with General Merid, who had written a separate message.

The oral message from Dejazmatch Kebede Tessema was that if what I had claimed in my note to him was true I should not fear to explain myself to the emperor in person, but if I wished to attach any conditions to giving myself up I must be criminally liable for my actions. General Merid's note was a safe passage for me and others who might be with me because it was assumed that I was with some of the bodyguard officers and would reach Addis Ababa unhindered.

My father informed me that my brother Melaku had been captured and was safe, but that 13 government officials had been killed inside the palace including General Mulugeta Bulli, Ras Abebe Aregai and Ato Mekonnen Habte-Wold. I was heartbroken by the news and ashamed that my name should be associated with this killing. In my grief, I blamed the emperor both for the coup and its failure. If he had appointed a sensible man as Bodyguard commander, none of this would have happened.

On 21 December, three of us set off back to the city and although there was a roadblock on the outskirts at Shola-Ber with every car being stopped in and out of the city, the soldier who stopped us merely glanced inside the car and told us to proceed, so there was no need to produce the safe conduct. We reached the home of my in-laws without any incident and since I had not shaved or changed my clothes for nine days I asked my wife to get me clean clothing while I bathed.

That night, there was a volley of shots and then sporadic shooting which was reported in the media as an attempt to capture me and Captain Asrat Defaresu. It was impossible for me to assess the significance of the reports, so I decided to give myself up the next morning. My father-in-law drove me to Dejazmatch Kebede's house which was only a kilometer away and we drove right up to the front door. An attendant ushered us into an anteroom and

7. Attempted Coup D'Etat

immediately the Dejazmatch appeared and we exchanged greetings. My father-in-law left us and the Dejazmatch led me to his study where he told me that although my note was clear, he wished to know whether I had anything to add. When I said the note explained everything, he asked me: "Were you forced in any way to cooperate with them because you found yourself in an unexpected situation?" I replied: "There was no force at all. My immediate concern was to make any contribution I could to a peaceful conclusion to the matter. I was quite aware why the situation arose and on many occasions I have openly criticized the irresponsible way that the public service and government affairs have been handled and the glaring need for a more responsible government. On any occasion which presented itself, I expressed to the emperor my feeling that there was need for a change of government. So although I did not subscribe to the coup or agree with the way it was carried out, in principle I was with them so I cooperated to try to save the situation."

We were driven to the Jubilee Palace, where we parked about 100 meters away from the building. In the middle of a beautiful lawn stood a circular stone-walled building with a thatched roof which housed the emperor's office and several others. The area was crowded with generals and all ranks of the services and civilians. The Dejazmatch left me with his driver and walked across the lawn to look for the emperor, bowing to the people as he went. He came back and then escorted me across the lawn. We walked past the crowd, many of whom knew me and were wondering about my fate. General Tedla Mekonnen stepped out of the crowd to greet me and asked: "How did you come to be involved in this?" I responded with a smile: "You have heard it from the radio." We continued on our way.

At the main entrance of the palace stood Girma Belew, the principal secretary of the Department of Marine. He had been one of my most trusted assistants. I greeted him brightly, but I saw from the look on his face that he did not want to have anything to do with me. I dismissed him in my mind as an opportunist. In the lobby I met Daniel Abebe, who also gave me an evil look. In his case, the reaction was understandable since he had lost his father, Ras Abebe Aregai, the minister of defense, in the events which I stood accused of having instigated. Even if he had chosen to shoot me there on the spot to avenge his father's blood, he could not have been blamed.

Through the right door of the lobby we entered what must have been the emperor's study. I was not sure since it was the first time I had visited the Jubilee Palace. It was a large, carpeted room with a writing desk at the far end. There, in front of it, stood the emperor wearing a khaki cape. On the left, leaning against the wall was General Isayas with a pen and writing pad in his hand, which I assumed was to record what was said. The Dejazmatch was on my right-hand side as I bowed and faced the emperor, who looked exhausted and

111

colorless, with his hair reddish. He intoned: "Tell us how you got involved in this affair." I repeated what I had written in my note to the Dejazmatch and repeated what I had added in his study about the way in which I became involved without being forced to cooperate. The emperor listened quietly then walked back to his desk and picked up the note which I had sent to the Dejaz-match and handed it back to him. He said: "Well, we do not think there will be any more you can tell us. You can go now."

I bowed and walked out of the room to the lobby. The Dejazmatch remained behind with the emperor and while I was standing waiting for him, along came the prime minister, Aklilu Habte-Wold, and the foreign minister, Yilma Deressa. The prime minister's elder brother, Mekonnen Habte-Wold, had been killed as a result of the events of which I had been accused, but he still came to greet me and say he was sorry to hear of my involvement. But Yilma gave me a grim look and walked away.

I was waiting for the Dejazmatch because traditionally I was under his charge until the matter was clarified. As I waited, along came an army colonel who told me: "You will follow me to General Merid's office where he wants to see you." He led me to an army jeep with two armed soldiers sitting behind the driver. I realized I was being detained because the general's provisional office was right there in the palace. As we drove out of the main gate of the Jubilee Palace. I saw a large crowd and waved to them cheerfully. On the way to the First Army HQ where I was being taken to be detained, I saw Colonel Tadesse Melke, who had been the best man at my wedding. I waved to him cheerfully, but he made up his face to express his disapproval of me. Another cowardly opportunist, I concluded. The list was growing. There is an old Amharic proverb: "kifu qen ayimtta wodaji endalatta," which means "let not bad days come so that I will not lose all my friends." In my mind I turned it round to: "Let bad days come so that I can know who my real friends are and not waste time with cowardly opportunists."

I had driven past the First Army HQ every day between my home and the office, but had never been inside. It was in a large compound with many build-ings like transit sheds on either side of the driveway with a villa at the far side like an office block. I was handed over to an army Major Asefa, who was well-known both to me and to my in-laws who had helped him out when he was sick in the hospital with no friends or relatives to care for him. He was the one who was to ransack our house and take away much of the property. My in-laws assumed he was storing it so nobody else could loot it. He was in charge of the detainees and greeted me with the now familiar: "How on earth did you become involved in this affair?" He led me to my detention quarter which was an office room with a desk and nothing else at all. He suggested going to my house to collect a canvas bed, which became my sleeping and sitting furniture.

7. Attempted Coup D'Etat

Fortunately for me, Major Asefa was replaced that day by Colonel Belete, who was to become a general and later a victim of the massacre of 60 government officials by the Derg on 23 November 1974.

The door of the room was left wide open with two soldiers armed with a machine gun outside guarding me. I was laying on my back gazing at the ceiling two hours later when Negatu stepped over the machine gun and sat on the foot of the canvas bed. I was amazed and asked how he had managed to gain admission. "Nobody stopped me," he said. "When I was told that this was where you were being detained I asked in which room and walked right in." He gave me encouragement and left. Apparently the soldiers were new to Addis Ababa, having been posted from the provinces. They took Negatu for an officer in mufti. With his upright stature and military bearing, he looked like the commanding officer of the place. As he was walking back to the main gate, he was stopped by an officer who demanded to know how he got into a security zone. Negatu responded that he should have been asked the question as he was going in, not as he was leaving. As for how he got in, he had used the main gate, what else? As they were arguing, along came a Captain Kibe, who knew him well and told him to hop into his jeep. Otherwise Negatu could have been in trouble.

On Friday, 23 December, I was taken in an army truck with Bodyguard officer detainees and my brother Melaku to the palace, where we were unloaded on the lawn and given foolscap paper and pens to record and sign the same statements we had made to the emperor. These documents were to be used by the attorney general to draw formal charges against us. There was no doubt in the mind of the emperor that I was guilty of treason and deserved to die. I admitted having said to Worqneh that they should not have taken action when the emperor was out of the country, which the emperor construed to mean that I would have wanted him to be killed. This was not what I had meant and I was never asked to explain.

The attorney general, Judge Marain, was an Israeli appointed to the position in recognition of services rendered to the emperor while he was in exile. When he was handed that handwritten Amharic document to formulate charges against me, he asked his assistant Nerayo to translate it and found that it raised so many questions that he needed to clarify before he could consider it as the basis of formulating charges against me. The attorney general appointed two police officers to investigate my case, Colonel Dawit Gebru, who is still alive and lives in Washington, and Colonel Tadesse Gebre, who died in September 1988. They took statements to clarify the points which were not fully answered in my own statement. For the first time I was asked what I meant by my question to Worqneh: "Why when the emperor is out of the country?" I explained that if I had been in the position of General Mengistu

113

and wanted to make a change I would have done so without bloodshed by forcing the emperor to accept a constitutional monarchy. I went into detail of how I would have done it.

When Judge Maraine received this clarification, instead of drawing treason charges, he closed the case and recommended to the emperor that I should be reinstated to serve my country. When the emperor received the letter he was furious and called the minister of justice, Dejazmatch Zewde Gebre Selassie, who later became deputy prime minister, then foreign minister, and now lives in New York. He was ordered to terminate the contract of the attorney general and expel him from the country. The minister of justice waited until the emperor had cooled down, then pointed out to him the consequences to Imperial prestige of terminating the contract. He suggested that since the contract had just half a year to run it should not be renewed. So Judge Maraine left Ethiopia after 20 years of service without any thanks, all on my account.

Then the emperor appointed a Ministerial Committee, chaired by the minister of justice and composed of Leul Asrate Kassa President of the Senate, Minister of Defence General Merid, Chief Justice Blata Qitaw and Teshome Haile-Mariam to review the case which the attorney general had turned down. The chairman explained the background of the case as far as legal questions were concerned. This was so the committee had no power to reverse the decision of the attorney general and that the case should be dropped. Leul Asrate Kassa expressed the view of several of the members that what mattered was not the law, but my attitude. Just talking about a constitutional monarchy and wanting change had to be an offense and the person who committed it should not be allowed to get off scot-free. The chairman insisted that the matter should be considered dispassionately and not emotionally. The committee was constrained to find that, although there was no offense under the law, the emperor had the traditional right to banish me to a remote province at his pleasure and to restrict my movements to whatever extent he felt necessary. The chairman presented the decision of the committee to the emperor for a decision on which province I should be sent to. The emperor's first choice was Gonder, where the governor was Amha Abera, the grandson of Ras Kassa, who now lives in the United States. The chairman, knowing the problems I would face there, persuaded the emperor to change his mind on the grounds that I was known to be in ill health and if I was sent far from home I might fall sick and the emperor would be blamed.

The chairman suggested Wollisso, 120 kilometers from Addis Ababa, a small town in Shewa province. The emperor never visited the area. The chairman knew my father had been a judge there for many years and also that Mr. Clewer had built a cottage on a plot which I owned for the use of his father and that the cottage had reverted to me when the family left the country.

7. Attempted Coup D'Etat

It took three months to reach a decision about my fate. During the first month, I was confined to a room in the First Army HQ. My friend and former boss, Mikael Imru, was allowed to see me after he returned from his ambassadorial post in Washington. I was delighted to see him. His brother-in-law, Colonel Tamrat Yigezu, was the chairman of the committee which the emperor set up to screen all of the Bodyguard officers and civilians involved in the revolt. The committee met in the conference room of the same building where I was detained. There were just two other detainees, Amde Wondafarsh and Ato Goytom Petros. Amde Wondafarsh was a blood relative of Germame and his brother, Germame Wondafarsh, was killed in the fighting. Amde is still alive and works with the International Livestock Center for Africa (ILCA) in Addis Ababa. Ato Goytom Petros was vice minister for foreign affairs and had been forced to transmit telegrams to Ethiopian missions abroad in the name of the takeover group. He was released, reinstated to his post, and died in 1983.

During the month I was detained in First Army HQ, I made a statement to the investigating commission but since it was the same statement which I had made to the emperor it brought no new developments. To my surprise and joy I found in the drawer of the desk in the room where I was held a copy of Plato's *Republic*. Inevitably I began translating those passages which dealt with the conduct of government officials. About the middle of January, the three of us were moved to the artillery division headquarters where other detainees were held, including General Mengistu, who had been imprisoned after he was wounded and captured. One of the detainees, Getachew Garedew, was an employee of the state bank from Dire Dewa. He had been badly beaten by the police and after three days he was taken to court where he was ordered to be released. When police tried to rearrest him, he fled to Somalia where he began to broadcast malicious propaganda against the emperor over the Somali Radio Amharic Service. When Somalia and Ethiopia became reconciled, he moved on to West Germany where he married a German girl and settled. Others of the detainees were held for offenses like dancing for joy in public when the overthrow of the emperor was announced. The fact that we were all held together was an indication that our offenses were not regarded as grave.

Relatives were allowed to approach the building and exchange greetings with us from a distance and the officers guarding us would come into our room to share tea with us or play games. We were allowed books and newspapers and there was an enormous accumulation of the food which relative and friends were allowed to bring to us each day. We distributed the surplus among our guards and this served to further build relations. I formed a close friendship with Balamberas Girma Yayeh-Yirad, who was full of vigor and had an impressive personality although he was about 60. He had been close to the emperor until each discovered the other's opposing characteristics. His offense was being an uncle of the Neway brothers. We spent two months together and they passed like hours. Each day when we were allowed out into the sun for two hours, we would sit close together and he would tell me stories of his time with the emperor.

He told me that when the Ethiopian-Italian war had broken out, he had been in prison and the emperor had sent an edict that he should be brought from Addis Ababa to Dessie in chains. He never discovered what was going to happen to him because before the order could be carried out, the emperor's army was defeated by the Italians and the emperor ran away. When the Italians entered Addis Ababa, he was released. The letter from the emperor ordering him to be transferred in chains was to save his life when an attempt was made on the Italian viceroy Graziani's life and the Italians began massacring Ethiopians indiscriminately in February 1937. Balambaras Girma was being led to execution by the Italian carabinier when he produced the letter to show he was an enemy of the emperor. He was immediately released and given protection. The manner of his fall from favor and the lessons he pointed out to his nephews as a result of it, bear recounting.

Eyasu, the heir of Menilek, had been detained at Fiche, 70 kilometers northwest of Addis Ababa under the supervision of Ras Kasa. Eyasu's father-in-law, Ras Hailu of Gojam, tried to organize his escape, but was placed in detention in Addis Ababa. His son Admasu, was governor of a province in the domain of his father, who was reputed to be the richest man in Ethiopia with his treasury overflowing with gold bullion and silver thalers. On hearing of his father's detention, Admasu rushed with his followers to Debre-Marqos, the capital of Gojam and the seat of his father. When news of Admasu's occupation of Debre-Marqos reached the emperor, he rushed Balamberas Girma to Debre-Marqos by small plane to persuade Admasu not to loot his father's treasury but instead to go to Addis Ababa to be formally appointed as the successor to his father. Girma, believing the emperor's words, convinced Admasu to fly back to Addis Ababa with him.

The evening of their arrival in Addis Ababa, Girma went to visit Admasu at the house of the Dejazmatch to which he had been sent pending his appointment. Girma was shocked to find Admasu in chains and complained to the emperor. The emperor promised that Admasu would be transferred to the home of Ras Desta, but when Girma went there he found him still chained. It was then he realized both he and Admasu had been duped. Girma was ordered by the emperor to fly to Debre-Marqos in the same small plane and ferry the contents of the treasury to Addis Ababa. It took several trips. Admasu was imprisoned in Ankober, the old capital of Shewa, 145 kilometers north of Addis Ababa. He died there from gangrene caused by the shackle on his leg.

7. Attempted Coup D'Etat

Girma was called back to Addis Ababa after two years in Debre-Marqos and accused of having embezzled the wealth of Ras Hailu. He was thrown into prison.

Girma had told his nephew, General Mengistu, if he did not take early action against the emperor he would be used and then discarded because that was the emperor's nature. He reminded both of his nephews of the words spoken against Emperor Tewodros by a woman whose husband and son he had killed, words which became an Amharic proverb: "If you fail to uproot this one piece of chili stock it will burn and finish you all off." I only wished I had a tape recorder to preserve Girma's words for posterity. I was in Haiti in 1963 when I heard of his death and felt sorry that he had gone forever without leaving behind his wisdom. He was typical of the born leaders of the old generation whom the emperor frustrated, depriving the country of their valuable service and instead setting out to ruin them.

Another nephew of Girma's was detained with us. The manner in which he toadied up to every soldier and officer sickened the rest of us and irritated his uncle. Ato Goytom, the vice minister for foreign affairs, and myself were so openly critical that this nephew of Girma's formed the conclusion that we must be agents provocateur planted by the emperor to gather evidence against the others. He was foolish enough to venture this opinion to his uncle, warning him that his close association with me in particular was going to land him and the rest of the family into serious danger and that he should have as little as possible to do with us. Girma was so enraged that he used an Amharic term, which means somebody so lacking in judgment that they pick up the afterbirth instead of the child, against his nephew.

From time to time we would get information about the progress of our cases and we had been told that this nephew of Girma's would be the first to be released. This seemed reasonable to us since he had not been involved in the coup, being too pusillanimous in nature to have any part in it. The day he was due to be released, he was instead taken to be tortured and then imprisoned for 10 years.

It turned out that Bezuneh Shifferaw, who worked at the Coffee Board where Girma's nephew was general manager, had been caught with pamphlets which eulogized the coup attempt. When caught and interrogated, he had named his general manager as the mastermind, which was almost certainly false. He served a year of his sentence before the new chief justice, Afe-Neguse Tadesse, allowed his appeal and he was released. Tadesse was immediately removed from his post and appointed vice governor of Tigre Province. The emperor was most unlucky in his appointment of judicial officers. Instead of yes-men, he got men of principle and justice who were prepared to defy his wishes and face the personal consequences. Girma was released and confined to house arrest with all of the others except Belete and myself. Four days later, I was taken to the Senate House, where the president, Leul Asrate Kassa, told me that despite my disloyalty to the emperor who had educated me and promoted me to the rank of assistant minister, I had been forgiven and instead of the severe penalty I deserved, I was to be banished to Wollisso.

I was sent to the Ministry of the Interior where again I was in luck. Before the revolt, the minister of the interior had been Ras Andarge and things would have gone ill with me if I had fallen into his clutches. However, after the revolt Ras Andarge was dropped in a Cabinet reshuffle and replaced by my good friend, General Abiy Abebe. Ras Andarge was one of those who miraculously survived the shooting committed by the insurgents in the last desperate moments in the Palace. General Abiy received me in his office with his usual friendly smile and greeted me with the Ethiopian customary kiss on both cheeks before sitting me down and chatting with me for an hour about the events which had been brought me to his office. He advised me as a sincere friend to be patient and wait my turn to serve my country. In the traditional system of banning somebody who had offended the emperor, the offender was handed over to the minister of the interior who had instructions as to the province the emperor wanted him confined to and what kind of treatment the emperor wanted him to receive.

In my case the emperor's first choice was Gondar. The governor there, Amha Abera, had been affected by the revolt. Under persuasion by the minister of justice, the emperor agreed on the second choice of Wollisso where the governor was Dejazmatch Tesfaye Inqo-Selassie. But what amazes me when I recall these events, I never worried and burdened my mind with thoughts of what might happen to me. I prepared myself to accept whatever came if I could not help it and in all cases God had been helping me.

At the end of our conversation, General Abiy called a police colonel and gave him instructions that I could spend that day and night in Addis before leaving. I went to the house of my in-laws where my wife and child were living and it became a day of rejoicing. At one point during the three months of my detention, it had been rumored that I was condemned to death and I was going to be hanged on a particular day which alarmed my father-in-law who rushed to collect my wife from her office to save her from the sudden shock. My friend Negatu spent the whole day waiting there with a revolver in his pocket, but fortunately the rumor did not materialize. So for my family and close friends that day was a day I had risen from death. The whole afternoon till midnight people streamed to my in-laws' house. Even those who had returned my greetings with disapproval came to congratulate me.

The next day, after breakfast with my police escort, I left Addis for Wolliso driving my own car. The route from Addis is a very good asphalt road, two hours' easy drive. The governor, Dejazmatch Tesfaye, received us in his office. He remembered that many years before when I had been a student and part-time assistant to Mr. Clewer, the chief architect of the Ministry of Education, I went to Jimma with Mr. Clewer to supervise the construction of a school. On our way back, the governor was standing by the roadside just at the outskirts of Jimma to ask for a lift to Addis Ababa. Mr. Clewer was driving an old Italian Ardita Convertible and we gave him a lift to Addis. He briefed me on the basis of the letter he received from the Ministry of Interior on what my rights and obligations were. I was free to live and move wherever I wanted within the town limits and I would be paid Eth$100 per month for support. I must not go beyond the town limits. With that briefing, I took leave of the governor and drove to Wollisso Ras Hotel where I knew everybody. I arranged with them for my meals, paying my banishment allowance of Eth$100 per month.

The following weekend, two days after my arrival at Wollisso, I was visited by Mikael Imru and his brother-in-law, Colonel Tamrat (chairman of the investigation committee), and the whole staff of the Department of Marine. This reached the emperor's ears and he immediately called the new commander of the police, General Deresse Dubale (killed during the November 1974 massacre), and ordered that I should be removed from Wollisso and taken to Jimma, 230 kilometers southwest. The following Saturday, the governor came to my cottage and informed me he had instructions that I had to be taken to Jimma the next morning, accompanied by one police officer.

I left Wollisso after exactly 10 days. It was 6 p.m. when we reached Jimma. All government offices were closed so the police officer said he would spend the night with friends and meet me the following morning wherever I was going to spend the night. I told him I did not know anyone in Jimma, but I knew Ghion Hotel so I would go there for the night. There are only two modern hotels in Jimma: Ghion and Ras Mesfin. Ghion is considered first-class and is used by foreign visitors from Addis Ababa and Ras Mesfin is second-class. After a quick shower, I decided to take advantage of the pleasant evening climate of Jimma by sitting on the veranda. There I met Kifle Inqo-Selassie, the younger brother of the governor of Wollisso and head of the Town Council of Jimma. Sitting with him was Tesfa Bushen, the principal of Jimma Agricultural College. Both were surprised to see me so I told them my whole story.

At dinner, the manager of the hotel, Bezabeh Ayano, came to chat with me, telling me he knew of me and was delighted I was out of danger. He offered me full accommodations at the hotel for my monthly allowance, which was a considerable discount on the regular tariff and a great concession. I thanked him and felt my greatest problem was solved.

The next morning, the police escort took me to the office of the governor general of Kefa Province. The governor general, Colonel Tamrat Yigezu, was chairing the committee investigating the revolt and his deputy, Fitawrari Zekaryas Tekele whom I also knew well, was in charge. His office was a large room on the first floor of a spacious Italian-built block. As I entered it, I saw from the look on his face he wished to pretend he had never known me and held me in contempt. The police officer handed him the letter from the governor of Wollisso which enclosed the original letter from the Ministry of the Interior, stipulating the conditions of my banishment. Zekaryas did not even care to look at the letter and immediately asked me where I was going to stay. I told him of the arrangement I had made at the Ghion Hotel. He responded brusquely: "That is impossible. It is frequented by many foreigners and I cannot allow you to stay there. You will have to find a small house in a more secluded place." I told him that before trying to dictate his whims he should read the letter from his superiors since I knew my rights and would stay at the Ghion Hotel whether he liked it or not. From his attitude it was clear he had received telephone instructions from Addis Ababa. It did not help that the minister of the interior, General Abiy, had not been informed of my transfer from Wollisso to Jimma, since it was the result of a direct order from the emperor to the commander of the police.

When I insisted that I had the right to stay anywhere I chose within the town limits, he called in the chief of security, Major Bekele, and the area police commander to back him up. I insisted that he call the minister of the interior and I spoke to General Abiy on the telephone myself, then passed it to Zekaryas. The argument lasted from nine in the morning until two in the afternoon and finally Zekaryas ordered the Italian manager of the Ras Mesfin hotel to give me the small house in the backyard of the hotel with full board and all services for Eth$100 per month. It represented an 80 percent loss of income for the poor Italian. The room was much better than the one at the Ghion Hotel, with a connecting bathroom and dining room. Zekaryas, the colonel and the major escorted me and it was clear that instructions had come from Addis Ababa to watch me day and night. I was to be excluded from the public rooms of the hotel and on the first night, a police lieutenant was sent to sleep in my room. I told the police lieutenant there was no way he was going to sleep in the room which I had paid for and that he was welcome to sleep in the corridor. Evidently sympathizing with my stand, he went away.

Two weeks later, the new governor general arrived and it seemed good fortune was following me wherever I went. Dejazmatch Kifle Dadi was a close relative of Balambaras Girma, my dear old friend and erstwhile cellmate who had warmly recommended me to the governor and told him to do whatever he could to help me. Four days after his arrival he pulled up in his car as I was walking down the street and asked: "You are Gaitachew Bekele, aren't you?" I replied that I was and he asked where I was staying, telling me: "I will come to see you during the course of my visits to the establishments of Jimma. Have a good day for now." Two days later he came with Zekaryas and I told him how I came to be there. He said if I wished to move I could do so at once and that there was no need for a police guard. He would send his chauffeur to carry me to his house for breakfast and on festive days would always send food and drinks. It was through his efforts that I was finally released and appointed governor of Bahr- Dar.

He had requested that I be released and allowed to work under him as head of Jimma Town Council. The appointment as governor was a surprise for him and he was happy for me. He did not understand the thinking of the emperor, who did not like to have two friends working together. People who did not get on well together would watch each other and the emperor knew I would never get on with the governor general of Gojam, Dejazmatch Tsehayu.

In former times, banishment meant exclusion from society and civil rights, and being thrown at the mercy of the governor of the province of banishment. The general public, being ignorant of the reason for the banishment, would shun the individual concerned in order to avoid being tarred with the same brush. An example is a former deputy chief justice of the Supreme Court, Afe-Negus Gebre-Medhin Haile-Mariam, a key person in the resistance movement who had been banished in 1943 to Gore. In 1961 he was still in banishment, his spirit unbroken, and I came to know about him through Fitawrari Gebre-Kirstos Mekonnen who took me to see the old man at the Russian Hospital in Addis Ababa the day after my appointment as governor of Bahr-Dar. The former chief justice was undergoing treatment for the loss of his hearing and he said he had received the consideration of treatment because of the attempted coup.

When Afe-Negus Gebre-Medhin had been banished, nobody questioned the emperor's actions and the reasons were a mystery to everyone except the emperor and the victim. Everybody assumed he had refused to accept instructions from the emperor concerning a judgment but, when I met him he told me the real reason. He had been a patriot and when the question of decorating patriots with service medals arose, a commission was set up to evaluate those who deserved medals and the grades. Gebre-Medhin objected to those who had gone into exile getting the same medal as those who had stayed to fight. The emperor chose to interpret this as a deliberate slight, although Gebre-Medhin insisted to me he had not thought of it that way. He regarded the emperor as a patriot who had gone to Geneva to appeal for international help. The reason why my banishment was light in comparison was that the sword arm of the emperor, his security men and the bodyguard which he had used to enforce his whims, revolted against him.

I had been widely publicized as one of the ringleaders of the revolt and after two generations of rule by the emperor the country was sick of him, which made me popular for being seen to oppose him. Instead of being shunned, I made friends in Jimma. One such new friend was Shibru Wolde-Mariam, an instructor at the Jimma Agricultural School, who had been in the governor general's office on official business the first day I was taken there. He took the trouble to find out who I was and where I was being taken and followed me to the hotel. As soon as my escort had left, he walked in and introduced himself, saying he knew me by name through his brother Dr. Atnafe, and also my brother Daniel who had been one of his students there. He never missed a day to visit me and two or three times a week he would invite me to his house for meals. I became a frequent visitor to the school and a friendship was forged which has lasted to this day and has been cemented by our children.

The chief of security, Major Bekele Manaye, was required to submit monthly reports on me to Addis Ababa. He would visit me and I would try to educate him on my views on public administration. His secretary was Lieutenant Feleke, a close friend of one of my young brothers, and he would visit me at night to inform me of the contents of Major Bekele's security reports on me. They were fair, and accurate and contained no malice toward me, but he would include in the list of those who had visited me enemies of his who had never been to see me at all. Major Bekele was well-aware another new Jimma friend Abate Mulat, Ras Mesfin's nephew, would drive me beyond the city limits to the home of Aba Jifar, who had been hereditary ruler of Jimma. One of his sons, Aba Jobir, had been under house arrest for 20 years because of collaborating with the Italians.

One weekend a month, Negatu would bring my wife and our son Tewdros, who had been five months old at the time of the revolt. I also received visits from my parents and I could see my mother was being worn out with worry about my brother Melaku, who had been sentenced to eight years in the main prison in Addis Ababa. I was also visited by staff of the Department of Marine, including the German engineer, Mr. H. D. Hoeft, who came to bid me goodbye at the end of his three-year contract.

We Amharas are not tribally orientated and have no tendency to form racial or tribal associations. This has been clearly demonstrated in our current political upheaval. After our symbol of national unity had been savagely removed and replaced by a veritable thug, it became a fashion for every tribe, except the Amharas, to form a tribal grouping, and declare a liberation front. The reason for this is that we are a composite of all the races of Ethiopia and our society is structured not on the basis of race, but on the assimilation of our culture. An episode from my time in Jimma demonstrates this. One day, during the morning walk I always took through the coffee farms and forests, I met a Jimma

7. Attempted Coup D'Etat

Gala boy called Haile-Mariam, collecting firewood which he sold for a living. I asked him how much he earned and what he did with the money. He told me he made 20 cents of which all went toward food, forcing him to sleep on verandas with guards. Sometimes he would be donated secondhand clothing. All he owned in the world were the rags in which he was dressed and the string which he used to tie firewood. We talked for two hours and then I told him that since I had taken his collecting time I would pay him the 10 cents for his dinner and share my lunch with him. I told him if he would go to school I would give him 20 cents each day for his food or share mine with him and that he could sleep on my veranda. He agreed and went to school for three months before I was released, when he asked to be allowed to go with me. I took him to Addis Ababa and then to Bahr-Dar, where I acquired employment for him in a cotton factory. He married a Gojame girl and is now a Gojame Amhara by cultural assimilation.

The other episode which clearly demonstrates this fact took place during the Italian invasion of Ethiopia. Some disgruntled Oromo individuals approached the prominent chieftain Aba Doyo and sought his consent to take advantage of the situation to eliminate the Amhara living among them. Aba Doyo said: "Bring me a handful of teff grain and I shall give you a decision." When they brought the teff he commanded them to separate the brown grain from the white. They saw at once the task was impossible and said so. "Then why ask me to do the impossible?" he responded. "The Amhara and Oromo are totally intermingled through marriage and cultural assimilation." He gave the example of his own family, a union of the Amhara, Tigre and Oromo, but all had Amhara names and were identified as such. "Would you have me kill my own family members and the whole of the rest of the population to get rid of the Amhara?" He ordered them to come to terms with reality and get on with their daily work in peace.

While in Jimma, I had time to write a little book in Amharic called "Ye-Aggelgay Mestewat," which means the "Mirror for a public servant." It explores the relationship between the public and public servants, taking as an example the office of provincial governor and explaining the relationship of each branch to the public. To get authority for the book to be published, I wrote a letter to the emperor explaining the main theme of the book and requesting him to read it but not to give it to any of those around him since I was sure they would find all sorts of reasons why it should not be published. I urged him that since no one was wiser than himself, he alone should decide. The same day the letter and manuscript went to the emperor, I was telephoned by the minister for foreign affairs, Ketema Yifru, who told me the emperor had agreed to the publication of the book provided the letter was published in it. I agreed to the stipulation because I had known when I drafted the letter that was how the emperor would respond. The letter revealed my contempt for those around him and he wanted it published to make them my enemies. Besides, there was no other place in the book where his name was mentioned.

The book was published by the Tesfa Gebre-Selassie Printing Press, four months after the emperor gave it his blessing and paid the expenses. However, soon after it appeared it went out of circulation and I was told the reason. The Minister of Health Ato Abebe Retta understood the message of the book, especially the letter, and explained to those around him that a person can only agree to have people near him who are like himself.

8

Governor of Bahr-Dar

Bahr-Dar means "by the edge of the sea" and is a small town on the southern tip of Lake Tana, the capital of the district which has taken its name. It is one of the seven districts in Gojam province bordering Begemdir 611 kilometers northwest of Addis Ababa. Bahr-Dar's importance stems from its history, the lake, and the Blue Nile waterfall, Tiss Isat, 35 kilometers outside of the town. The varied bird life includes silvery checked hornbills, herons, hoopoes, ospreys, and weavers. The lake, besides being home to many kinds of fish, is the habitat of crocodiles and hippos. The islands of the lake are famous for their churches and monasteries, some of which date back to the twelfth century. Bahr-Dar lies at an altitude of 1700 meters above sea level. Therefore its climate is suitable for all types of tropical fruits, vegetables and other crops, and for raising livestock.

I was no stranger to Bahr-Dar, having visited there a number of times and having started development activities related to lake transportation when I was with the Department of Marine. The only buildings with electricity and piped water were the port manager's office and residence which the department had built. The chief administrator of the town council, Meriggeta Mezegabe Tibebe, knew me well, as did Ato Kebede, the manager of the Ras Hotel and Manbegroh the port manager who was one of the eight Addis Ababa technical school graduates recruited as tugboat mechanics. When I arrived in Bahr-Dar in November 1961 as governor of the district, I was welcomed with great enthusiasm by a large crowd of local officials and townspeople.

The appointment had created the suspicion among some people that I had been the emperor's informant all along because it was announced before my release. Even the governor of Kefa, Dejazmatch Kifle, was pleasantly surprised because when he took me to the palace that morning he had no idea I

125

was to be released. He told me he had interceded with the emperor on my behalf and my best strategy would be to fall on my knees before the emperor and beg his forgiveness. I thanked him sincerely for all his trouble, kindness, and advice, but told him that since I had done nothing wrong I would never ask for a pardon. He spent an hour trying to persuade me, but seeing his good efforts were about to be wasted, he told me to go to see my in-laws and get back to him in the morning.

He took me in his chauffeur-driven car to the Genete Leul Palace, where he told me to wait under the shade of a tree while he passed into the second enclosure. Half an hour later I was told by a palace attendant to join a line of people standing in front of the same building I had entered when I had been appointed an assistant minister. The three people I found standing in the middle of the room to confer appointments were all different. I was told by the prime minister, Tsehafi-Tezaz Aklilu Habte-Wold, that His Majesty graciously appointed me as governor of Bahr-Dar. From there we were led to the left-hand wing of the main palace where the emperor was to be found. I bowed and left the room to be confronted by Dejazmatch Kifle who was with some ministers. He bounded forward with a great smile on his face, hugging me and kissing me on both cheeks, congratulating and praising the emperor for his graciousness. The others, who had passed me by without a greeting while I was waiting outside, now came to kiss my cheeks and congratulate me.

It was at that time rumors began that I had been the emperor's man all along. Araya Equba-Igzi told my friend Goytom Petros, who had been detained with me that I must have been a planted informant. Goytom defended me and replied that the unprecedented appointment must be a ploy on the part of the emperor to create suspicion of me among the reformers and isolate me from them. I felt he was right but the emperor went even further than that in his deviousness. The emperor thought I would be reluctant to leave Addis Ababa for an appointment in such a remote province and would instead loiter around the capital trying to lobby for a more congenial posting, as others had done before me. He expected that I would go through dej-tinat, the process of showing my face at the Court every day without fail, idly spending my time and gossiping.

The day after my appointment I went to see my good friend General Abiy, who was now my boss. He congratulated me on my appointment and advised me to curb my overt radicalism. He referred me to his vice minister, Asefa Gebre-Mariam, to make administrative arrangements. I told Asefa, another close friend, that I wished to leave for Bahr-Dar as soon as possible. His assistant, Mekuria Worku, was called into the discussions and it was proposed that I should fly to Bahr-Dar. Being told that my predecessor, Ato Belete, had no service Land Rover, I asked if I could be given one of the old Land Rovers from the ministry since I preferred to drive to my district rather than fly. They loaned me a short wheelbase model with worn-out tires. It was the only one available, and it took me a week to get the tires retreaded and have the vehicle made road-worthy. In this I was assisted by an old friend, Negussie Habteyes, although he had been illiterate he spoke Amharic, Galigna, English, and Italian fluently. He had been employed as a driver when the Department of Marine was established and I was so impressed by his diligence and energy that I recommended to Director General Zewde that he should be put in charge of the other drivers. He was also encouraged to learn to read and write, which he did in no time. He proved a reliable driver and expert mechanic, and was promoted to be in charge of general services indispensable to every head of the department. He died of a kidney complaint in 1987.

Two weeks after my appointment, I left for Bahr-Dar with Zewde, my houseboy and Negussie, carrying a tent, air mattress, and sleeping bag which I had bought with two jerry cans of fuel. We made overnight stops at Gohatsion and Debre-Marqos, the capital of Gojam province, and passed Merawi where the subdistrict governor, Balamberas Kelkay, met us. We arrived in Bahr-Dar at nine in the evening to be welcomed by a large crowd who had been waiting for us since six. I thanked them for their welcome and expressed my regret that they had to wait so long.

The next morning I made arrangements for Negussie to fly back to Addis Ababa, then set off for the office noting on the way that one of the first development priorities would be public latrines for the town. I found a large crowd was gathered at the office, not just to greet me but to complain about the administration.

It was a clear indication of widespread injustice and maladministration. Rural people cannot be easily taken for a ride, since they know their rights as well as their obligations. Any deviation from what they know to be just will be taken up with higher authority. This was simply achieved under the traditional system because all administrators took a solemn oath before God that all decisions they reached would be with a clear conscience in the face of incontestable facts. The oath had been abolished with the traditional practice of recruiting local natural born leaders as administrators. It had been substituted with a supposedly modern system of centrally appointed officials, bureaucracy, and a rigid and complicated hierarchy.

Traditionally, administration and adjudication of minor disputes were carried out by the chiqa-shum or atbia-dagna, the local chief and judge. The next level was the subdistrict governor who had wide administrative and judicial powers, but could not impose a death sentence which was the prerogative of the governor general. Then came the district governor, followed by the supreme power next to the emperor, the governor general. All were local men.

The Emperor's Clothes

There was no need for a police force since local people maintained their own security. There was no need for a separate court system because the administrators dealt with civil matters at a local level. In a criminal case, the accused would be put in chains and taken to the subdistrict.

Under the new system it became necessary to travel to the district capital to pay taxes. The tax collectors would demand to be bribed to collect and record the taxes. Proper recording was necessary because if taxes remained unpaid for some years, peasants could forfeit their land.

Knowing what had been going on, when I saw the crowd outside my office I decided to deal with the matter the way my forefathers would have done. I would stand among the crowd, hear each complaint on the spot and give a decision at once. I began by telling the crowd: "I came to Bahr-Dar to serve you. So did the others here. The salaries we are paid come from your taxes, just as a servant is paid by the master, so you are our masters and we are your servants. If any one of us fails to meet your just demands for service, come straight to me and tell me. My door will remain open at all times so that I can hear your grievances and redress them at once. I shall issue directives to subdistrict governors to deal with your cases at the subdistrict level and if any of you are forced to come to the district headquarters unnecessarily, your travelling expenses will be reimbursed and deducted from the salary of the subdistrict governor who had failed to serve you." I started my work with this open declaration of adherence to traditional values, hoping my colleagues would take the warning. It was our only guarantee of peaceful progress and national unity.

The staff of the district office consisted of the principal secretary and his assistant, a registry clerk, a typist, and a messenger. The subdistrict governors were Fitawrari Demlew, Fitawrari Kelkay, Fitawrari Tafer, and Fitawrari Anley. I issued administrative directives to the subdistrict governors along the lines which I had promised the crowd on the first day and that stopped the flow of people to the district office with all sorts of complaints of injustice and disputes.

However, petty crime and cattle theft were giving the police and the local courts the excuse to pester and extract bribes from the local people. I decided to say this without criticizing the government machinery. So I prepared self-rule administrative guidelines on the lines of urban self-help institutions called Idir. I called a meeting of all subdistrict governors to discuss the problems and to hear any suggestions to abolish or minimize them. Since they had no suggestions to offer, I asked them: "What about organizing the community so that they can carry out the policing of their own localities and settle minor disputes among themselves?" They all agreed with this proposal so I continued: "Since you agree, go back to your subdistricts and advise the people to select three representatives from each Atbia-dagna and send them here for a meeting to see if they can come up with their own proposals to solve these problems. If they have none, we shall ask them to organize themselves on the lines of the urban Idir. In February 1962, four months after my arrival in Bahr-Dar, we held a gathering at the district office of 1455 representatives from the 485 Atbia-Dagna and the subdistrict governors. I told them I wanted to minimize, if not eradicate, the political and social problems that were disturbing peaceful development. Since they were the people affected, I wanted suggestions from them.

They all said cattle theft was the major problem, but that a solution was the responsibility of the government. I said: "Quite right, but for the government to set up 60 police stations would mean increases in taxes. But let us recall how our forefathers maintained the security of their localities before the modern system of police. What about the three representatives from each atbia-dagna acting as Idir Dangnoch and coordinating among themselves the policing of their own localities and solving minor social disputes?" The gathering unanimously agreed. I asked the secretary to read out the directives which they would have to follow, and from that moment on there was little work for the police or the courts.

During my second week at the district office, the chief administrator of the town council asked for a police escort to carry Eth$20,000, the surplus from the previous year's operations of the town council, to Debre-Marqos. I asked why money collected from Bahr-Dar should go to Debre-Marqos and was told that it was in conformity with instructions from higher authority. I told him: "Not one cent of the money which belongs to the people of Bahr-Dar will go to other towns. It is the money contributed by the people of this town to be used for the development of this town. I shall write a letter referring to your request for a police escort and give my reasons for refusal to Debre-Marqos, copying my letter to the governor general and the Ministry of the Interior."

I asked the leader of the German town planning group, Professor Max Guther, to work out a project on which I could spend the money. They worked out a plan for the house of the future mayor of Bahr-Dar, which could in the meantime be the residence of the district governor. The two contractors in Bahr-Dar were asked to bid and Orsini won the offer for Eth$30,000. The cost of the sand which was to be brought from the other side of the lake by Navigatana wae Eth$10,000 of this. Since Navigatana owed the town council more than Eth$15,000, I ordered the chief administrator to negotiate with the contractor so sand would be provided by the council and the cost credited. So Bahr-Dar got its first house to be constructed as part of a town plan.

Bahr-Dar town had no paved roads. During the dry season it was all right except for the dust; during the rainy season it was going to be really messy.

And the contractors with their heavy lorries were going to make it worse. So two months before the rainy season was expected, I asked the town council to put up a public notice saying all roads would be closed to heavy vehicles from June until the end of September. The contractors worked together and paved the road before the onset of the rains.

As a rule, the salaries of the government officers were miserably low, e.g the subdistrict governor's salary was Eth$100 per month and the registry clerk and typist were paid Eth$25 each month. The subdistrict governor, it was understood, had other sources of income from land and house rents, but the young officers had just their salaries on which to live. It was difficult to support a family on an income of Eth$25, so my predecessor allowed them to charge Eth$0.25 for every official letter issued to an applicant.

During my tenure of office, the number of applicants drastically decreased and those few refused to pay. So the matter was presented to me for my ruling. I explained to the poor officers that I sympathized with them, but would not allow the practice to continue. It was corruption and an unlawful tax against the public who was entitled to free services on account of the tax legally levied. I had to think of another way for them to be compensated, so I called the district treasurer to find a way to assist these underpaid officers. He pointed out that the staple diet, Teff, which cost Eth$10 per 100 kilos in Bahr-Dar, cost only Eth$5 in the subdistrict. So if the junior staff could be given advances of Eth$10 each and the subdistrict governor requested to purchase teff and dispatch it to Bahr-Dar, that would feed them for four months and solve their problem. So it was arranged in that manner.

The emperor wanted to build a new city at Bahr-Dar. In one of his letters, he mentioned that the new city should be given his name. The population of the Bahr-Dar town then was 20,000 and the new city was being planned for a population of 300,000. When the emperor went on a state visit in 1954 to the Federal Republic of Germany, one of the aid package agreements made was for an assistant to prepare the plan for the new city at Bahr-Dar and to study economical development projects for the area. On the basis of this agreement, a team of German town planners was to come to Bahr-Dar in 1959. The team consisted of Professor Max Guther, the team leader who was expert in town planning from Darm Stadt University, and three assistants, Petzoid, Mueller, and Fautz. Professor Guther explained to me that with the existing land allocation system in Bahr-Dar, which encouraged speculation in the land instead of development, it would be difficult if not impossible to implement the new city plan his team was preparing.

The city council had already sold out the plots within the present town limits to high officials in Addis Ababa, including the emperor and his son-in-law, Ras Andarge. Those sold included the best plots along the border of the lake.

8. Governor of Bahr Dar

In order to develop the new city according to the plan, the title deeds of the land must remain the property of the town council and should be allocated to people who would build commercial premises. Plots in the appropriate zones should be allocated with the condition that unless they were developed within a year, the right of tenure expired and the city council would allocate the plot to another developer.

I told Professor Guther I would issue an administrative order to the town council to follow the policy for the future and, to annul the mistakes committed before, the town council would issue a notice through the mass media informing the general public of the new policy. The notice would give the owner of the allocated plots in Bahr-Dar three months to start developing. Those failing to comply with this time limit would forfeit the plot and it would be allocated to a new developer. So this administrative directive was issued immediately and the town council put the public on notice accordingly.

Part of the plot allocated to Ras Andarge was in the zone for hotel development according to the new city plan. After the three-month limit expired and the previous owner did not start development, a big transportation operator, (Gosh Gonder) Ato Ferede Zerihun, applied for a plot to build a motel and was allocated part of the Ras Andarge's plot bordering the main road to Gonder with the condition that he started development immediately. The motel was constructed according to plan.

The plot reserved for the emperor according to the new city plan was for the official residence of the future mayor of the city. Therefore, the house designed to be constructed with the Eth$20,000 became the official residence of the district governor. The administrative directive was put into effect immediately, so no one entertained any doubt of its being law.

In the package of German assistance, a 60—bed hospital was included and the construction began immediately. The development activities such as the construction of a polytechnic by the Russians, a textile factory by the Italian war compensation fund, a hydroelectric project at the Tissisat Falls by ELPA, and a teacher training school by the Ministry of Education were all progressing without any problems.

Everything was peaceful except for some of the Italian community who had been exterminating the population of wild animals as a pastime. I gave instructions to the police to catch them red-handed and confiscate their shotguns and so brought an end to their lawlessness. Around that time, there was a German technician working for ELPA [Ethiopian Light & Power Authority] who was noted for his unruly behavior. When he tore up an Eth$10 note which bore a picture of the emperor, I had him thrown in jail.

In the subdistrict of Mecha, there was a notorious outlaw called Semeneh. He had managed to outwit every government effort to capture or kill him. He was known to be a crack marksman and was the terror of his victims and the police. He had become an outlaw after shooting and killing another man in a quarrel. Semeneh came to be blamed for all the robberies and thefts in the sub-district so to avenge his name, he went after all the robbers and thieves who crossed his path.

His wish was to be left alone by the authorities to settle the matter of the original killing by the traditional formula of paying blood money. After the killing he had given himself up, but when he found out the traditional way of settling the matter was not going to be followed, he went on the run. The authorities, especially the governor general, felt the only answer was to take him to the gallows. When they failed to catch him after his escape from prison, they took his wife and father hostage and put them in Bahr-Dar prison in his stead. When I made my first visit to the prison, these two innocent people appealed to me and I ordered their immediate release. On hearing this, Semeneh sent local elders to me to plead for the government to give its blessing for him to settle the matter traditionally.

I told the elders openly that although government policy stated that he should be destroyed, I saw no reason why such a brave man should die so I would make sure no police action was taken against him. During my tenure as governor, Semeneh lived peacefully with his family, but a year after I left he was killed fighting. I felt it was sad that a great nation which had ruled itself through the common law for thousands of years was abandoning its traditions to try to apply foreign laws which had no meaning to the people. The so-called modernization process of five decades for which superficial observers both foreign and local gave His Majesty credit, served only to promote demoralization, deculturalization, divisions, and the abandonment of traditional values.

If Ethiopia could but have had a leader who was proud of his heritage during those five decades, the country could have progressed like Japan, without losing her cultural heritage and identity and compromising her national dignity.

I here wish to take issue with the comments of John Spencer in his book "Ethiopia at Bay": "a society aging in modern terms of reference and beset with inner rivalries and contradictions, yet at the summit, this society presented to the world a robust coherence which, from my vantage point in the Ministry of Foreign Affairs I could observe in all its manifold and pyramidical complexities."[1]

Although Mr. Spencer's connection with Ethiopia spanned 35 years, his understanding of the people appears superficial. This is proved by another passage in which he describes an encounter with an old Ethiopian woman while he was walking in the countryside with two Ethiopian officials of the modern hierarchy.[2] He claims the woman, on seeing his white skin, fell on her knees and worshipped him as Christ. If this passage is to be taken at face value, the sanity of either the old woman or Mr. Spencer must be called into question. Ethiopians had been Christians before Mr. Spencer's countrymen and had never believed Christ had white skin. Besides, they had seen plenty of whites during the Italian invasion and the old woman could not have been surprised to see a white man. What had really happened in the encounter Mr. Spencer describes was that the old woman, seeing two officials, appealed to them in the customary manner for a solution to some problem she had.

I know my interpretation is right because the same thing once happened to me during my time with the Ministry of Communications when I had gone into the interior with a Land Rover to inspect the construction of some rural roads. An old woman stepped from the side of the road and spread her Netela, a toga-like garment, in my path. I stopped and asked her what was wrong. She told me that for some unknown reason her only son had been taken by the police and thrown into prison in Sheno, the capital of Qinbebit.

I took the name of the son and found the son was being held as a suspect in a murder case on very flimsy evidence. I took the matter up with the police commander, General Yilma, in Addis Ababa and he sent an inspector to investigate. The inspector could find no evidence against the boy, so he was released. Although the modern view of my action would be interference in somebody else's jurisdiction, traditionally all officials had a common responsibility to ensure that justice was done. Mr. Spencer comments on a discussion with the former prime minister, Tsehafi-Tezaz Aklilu Habte-Wold, who expressed his disgust for "ignoramuses lifted by Imperial appointments into positions of power." Mr. Spencer quotes the prime minister as "by no means convinced that Ethiopia had reached the stage where parliamentary democracy could be viable." It needs to be remembered tht the prime minister was himself a product of the Imperial system and was regarded by many as an ignoramus lifted to power.

Since my office door was always open, one day a monk named Aba Wole-Tensay walked in. He was barefoot, blind in one eye because of cataracts, and dressed in the traditional gabi. I got up, went to meet him in front of my desk, kissed the cross and went back to my seat. He told me he had come to seek permission to visit the monastery of Deqe Istifanos. I was surprised and asked him how a monk could be seeking permission from the secular authorities to visit a place which was the rightful abode of those who had devoted their lives to God? He then started to relate his story, but first let me explain of the background of the relationship between the church and the state.

The biblical heritage of Ethiopia dates back to the time of the Old Testament and in the middle of the fourth century Christianity was introduced. At this time, the Axumite kingdom, the cradle of Ethiopian culture and civilization, was at its height of political supremacy in the region. Its capital, Axum, was the center of diplomatic, commercial, and social activities and its Red Sea port, Adulis, was an important commercial center for trade on the African coast. Much of the Greek and Roman cargoes for the Mediterranean and the East passed through Adulis.

These strong commercial links led to the conversion of the king to Christianity. The Axumite king Ezana made Christianity the state religion and established the tradition of the church as the spiritual head of the kingdom. The leadership in spiritual and cultural matters was gradually consolidated through the establishment of monastic centers which served as permanent repositories for Christian learning and cultural development throughout the empire.

The active expansion and development of the church and its strong political influence were not limited to the boundaries of the empire, but extended across the Red Sea to the Arabian peninsular. During the sixth century, the strong position of the Axumite kingdom made it a champion of Christianity in the whole of the Red Sea area. King Kaleb occupied part of the Arabian peninsular through military intervention against the persecution of Christians.

With the establishment of the church in the Axumite kingdom, the process of parallel development of the church and state and political and territorial expansion of the kingdom took on another dimension which was carried on throughout the Medieval period.

This expansion and development was checked during the ninth century when the political power and vitality of the Christian kingdom started to decline, drifting into a state of anarchy. Some tribes had remained faithful to the teachings of the Old Testament and a woman leader, Yodit, of the Felasha tribe succeeded in destroying the Axumite dynasty and dealt a devastating blow to the church and the Christian community from which it took 40 years to recover. The church was revived under the Zagwe dynasty and ruled the country for the next three and a half centuries. The epitome of the culture of that period was the rock churches at Lalibela.

With the return to power of the Axumite dynasty in 1270 in the person of Yikono Amlak, there recommenced an active development of both the church and the state. It was the leaders of the church who negotiated the transfer of power from the Zagwe dynasty back to the Axumite dynasty through the good offices of the founder of the Debre-Libanos monastery, Abune Tekle-Haymanot. The Bible was the cornerstone not only of the Christian principles of the kingdom, but also of the culture and politics.

The monasteries produced great religious and political leaders. One of the priorities of each monarch was to establish more monasteries and expand culture and learning, most notably during the reign of Zera-Yaqob between 1434 and 1468. There was a growing sense of national independence from the religious suzerainty of the Patriarchate of Alexandria, but the clergy was divided on the issue and it was not until the Italian invasion that the schism was to take place. At the time of the introduction of Christianity, a practice was introduced which became the tradition that the archbishop of the Ethiopian church would be appointed by the Patriarch of Alexandria from among the monks of Egypt. During the Italian invasion, the Egyptian archbishop quietly submitted to the invaders, although he was later removed from office.

The Ethiopian bishops, such as Abune Petros and Mikael, publicly condemned the invaders and excommunicated any Ethiopian who cooperated with them. For this defiance, they were publicly executed by the Italians, along with the monks of Debre-Libanos. So in 1948 the age-old tradition was discontinued and the new Ethiopian archbishop was appointed by an electoral college of clergy representing monasteries and churches from among a short list of three nominated by the church synod.

Just as Ethiopian Christianity was started and spread through commercial influence, so it was with Islam. Merchants from across the Red Sea converted the coastal tribes whom the church had neglected to evangelize because of the inhospitable terrain. During the period of the Ottoman expansion of the last years of the fifteenth century, the Moslem community, led by Mohammed Gragni and armed by the Turks, invaded the whole of the Christian empire supported by mercenaries from Arabia, Iran, India and Turkey. The country was laid waste and there was wholesale destruction of the rich Christian culture with the massacre of church leaders and monks as well as the Christian community at large. This continued for 15 years until, with military assistance from Portugal, Mohammed Gragni was killed. The Christian kingdom regained all of its territory and work began on the restoration of churches and monasteries.

But with the Portuguese military assistance came Roman Catholicism. However, the young Emperor Gelawdewos (1533-1556) stood firm against all attempts to convert Ethiopians to Catholicism, even under the threat that Portuguese support against the Moslems would be withdrawn unless he accepted the Pope as the spiritual head of the church.

Throughout Ethiopian history, strong leaders resisted all attempts to subordinate Ethiopian culture or leadership to that of any other nation. However, half a century after Gelawdewos, the Roman Catholics managed to find a weak-minded leader in the person of Emperor Susenyos (1607-1632) who converted to Catholicism and was excommunicated by the church. There was much bloodshed in the country until he fell seriously sick. It was said his illness was divine retribution for abandoning his heritage. He then renounced Catholicism and abdicated the throne in favor of a strong character, his son Fasiledes, who became one of the country's greatest leaders. He was responsible for the founding of Gonder as the capital of the empire and the construction of Gonder Castle.

An interesting episode occurred while Fasiledes was out hunting. In those days, hunting was regarded as sissy if firearms were used and therefore was carried out with spears. After spearing an elephant in the jungle and following it on horseback, Fasiledes became lost when he was separated from the rest of the party. He met a peasant gathering gesho, a type of hops used in the brewing of beer. He asked to be shown the way and the peasant, who was on foot, asked how that would be possible when Fasiledes was on horseback. Fasiledes replied that the peasant should leave behind his gesho, for which he would be compensated, and hop up behind the emperor. As they rode on, they came upon the royal party. Fasiledes told his guide: "You see those people over there? They are the Royal Court." The peasant replied: "How I have always wished to meet our kind and God-fearing emperor." "Well," said Fasiledes, "when we reach them they are sure to dismount and whichever man remains mounted must be the emperor." Sure enough, the court dismounted, leaving just the two men on the horse. The peasant said merrily: "Well, that means that the emperor must be either you or me." For his wit he was handsomely rewarded for those were the days when a leader did not regard himself as exalted above other people and expect to be worshipped. Unfortunately, the days when Ethiopians were proud to be known as such are gone and today every tribe wishes to be known by its tribal name.

If it had not been for the church, our literature would never have been developed. It played a dominant role not only in the spiritual and cultural life, but also in the social and political life. Church schools were among the important institutions which produced and molded both spiritual and secular leaders. In time of war, church leaders were in the van of the army, carrying the Ark symbolizing St. George and regular masses were said to meet the spiritual needs of the army.

Every adversary who rose against Ethiopia regarded the destruction of the church and the monarchy as vital objectives. Whenever the country found itself under a weak leader, it was thought that Ethiopia had lost the favor of God and the answer was always prayer. It is significant that since the present regime came to power, church attendance has increased tenfold. Just as Yodit tried in the ninth century, Mohammed Gragni tried in the fifteenth century and the Italians tried in the twentieth century, so the present regime employs the slogan "sir-neqel lewtt," which means "change which is uprooting the foundations." I doubt whether any of them understand the damage they have done to national pride, unity, and integrity.

Archbishop Abune Tewoflos, although he was powerless as a spiritual leader, should have spoken out against the disgraceful deposition of the emperor by a bunch of army personnel and against the barbarous massacre of 60 government officials. He had a responsibility, according to our traditions, to excommunicate the culprits and to call upon the general population to take arms against them. In spite of his silence, he was detained for five years at the end of which, in May 1979, he was taken out of his cell and has not been seen or heard of since. Individual monks who publicly condemn the regime are hanged in the country markets therefore the regime is doing everything it can to undermine the church by interfering with the appointments of the archbishop and other church personnel.

However, people within the country are finding renewed faith in the face of persecution and wherever Ethiopian refugees find a haven in the world, they establish a church which becomes the center of the lives of their community. Even in exile they are sustained and find dignity in their culture. One's culture should never be abandoned and the present leader of Ethiopia is no exception to swallowing foreign culture without thinking. After a visit to North Korea, he decreed that everybody in Ethiopia should wear North Korean costume. This new, self-appointed emperor is culturally naked.

Until the present regime took power, kings or emperors always had to be anointed by the church to be recognized. One of the main factors for the failure of the December 1960 uprising was the support of Abuna Basileos for the opposing camp and his excommunication of those officers and soldiers who supported the revolt. A small plane dropped leaflets on the field of battle announcing the excommunication. It was a powerful weapon.

From the time a simple monk from Bulga restored the Axumite dynasty in the thirteenth century and the church was rewarded with one-third of all the lands of the kingdom, the monastic superior of Debre-Libanos became the premier monk of the kingdom and counselor and confessor to the emperor. Each Christian household would have a priest or monk who was described as the father to the soul.

The administration of the church has always been separate from that of the state and the monasteries always administered themselves with neither the emperor nor the Archbishop having power over them. This long-established rule was broken in the case of the Deqe Istifanos monastery by the bishop of the province. The irony was that he did not only violate the autonomous status of the monastery, but also subordinated the spiritual power of the church to that of the state. To achieve his selfish aims, he used the secular arm to remove the head of the monastery who was opposing him.

The Deqe Istifanos monastery had a large tract of coffee under its jurisdiction and the bishop of the province, Abune Marqos, wanted control of the revenue. There was no way he could get it without flagrantly breaching the autonomous status of the monastery, which he did. He sent a monk of dubious

character named Aba Tekle-Haymanot to join the monastery and start causing
trouble among the other monks for the head of the monastery, Aba Wolde-
Tensay, who was the monk who had come to see me. The bishop used the
excuse of the fabricated disaffection against the head of the monastery to sum-
mon him and accuse him of abuse of power. Aba Wolde-Tensay refused the
summons on the grounds that the monastery was autonomous and the bishop
had no jurisdiction over it.

The bishop was then forced to call on the governor general, Dejazmatch
Tsehayu, to order the district police into the monastery to arrest the abemnet,
head of the monastery. This action on the part of the bishop demeaned the
church, but the poor monk was brought 245 kilometers to Debre-Marqos, the
provincial capital, and thrown in jail with common criminals. The bishop then
sent his own man as abemnet of the monastery, another flagrant violation of
the constitution of the monastery which stipulated that the abemnet must be
elected from the members of the monastery by the monks themselves.

It was necessary to get rid of Aba Wolde-Tensay so the bishop could have a
clear field. During one of the emperor's visits, he was informed jointly by the
governor general and the bishop that the monk who had been disturbing the
peace of the monastery was criminal and merited Imperial banishment.

He was taken to Bahr-Dar in June 1960 to be read the Imperial order banishing him from the district and the monastery. The frail monk demanded: "Is
this how Imperial justice is administered, without listening to both sides? God
will remember this judgment." I had arrived in the district in November 1961
and in April 1962, during a tour, I was informed that Aba Wolde-Tensay had
been a good administrator responsible for a lot of good things in the
monastery, and since his banishment the monastery was in sorry shape. Since I
had no right to interfere in the affairs of the monastery, I made no pronounce-
ments on the subject, but remembered what I had been told.

So when I found Aba Wolde-Tensay before me, I knew all about his good
work. He was seeking an assurance that if he returned to the monastery and
the bishop sought my aid in having him removed, I would not assign police-
men. I assured him I was aware that even a common criminal could seek sanc-
tuary in a monastery by ringing the bell and that once he did, the secular
authorities had no power over him and it became the duty of the monastery to
have the matter settled by a panel of local elders.

Two days later, the first person to enter my office was the original representative of the bishop in the monastery, Aba Maza, who informed me that a
monk banned by Imperial order had returned to the monastery. I dismissed
him with the admonition that he must be confusing secular and ecclesiastical
authority and that he should take any complaint to the right place. The next
day I was telephoned by the governor general, Dejazmatch Tsehayu, who told

me that although he had already sent me a telegram on the matter, he wished to emphasize it since: "You must have given the monk permission to enter the monastery without knowing the background. He is a criminal who has been banned from entering the monastery by the emperor and the subdistrict governor, Fitawrari Demlew, has been alerted to the fact. You now send police to arrest him and bring him to Debre-Marqos."

I told the governor general I had no power over the monks or the monastery and could not obey his instruction. In the meantime, Aba Wolde-Tensay, who merely wanted to visit the monastery for two or three days, was persuaded by the monks to remain. This caused a panic in the office of the bishop and I kept receiving telegrams from the governor general which I ignored.

Two weeks later I was telephoned by the governor general who told me the bishop was on his way to Bahr-Dar and that I should meet him at the airport. Since the airport was in the center of Bahr-Dar, next to the office, I set out to meet the bishop on foot when I heard the plane landing. However, as I approached the aircraft I found he had come with an armed bodyguard and I decided I had no business meeting a spiritual leader who wished to enforce his usurped authority with a gun. I went back to the office and an hour later the bishop sent a messenger to announce his arrival. I sent back a message that I would call on him after work.

It was a long-established practice that at the end of the working day the district governor would be accompanied either to his residence if he was walking or to his car by a retinue of district officials—Fitawrari Demlew subdistrict governor; Captain Shewa-Regged Desta, district police commander; Meri-Geta Mezgebe-Tibebe, the town council chief administrator; and Ato Wube, the district treasurer. That day I told the group of the bishop's arrival and the need to go to welcome him.

The next day, the bishop sent a message that he would like transportation to see the Tissisat Falls. Since I had no driver, I took him myself after work, accompanied by the district officials. On our return, we were offered honey wine and the bishop broached the subject of Aba Wolde-Tensay. I told him I was disgusted that he should be trying to involve the secular administration in church affairs and that I wanted no part of it. We bid him good night and left.

The next morning the district police commander walked into my office with a gloomy face and informed me that the governor general had been on his telephone, ordering him to give the bishop a police escort and take him to the monastery. I told him the governor could only act through me and had no right to give direct order to my subordinates: "The moment you take action to carry out the order, I shall suspend you." I could see from the look on his face that he felt he was caught between a rock and a hard place, so I gave him a letter stating what I had said, copied for the governor general.

The Emperor's Clothes

The bishop was then driven to commit another disgraceful act. He rented a motorboat from the port office and set off for the monastery with three or four followers. The monastery was in the middle of Lake Tana, 45 kilometers from Bahr-Dar. Arriving at the landing stage, the bishop sent a message to Aba Wolde-Tensay that the district governor was waiting for him in the boat. It was absolutely disgraceful that a religious leader should use subterfuge to unlawfully arrest a monk. He chose to break the Ten Commandments on the doorstep of a monastery instead of visiting the monastery as a pilgrim. Poor Aba Wolde-Tensay, thinking it was me waiting for him, was unceremoniously grabbed by the bishop's followers, stripped of his qob or head cover which denoted him as a monk and carted off to Bahr-Dar, where he was handed over to the police as a common criminal.

It was my practice to take a walk at daybreak in the courtyard of the district governor's new residence, enjoying the beauty of the lake and the islands. In front of the garage I found 10 men dressed in white shema with covered heads. As I approached them they all bowed in salutation. I reciprocated and asked them what their problem was. They told me they were from the Deqe Istifanos monastery and were appealing against the unprecedented act of the bishop. I asked how many of them had been present when the bishop's messenger claimed he had been sent by the district governor. Four of them said they had heard it. I asked them to go to the district governor's office and wait for me there.

I immediately convened the district board of commissioners, whose duty it was to assist me in the exercise of the district governor's powers. They happened to be the same officials who had escorted me on my visit to the bishop. I briefed them and called the monks to tell their story. I promised the monks I would take every step to ensure that justice prevailed, but that on their part they must warn every other monastery of the character of Bishop Marqos.

I told them I would tell the clergy where I went for Sunday prayers and that I would stop attending if I heard the mention of the name of Bishop Marqos. The board agreed that the action of the bishop was deplorable and that the statement of the monks should be forwarded to higher authority.

The report went to the emperor, the minister of the interior, the prime minister, the patriarch of the Ethiopian Orthodox Church, and the governor general with a cover letter from me stating that if the church failed to take the appropriate remedial action, I would feel constrained to resign.

At the end of the board meeting, I went to the police station and found Aba Wolde-Tensay waiting for police transportation to take him to Debre-Marqos. I found him in great spirits. Although his qob had been stolen from him, he had covered his head with a shema. The news spread like wildfire and the monks of Gonder went to the governor general, Nega Haile-Selassie, to protest against the bishop of Gojam and to ask that their complaint be transmitted to the emperor.

I was called to Addis Ababa. As soon as I arrived, I was ushered into the office of the emperor where I found the bishop and the emperor's secretary, Ato Solomon. The emperor asked what happened between me and the bishop.

I related everything in detail, including how the bishop misused the emperor's name to banish the monk from the monastery and how this had embittered the people of Bahr-Dar toward the emperor. The emperor rounded on the bishop, whom I saw wished that the floor could open up and swallow him. The emperor railed: "Is this what you were sent there to do as head of a religious organization? You have disgraced your office." Taking my cue, I said: "Your Majesty, the poor monk is thrown into Debre-Marqos prison with common criminals, all in your name. I would like a letter from Your Majesty to the governor general so that I can bring him here to tell you of all the injustices he has suffered." He ordered the secretary to give me the letter.

I flew to Debre-Marqos and returned with the monk, who spoke magnificently. The emperor said he was very sorry for the injustices he had suffered and would appoint a commission to set things right. The commission recommended that Aba Wolde-Tensay be reinstated and the autonomy of the monastery be respected. Governor General Dejazmatch Tsehayu informed the emperor that he would no longer be able to command the respect of the people of Gojam if I remained as district governor, so the emperor must choose between him or me. Two weeks after the reinstatement of the monk, I was called to Addis Ababa and appointed Ethiopian ambassador to Haiti. I was furious since I had no desire to leave my country. On the same day, two others were appointed with me. We were led to the presence of the emperor to kiss his feet, which was regarded as a great honor for all of us. The other two did so, but when they departed I pointedly remained standing. I could see from the look on the face of the emperor that he understood my feelings as I turned and walked away from him.

The next day I flew back to Bahr-Dar to pack and took little comfort in the farewell party which was organized for me. My one year and two months had been the most gratifying period of my life and I felt it would have been better to be banished on the soil of Ethiopia than to be exiled to a foreign land. I expressed the view to General Abiy, but he advised me that since I had family responsibilities it was no way to talk. His kind, fatherly advice convinced me to go to Haiti.

Ethiopia and Haiti are so far apart that there was no justification for an embassy. Like so much else that went on in Ethiopia at the time, the establishment of an embassy in Haiti was based on emotion rather than reason. When Yilma Deressa had been Ethiopian ambassador in Washington, he had gone to

Haiti on vacation and met the playboy president who entertained him lavishly. Yilma boasted that he would work for the establishment of diplomatic relations between the two countries; and, when he was appointed foreign minister, he felt he had to do so or lose face.

When Lij Mikael Imru became foreign minister in 1961, he saw no reason for the embassy and closed it. He had been replaced by Ketema Yifru as minister for foreign affairs when I was appointed in 1962. Mikael, with his independent mind, had not lasted long as foreign minister before being posted as ambassador to Moscow.

A year after I left Bahr-Dar, the people of Gojam revolted against the government and the governor general, Dejazmatch Tsehayu, was removed from there and appointed Governor of Kefa Province.

Note

1. John H. Spencer, *Ethiopia At Bay* (Algonac, MI: Reference Publication Inc., 1984).

9

Ambassador (1963-1969)

My appointment as governor of Bahr-Dar subprovince was a demotion in rank from assistant minister, due to my involvement in the December 1960 abortive coup and the fact that I was given any position at all was intended to mollify me. It was also a calculated move on the part of His Majesty. The attempt to have me hanged had failed as did the attempt to ruin my morale by banishing me into a remote province. The governor general, who was supposed to make life miserable because I was one who was disgraced and banished by the emperor, became a supplicant on my behalf for my reinstatement.

It was not in the nature of His Majesty to override the best judgment of his close associates. Whenever he wanted to disgrace somebody, he always sought their cooperation. Therefore, when the governor general of Kefa, Dejazmatch Kifle Dadi, spoke favorably on my behalf, requesting His Majesty to release me so I could serve under him as the chief of the Jimma town council, His Majesty had to manipulate the situation in order to make the best of a bad job. If he agreed to the exact request, the credit was going to go to the governor and the emperor would lose face. Therefore, he had to diminish the efforts of the governor to ensure he got the credit for my release and appointment.

The position the governor requested for me, the chief of a town council, was incomparable to the position of subprovincial governor which His Majesty had granted me. To be called from banishment to Addis Ababa and to be appointed as governor the same day was the work of an emperor and all the credit must go to him. At the same time, he was also hoping that after he bestowed all this favor upon me, I would be inclined to ask for more by following the established system of constant attendance at the palace, seeking an appointment in Addis Ababa and reinstatement to my previous position.

It was a trap to discredit me in the eyes of my supporters by demonstrating that I was shy to take up my position in the provinces and was seeking an easy position in the city. Such behavior would provide him with public support to take drastic action against me, to dismiss me with disgrace. This also failed because I left the city two weeks after my appointment and the expectation that the banishment would have a mollifying effect in my dealings with my superiors did not work. The governor general of Gojam, Dejazmatch Tsehayu Enqo-Selassie, to whom I reported, was a very close associate of the emperor and the most feared governor general in the country.

The incident of that poor monk discussed in the previous chapter brought to a close all the strategies designed to disgrace me in the public eye and bring me under control. Now the only alternative left for the emperor was to banish me out of the country to a place where I could not meet any Ethiopians except one third secretary, Abdulahi, and his wife and two children. Abdulahi was an Ethiopian Somali from Nazret who, after he finished his secondary education there, had managed to get employment as registry clerk in the Ministry of Foreign Affairs because of his acquaintance with the minister.

He was a good Ethiopian, a man of integrity and principle, but he required constant guidance and support in his work. As third secretary of the embassy, he was responsible for accounts and typing the ambassador's correspondence with the foreign office. He always came to me with his accounting problems and I had to help him out. On another occasion, he left the cash safe unlocked while he went to the bathroom and when he returned he found about U.S.$100 was missing. He accused the messenger of stealing it, but had no evidence to prove it so I was obliged to take extra measures to guard him from falling into more problems innocently.

When I was transferred to Mexico, I warned the foreign office that if they left Abdulahi in charge of the embassy they would have to face the consequences. They did not take notice of my warning and left Abdulahi there as charge d'affaires. Three months later, Abdulahi wrote informing me that he found himself in debt for more than U.S.$1,000 which he could not account for in balancing his three months' expenses. I felt very sorry for poor Abdulahi and immediately wrote to the foreign office reminding them of my warning and now they had no one to blame but themselves. However, six months after I left, the embassy was closed.

I had served as governor of Bahr-Dar subprovince one year and three months when I was called to Addis Ababa in early January 1963. When I went to the palace to report, I was ushered into one of the rooms adjoining the emperor's private office, where the Prime Minister Tsehafi-Tezaz Aklilu Habte-Wold, the Minister of Defense General Merid, the Minister of Interior General Abiy and His Majesty's private secretary, Ato Tefera-Worq, were standing. I bowed to salute them and then the prime minister spoke saying that with the grace of His Imperial Majesty I had been appointed ambassador to Haiti. It was something which I had not expected. Demotion or imprisonment I could have taken easily, but to be exiled from my country really shocked me to the extent that I could not control expressing my feeling of shock. My sincere friend General Abiy tried to calm me down, reminding me of my responsibility to my family which he said I must always take into consideration before I jumped into precipitate action.

The fact that the appointment shocked me had achieved one of the expected goals. The emperor wanted to turn me into a demoralized diplomat and a slave of luxurious life, which would force me to fall into line as a sycophant. After analyzing the aim of the appointment, I felt the challenge to disappoint them, so I prepared to take up my new career. I went to my new ministry, foreign affairs, to be briefed in a completely new field to which I had never had any inclination. When I asked for a formal briefing, I was advised to read books on diplomacy. As for information on Haiti, there was very little in the file. I was advised by Ato Zewge Wolde-Mariom [now deceased] that the administrative officer of the foreign office to request for the Eth$5,000 which he said was an established practice to grant a newly appointed ambassador to cover personal expenses necessary to buy clothing and other necessities. This was denied to me, even when I pointed out to the minister (Ketema) that during the abortive coup the army had ransacked my house. Both my wife and I lost everything we had so I needed the money to replace what we had lost and since I was going to represent my country, everything had to be seen in that light. He informed me that the practice discontinued, there was nothing he was going to do about it, and the only thing he could authorize was an advance on my salary to be paid back in installments.

Another established practice which was denied me was the first-class air ticket for ambassadors traveling to their new post. That I did not question. Somehow I felt guilty that I was going to cost my country expense just to keep me away from serving it. However, I left for Haiti in February 1963 with my family: my wife, who was five months pregnant with our third child; Tewdros, our eldest son who was two and a half; Heywote, our daughter who was one; and my sister Senayit, who was ten. I was disconsolate to think of these children being brought up in a foreign land away from their own environment, relatives and culture, and how they would take it when returning home after they had grown up because their memories and attachment would always be with the environment where they had passed their childhood, as it was with me and Qinbebit. All my plans to bring up my children according to the best traditions of my heritage were dashed.

To present my credentials to President Francois Duvalier, a morning coat was required by protocol. However, I informed the chief of protocol that I would dress in my national costume and it was agreed. The embassy, which had been opened two years ago and was in the process of being closed until I was appointed, was a seven-room house in Port-au-Prince. Three of the rooms were used as bedrooms and two as offices (chancellery), and the others were sitting-cum-dining rooms and kitchens.

Port-au-Prince is at the foot of rugged mountains at sea level about nine degrees north of the equator, therefore the climate was very hot and humid which presented a problem for my wife who grew up in the ideal climate of Addis Ababa.

The only African countries which had embassies in Haiti at that time were Liberia, which was long-established; Dahomey (now Benin) which was newly opened but eventually closed; and Ethiopia, which was recently established but closed in 1967. The Liberian ambassador, Bill Fernandez and his wife Laura became our friends in spite of our age difference (I was 37 and Bill was 58). Within a day or two of our arrival, even before I presented my credentials, the U.S. ambassador, Mr. Thurston, invited us for dinner. A close friendship between us, but unfortunately within two months of my arrival, there was an attempted coup and Ambassador Thurston left for home for consultations, only to be turned back from the airport as persona non grata on his return.

Apparently Ambassador Thurston must have been involved in the abortive coup because at most functions at the American embassy, there was quite a number of army officers. To get information on the day of the coup attempt, I drove to the American embassy and Ambassador Thurston informed me that the coup was all over. But at midday, an official announcement stated the reason for the shooting at 6 a.m. was that an army colonel who had been detained the night before had been shot while trying to escape.

According to my friend Bill Fernandez, who was well-placed in army circles and also close to Duvalier, the president was well informed of the plot beforehand and the colonel was caught and killed the same night. The morning shooting was a mockery to serve for the public announcement. That started a reign of terror in Haiti. Sporadic shooting and the burning of houses by the Tonto Macoute sent to net those army officers involved in the attempted coup became widespread in Port-au-Prince.

Once it was announced that the leader of the coup had been caught and killed, those who had been involved decided to take advantage of the treaty between Latin American countries, which allowed political refugees to seek asylum in the embassy of a signatory state. The Latin American embassies in Port-au-Prince were packed with refugees. One young chap who was terrorized ran into our embassy asking for political asylum, but Ethiopia was not a party to that special treaty so I was going to be in an embarrassing situation if the authorities asked to hand him over. I explained the situation to the young man and suggested that I drive him to one of the Latin American embassies and drop him at the gate so he could run in. I put him in the back seat of my VW Beetle and chauffeured him to the gate of the Brazilian embassy.

Later in the year, we had to give refuge to our former landlord, who asked if we could keep him in hiding for sometime until the situation settled down. He remained with us one month and when the situation which scared him settled, he left the embassy.

I have come to believe that no person has the power to change the fortune or the destiny of another. Everything that happened to me all along in my career made me come to this conclusion. Now I was exiled from my country under the pretext of being an ambassador, but by denying me the means to maintain that position it was hoped to make me suffer humiliation. The embassy budget for house rent was only U.S.$500 and it was quite impossible to rent a representative house for an embassy with this amount, so I was forced to suffer in that five-room villa in Port-au-Prince from February until April.

Since the heat of Port-au-Prince was affecting the health of my wife, I was trying to find a similar villa up on the mountain in places like Petion Ville. I asked my colleagues to help me to find one. After the April abortive coup when all MAG personnel were thrown out of the country, house rents slumped. In my case, something which I never expected happened. One Sunday there was a religious ceremony in which the president and the whole diplomatic corps were present.

After the ceremony, my friend, the German charge d'affaires Mr. Metternich, approached me and said: "I have found you a nice house up on the mountain. Come with me now to see it." So I followed him past Petion Ville and started climbing the mountain. The road ended by leading through an imposing gate way into a compound with a swimming pool at the far end. On the left stood a white palace-like building with marble steps leading to arched doorway. Getting out of our cars, we sat by the swimming pool under a parasol. An attendant came to greet us. Apparently Mr. Metternich had rented a room there for U.S.$50 per day when he arrived in Haiti, so he was familiar with the people.

I asked Mr. Metternich where the house was that he was going to show me. He said: "This is the one." I said: "Are you joking? I thought you were serious when you said you found me a house to be rented. I did not know you wanted to show me a palace!" While we were arguing, the owner, Mr. Frank Magloir, came along enquiring if I was the Ethiopian ambassador and commenting that I was very young for the job. He offered to take me around to show me his chateau. From the pool we entered the bar, a large hall with a mahogany counter and a big piano at one corner. We climbed a flight of stairs and came to a circular balcony from where one could see below a beautiful panorama of

Petion Ville, Port-au-Prince and the Caribbean. From the balcony we entered the dining hall where there was a massive mahogany table to seat 12 comfortably with heavy, upright mahogany chairs and a beautiful chandelier.

The dining room was at one end of the T-shaped room and the beautifully furnished saloon was at the other. From the dining room, crossing part of the saloon, a flight of stairs went up to the large landing leading to two bedrooms. The master bedroom with built-in cupboards and a large bed was in the middle of a big hall with an adjoining large bathroom, a small room for children and a large veranda overlooking the beautiful scenery. There were two large kitchens fully furnished and equipped and then six more self-contained bedrooms, fully furnished.

After he showed me around, we sat on the balcony of the master bedroom and I said: "Well, Mr. Magloir, I am sorry to disappoint you but I am not the type of ambassador to rent this property. You had better look for someone else. My budget for house rent could not even enable me to rent one room of this property, so I will not be interested." He said his main interest was not in the money. It could be U.S.$200 or whatever I could afford. What he was interested in was that I move into this house immediately to save it from Duvalier. He proposed we sign the contract immediately. He was going to erect the flag pole at that instant and said: "By tomorrow, you move in because I am in trouble and I want to leave the country immediately."

Mr. Metternich said the opportunity was God-given and I must take it. He advised that I pay U.S.$400 per month out of the U.S.$500 so we would be able to rent office accommodation at Port-au-Prince with the balance. The same afternoon Mr. Magloir came with the contract typed out and he drove us up to Montagne Noir to show the place to my wife, who fell in love with it. And so we moved from hell to paradise in one of the best embassy buildings in the whole of Port-au-Prince and were the envy of all the ambassadors.

All this was taking place contrary to the expectations of those in Addis who thought they had condemned me and my family to suffer from hardship. They made everything obvious when they transmitted the budget for the first month after my arrival in Haiti. They deducted the whole amount of my salary, which I had taken in advance for preparation, contrary to the agreement that it would be paid back in three months. I had to send a coded telegram to the emperor threatening to take the next plane back home if the foreign office did not keep to what had been agreed and transmit my salary immediately. I was representing my country and therefore had to maintain prestige. Whatever was directed against me was bound to undermine the prestige of my country and I would never submit to it.

I also had to fight to get an official car. After much correspondence, I received a note from the private secretary of the emperor informing me that the emperor had given orders for one of the Mercedes-Benz that had been bought for the OAU conference to be sent to the Haiti embassy. From the local Mercedes-Benz agent I found out how much a Mercedes 250 would cost. The freight cost of a Mercedes-Benz from Addis Ababa to Haiti turned out to be the cost of the car, so I sent a telegram to the emperor requesting his authorization for only the money they had to pay for shipping it to be transmitted to me so I could buy the official car. He agreed.

All this unconstructive fighting with Addis was time-consuming. I was feeling uneasy that I was wasting my valuable time and that I must do something worthwhile. So I started a correspondence course in Modern American Law with the Blackstone School of Law in Chicago. I read 12 volumes and passed the exams after three years to get my law degree [LLB].

In the diplomatic field, I managed to so interest President Duvalier in African politics that Haiti was to be represented in an observer capacity at the formation of the OAU in Addis Ababa on 25 May 1963. I also arranged for the chief engineer of the Ministry of Public Works Mr. Lion to go to Addis Ababa for consultation with the civil aviation authorities regarding the construction of runways for jet aircraft. Originally, this project was to be financed by the U.S. government and constructed by a U.S. company. When relations became strained, the conditions of financing were altered. The construction cost was doubled which made the Haitian government shelve the project. But President Duvalier instructed his minister of public works to undertake the project with their own means, which they did for less than half the cost offered by the U.S. construction company.

In 1966, the Ethiopian ambassador in Washington, Ato Berhanu Dinqe, defected and sent me a copy of his letter to the emperor. Since this was the first incident of this kind in the diplomatic history of Ethiopia it was bound to shock the emperor. I thought this was a good opportunity for me to be called back to my country, so I wrote a letter to the emperor complaining that I wasted my youthful time in vain when I could have served my country usefully: " I have wasted three of my best years just to comply with Your Majesty's wish, but from now on unless I am given the opportunity to return to my country, I will be obliged to take a step which may not please Your Majesty."

And I wrote to my friend General Abiy informing him of my letter to the emperor and telling him that unless I was called back, I would follow the example of Berhanu Dinqe. I knew he would talk to the emperor and convince him to call me back. Immediately I received a response from the emperor saying I would be accredited to Jamaica and Trinidad so as to occupy my time usefully. I immediately responded to this saying my request was to return to my country and I had no interest in diplomatic activities. A telegram came ordering me to Addis Ababa alone without my family. From Addis Ababa Airport I went directly to the palace and was received by His Majesty, who said: "The reason why we called you is that we are going on a state visit to Trinidad Tobago and Jamaica and we want you to go to these countries and cooperate in organizing our visit. At the end of the visit, you will be appointed as our ambassador to Mexico. As you know Mexico is one of the countries which remained a loyal friend of our country and I want you to go there and work for two years to strengthen the friendship."

I said I did not understand the reasons of his state visit to the newly independent Caribbean countries, leaving out the oldest, at which he has his ambassador. His response was that he was invited there. I told him that can easily be arranged, and took leave and went from there to Haitian Ambassador Elize and told him the emperor was invited by Jamaica and Trinidad, and he must communicate with President Duvalier for an official invitation. That came within a day or two. In the meantime, I went to see my friend General Abiy to be briefed on what he had done and also to tell him of my audience with the emperor and ask him his advice. As I had expected, when he received my letter he spoke to the emperor and was instrumental for what had taken place and he advised me to accept the appointment to Mexico for the time being. I only stayed four days in Addis Ababa and went back to Haiti.

I went to the foreign office and met with Minister Chalmers and Vice Minister Remonde to organize the emperor's visit before I proceeded to Jamaica and then Trinidad. President Duvalier was extremely pleased and wanted to make it an specially big occasion. We met two or three times with the president to discuss the detailed arrangements of the program.

For the emperor's scheduled 24-hour visit, I had to organize a state dinner or reception on his behalf in honor of his host depending on what the host country was going to do. It was agreed that the host country would organize the dinner party and the embassy, the reception. But when it came to the venue where the reception should be given, I insisted that it must be in the embassy. President Duvalier become adamant that it be given at the Imperial villa which he had assigned for the emperor. It was an ordinary four-bedroom house constructed on the slope of a hill in Port-au-Prince with no room for a reception at all.

By this stage in my career, I had long experienced dealing with the whims of despots, so I pointed out that it would be impossible to organize a state reception in that miserable place and stressed that it had to be at the embassy. If the president objected to this, the emperor's visit would have to be shortened. Instead of 24 hours, it would be eight to ten hours only so as to not necessitate the embassy's organization of a reception. The president strongly objected to this alternative also. We could not come to terms on this question because I did not deem it necessary to embarrass ourselves by trying to give a

9. Ambassador (1963-1969)

state reception in an ordinary small villa which could not accommodate even 20 people let alone more than 100.

I told the president the emperor would arrive in Port-au-Prince during the morning and would leave the same day so the program had to be adjusted accordingly and I would cancel the reception. He became mad at me and said "It cannot be changed." So with this decision on my part, I left Port-au-Prince and flew to Kingston, Jamaica, and everything went smoothly. After one week, I flew to Port of Spain, Trinidad, without problem.

The emperor's visit started there and I explained to him the change of program and the problem I had with President Duvalier. His visit to Haiti would last only a day and he would have to leave that same day. His Majesty agreed and the foreign minister, Ketema Yifru, was instructed to send a telegram informing President Duvalier to that effect. President Duvalier sent Ambassador Elize to Port of Spain to plead with the emperor not to change the program, but Elize did not have a chance to see him because the foreign minister told Elize he should not waste his time as the decision would not be reversed. Elize flew back to Port-au-Prince without success. I left Port of Spain for Kingston one day ahead of the emperor so as to meet him there. His reception in Kingston was chaotic due to Rastafarians storming the airfield as soon as the plane came to a stop.

The next day, I flew to Port-au-Prince to arrange for His Majesty's arrival there. Understandably, the president was mad about the change in the program and refused to cooperate with me. The protocol of the reception at the airport was muddled up because instead of meeting the emperor when he disembarked from the aircraft, the emperor had to walk halfway between the aircraft and the terminal building where the Guard of Honor was lined up to meet his host. Of course the emperor was affronted, and in the evening at eight when he boarded his plane to leave, I explained that the president alone was the one who decided on the reception protocol.

After the reception ceremony at the airport, the whole party drove to the national palace for luncheon. The emperor and his entourage drove to the Imperial Villa after the lunch. There were only three bedrooms there available for the emperor, Princess Sofia Desta, and Leul Ras Imru. The rest, like General Abiy, the foreign minister, and so on, had to sit in the small lounge. I offered to take them to the embassy which was nine miles out of Port-au-Prince. General Abiy accepted my offer and when he saw Chatele de la Montagne Noir, he was so surprised. He said he could not understand why I was complaining so loud to return home from such a delightful life here. He admired the views, the architecture of the house, the luxurious furnishing, the swimming pool, etc. I told my dear friend my accommodations did not give me any happiness and I would rather live like one of the peasants in my country. We argued on this point, but he accepted my contention that no luxurious living or material well-being can give happiness to a conscientious mind.

I waited for two and a half months after the end of the emperor's visit before I heard anything about my transfer to Mexico. The first coded telegram I received was instructing me to return to Addis Ababa. I reacted with great pleasure and informed the Haitian government and the dean of the diplomatic corps of my being recalled and the usual farewell parties become a daily affair. By about the middle of July, two weeks after receiving the instruction, I packed my personal belongings and had them shipped to Addis. Since my family wanted to leave ahead of me, I saw them off with the understanding that I was to follow them within a week. On the day after my family's departure, I received a telegram reversing the previous order. I was ordered to proceed to Mexico direct from Haiti after receiving my credential letter which was dispatched in the pouch.

Now, with my family in Addis and my going to Mexico, it was a very annoying arrangement. However, I left for Mexico the first week in August 1966. The Ethiopian mission in Mexico had been established as a legation in 1949 and it was raised to the level of an embassy in 1954. My predecessor, Ato Asrat Yinesu, had been there five years. The house I inherited from him in Colonial Polanco on Avenida Alehandro Dumas housed both the ambassador's residence and the chancellery. It had four bedrooms upstairs and the saloon, dining room, kitchen, and one tiny ambassador's office downstairs. Another room, two-by-four meters, was next to the ambassador's office to accommodate three secretaries.

It was very poorly furnished—one dirty sofa, two easy chairs, and no kitchen utensils or crockery. Fortunately for me, during the month of August the president of Mexico was busy compiling his annual statement to the nation called "Informa," due to be delivered in September. The presenting of credentials had to be done after this event which meant that for nearly a month I was free of any official obligation. This gave me a good opportunity to compile a report to the Ministry of Foreign Affairs on the state of the embassy. I clearly put my conditions in the report that if I was required to represent my country properly I would need a budget which would to enable me to do that. If the government was not in a position to meet my requested budget, then my conscience would not permit me to be a party of such an arrangement of humiliation and embarrassment for my country.

I gave the ministry an ultimatum of one month to let me know whether they agreed with my budget proposal. If I did not hear from them within that period, I would leave Mexico and go to Addis Ababa. I had the means to carry out my threat because when I was first recalled from Haiti they had sent me a ticket to Addis Ababa. Then, when I was sent to Mexico, I received another

9. Ambassador (1963-1969)

ticket. I sent copies of all this correspondence to His Majesty. I presented my credentials in September 1966 and left Mexico for Addis Ababa about the middle of October 1966. On arrival, I reported to the foreign office and also at the palace. Nobody said anything until I had been there for five months.

I thought I was forgotten and they might be thinking of my successor. I was planning to take up something privately when, in March 1967, I was called to the palace. His Imperial Majesty, in the presence of Foreign Minister Ketema Yifru, angrily asked me what I was doing in the capital away from my assignment. I replied that I thought I had made it clear in my report which had been copied to him. At this juncture, he turned his face toward the minister and said: "Hadn't we authorized the budget he requested?" The foreign minister responded positively and added that preparation was under way to send me off. His Majesty said I must leave the capital and be at my post before the end of the week. I bowed and left the room. The minister followed me and from there we drove directly to the Ministry of Foreign Affairs where he ordered the staff to take immediate action to meet my requirements and send me off.

Within two days, everything was ready and I left Addis Ababa for Mexico with my family to follow later, I had been given a draft for purchasing an official car for the embassy and furniture, so I stopped in Germany and ordered a Mercedes-Benz 250, and in London I went to Maples and ordered furniture. I used the embassy rent budget to buy a four-room condominium and converted it into a suitable establishment for an embassy. By September 1967, the Ethiopian embassy was on a level with other respectable embassies in Mexico City.

With the purchase of the condominium for the chancellery, after three years, when the last installment payment of the purchase price would be made, the embassy's recurrent expenses for renting office accommodation would come to an end. I worked out a long-term development plan, after paying for the chancellery, to purchase a three-bedroom apartment for the counsellor and then one for the third secretary. All this was going to be financed with the budget for renting a chancellery. But unfortunately, my successors did not follow the development plan so the Ethiopian embassy in Mexico, even today, owns only the building which I bought.

While I was busy organizing the embassy and putting it into shape, there was the political problem of the Olympic Games. Mexico was hosting the 1968 Olympics and the decision of the International Olympic Committee, which met at Grenoble in March 1967, was to allow South Africa to participate. The Ethiopian delegation, led by Yidneqatchew Tessema, protested against the decision, threatening the withdrawal of all the African countries. As Ethiopian ambassador in Mexico, the host country, I got involved in the issue and in September 1967, I was called to Addis Ababa for consultations on this matter and the Ethiopian participation, in general. In spite of support for South African participation from the president of the International Olympic Association, Avery Brundage, we were able to bring about a reversal in the Grenoble decision.

Ethiopia's team in Mexico consisted of 96 participants, 10 times the number sent to the preceding Olympics. Ethiopia participated in most of the track and field events, cycling, and boxing, a folk lyric display comprised of 40 persons, a children's camp, and painting and cultural exhibition. Mamo Wolde won the gold medal in the marathon and the 10,000-meter race.

The director of the National Museum at Addis Ababa, Ato Mamo Tessema, arrived in Mexico in July 1968, bringing with him 235 objects of art, both ancient and contemporary, to organize and arrange properly for the cultural exhibition. For the first time in the history of Ethiopian participation in this important international event, all the 96 Ethiopian delegates on the opening day ceremony of the Olympics paraded in their national costume, which was a unique presentation. The credit for this goes to Solomon Tessema [now deceased], the sports commentator of Radio Addis Ababa, who originated the idea of the project and got Ato Debebe Habte-Yohannes, the managing director of the Addis Ababa Bank, to finance it.

The embassy was expected to give an official reception in honor of the Ethiopian delegation, inviting officials of the Mexican foreign office, Olympic Committee, the diplomatic corps, and the leaders of the other countries' delegation. In order to carry out these official and diplomatic functions I had sent a request for funds amounting to U.S.$2,000 addressed to the emperor. I know the Ganian ambassador had been provided with 8,000 pounds sterling for a delegation one-tenth the size of ours. I received a negative response. I showed it to Ato Mamo who was one of the leaders of the Ethiopian delegation and I expressed my disgusted view of our leadership. I told him I was ashamed to represent such irresponsible and insensible leadership, incapable of recognizing the humiliation of its representative meant the humiliation of the leadership itself. Mamo sympathized with me and said: "Look here, I have carried with me more money than I could spend for my mission here. It is government money and I am willing to cover the reception expenses with the spare funds I have." I thanked him for saving me from humiliation and embarrassment. So the effort of the authorities in Addis to embarrass the ambassador by refusing to allocate funds for the official reception and entertainment expenses in honor of the Ethiopian delegation did not succeed. Thanks to the director of National Museum, Ato Mamo Tessema, who carried more than enough funds for his activities and expenses in arranging the cultural exhibition. As a whole, the Ethiopian participation at the Mexico Olympics turned out to be a great success.

9. Ambassador (1963-1969)

I returned to my country in June 1969 with the determination to retire from government service and take up farming. Since returning diplomats were entitled to bring in household furniture and a personal car duty-free, I stopped in Paris to buy a Peugeot 404 caravan which I was informed was the ideal car for a farmer. (When I joined Endalkatchew's ministry, I sold it and bought a VW.) I was returning home after seven years' absence, except for the brief visit mentioned in the last chapter. I found the face of Addis Ababa had changed dramatically. The thinking of the people had also changed, everyone talked about development in farming, industry and the building trade. Living standards had improved, with people well-dressed, well-fed, and living in clean, well-constructed houses and villas.

In the city center, many new and tall apartment and office buildings had risen. The city appeared to be bustling with commercial and economic activities, and new residential areas, like Bole, had developed with modern villas. I found most of my former colleagues living comfortable lives with personal cars and well-furnished villas. To maintain this living standard, most of them had taken up farming as an extracurricular activity to supplement their monthly incomes. They seemed to be doing well and contemplating retirement from their government positions to concentrate full-time on farming. I thought the situation was quite encouraging to start with my plan to go into farming. So without wasting time after my arrival in Addis Ababa, I started to investigate the possibilities of how and where to find land for farming.

Government policy for returning diplomats was encouraging for such activities because one was not required to sit in the office to earn his pay until reassigned a position. The foreign office paid the monthly salary one had been earning before taking the assignment of the diplomatic post. So I had all of the free time, but was paid the monthly salary of Eth$600 which I was earning when I was governor of Bahr-Dar. This went on from June 1969 until January 1970 when I joined the Ministry of Posts, Telecommunications, and Transport.

My investigation to find the land proved very difficult because most of the farming development that had taken place was along the Awash Valley. One of my former colleagues, Abebe Wolde-Sellassie, who was now an employee of Wonji Sugar Factory, and his friend Mulugeta Gebre-Wold had bought ten gashas of land [400 acres] along the Awash Valley and asked me to join them in that venture. So one day in October 1969, the three of us in a Land Rover went to inspect the site, visiting the farm of Leul Ras Asrat Kassa on the way. The farm was impressive with its modern farm buildings, residence, maintenance workshop, tractors and combine harvesters, an expanse of maize and cotton fields, and a few dairy cattle.

Then we visited the farm jointly owned by Ato Abebe Retta, minister of agriculture, and Ato Hadis Alemayehu, minister of planning. There was only a cotton field and no impressive farm buildings. We reached the site of our main objective and found no development work had been initiated. Yet all along the river, down the valley as far as we could see, was an expanse of cotton farm. A portion of this was the farm of Abebe Dessalegne, a former telecommunication engineer who retired his position and taken up farming as a full-time occupation.

This is the first time I had met Abebe, but he was well-known to my two colleagues. I was very much impressed by his achievement through sheer determination with little capital. He had started work on the farm a year ago and was living in a tent with his workers. Out of the ten gasha of total landholdings he had already planted cotton on two gasha which he expected to harvest in two months' time. Abebe asked us to stay for lunch. With no grocery store and restaurant nearby, we gladly accepted. We sat for lunch by the Awash River under the shade of a sycamore tree. The lunch consisted of roasted goat meat, vegetables from the farm, tomatoes, cabbages and potatoes, served on an improvised wooden table.

While we were having lunch, one of his workers passed by limping, and I asked Abebe why. Abebe told us the man had been shot by the Kereyu, the nomadic inhabitants of that area who used to graze their livestock all along the Awash Valley freely. Now they were deprived of it and looked at us with animosity. I asked how he and others like him came to own the land which had belonged to these people for generations.

He said it was the Bete-Rist (the Imperial landholders) who sold it to them. But how could Bete-Rist sell the land? This was a violation of the rist system (traditional system of landholding) by the very government entrusted to administer justice and uphold and protect traditional heritage. Abebe replied: "But it is the chief of the tribe who passed the ownership right of the land to the emperor (as inheritance)." I said: "This is even worse corruption. Before selling this land to people outside the tribe, the emperor should have allocated enough land to each household of the tribe for them to graze their cattle or to devise a project to settle them as sedentary farmers. What was left over from that could then be sold to others like you for commercial farming. That would have been the right procedure for a responsible government. Well, if this is the way this land was acquired, I am afraid my conscience will not allow me to own it and put my effort toward developing it, right in the face of the rightful owners watching me with animosity."

So my investigation into owning land and taking up farming came to an end. But what to do now with all of the free time I had? I decided to assist my mother-in-law, who was a widow, in developing her property. First, I discussed with her my idea of development on the empty plot she had in Addis Ababa and the half gasha of land in Debre-Tsigge, about 50 kilometers west from Addis Ababa on the Gojam road. Soon I was busy building a villa in Addis Ababa and a dairy farm in Debre-Tsigge. The villa was completed within four months and she moved in, leaving the old house which went to another child (born from the first marriage of her deceased husband) in the distribution of property of her deceased husband. The dairy project was well under way, the cow shed was constructed, and I had bought six heifers of reputed breed and one young bull from a nearby dairy farm. Three of the heifers gave birth within three months.

In January 1970, I started the self-help project to build the Sembo/Arerti Bulga Road project. The last time I had visited Qinbebit was in 1955 when I went there to bring my grandmother to Addis Ababa to live with me. So during the Epiphany, I asked my father and my younger brother Melaku if they would be willing to come with me to Qinbebit to spend the holiday there. The three of us drove there in a Peugeot as far as the track would permit us. We then parked the car outside a peasant farmer's house and walked about 15 kilometers to my grandmother's house. We were warmly welcomed and spent the night there. The next morning we attended the Epiphany celebration. What I noticed during this celebration was that there was not a single student, church school or otherwise present. All the children who were present had no opportunity of going to school. The traditional church schools had ceased to function during the Italian invasion and their revival during the postwar period was not encouraged because government schools were taking their place.

For the inhabitants of Qinbebit, the nearest government school at Shola Gebeya was about 25 kilometers away. I brought this shortcoming to the attention of the authorities in the Ministry of Education and requested a school be built for the inhabitants of Qinbebit. I raised this question with the people who were present for the celebration and they were willing to provide the plot for the building of the school. I asked them to show me the plot so I would be able to take up the matter immediately with the ministry. Fifteen thousand square meters of land was allocated for the building of the school.

On returning to Addis Ababa, I went to the Ministry of Education the next day where the official Ato Abebe Tilahun (a good friend of mine), who was in charge of school development for Shewa region, pointed out to me that since the budget for school construction had already been committed, he could not consider this project. I asked him to give me the drawings for standard school construction, which he did. I decided to build the school with locally available material as cheaply as possible, so I calculated a rough estimated cost of Eth$3,000 on the basis of the standard drawing of three classrooms, each class to accommodate 50 students. I managed to raise this within our family and the three-classroom school was constructed within a period of three months. I then went back to my friend Abebe and informed him that I had constructed the school and now needed a teacher. One was provided. In less than two months after the school at Sekoru was opened, all of the three classes were full.

In one of my periodic visits during the weekend, an American friend of mine, Mr. Khurman, the director of Pfizer International, wanted to come with me to visit this project. The next morning when we come out from our tent, we saw many people sitting outside. They mistook Mr. Khurman for a doctor who had come with medical help. Fortunately, Mr. Khurman was representing a pharmaceutical company and he always carried with him a first aid kit. Most of those who had come for medical assistance suffered from eye diseases and foot sores. So he spent the morning doctoring and then donated Eth$1,000 toward a project for building a clinic.

I asked my friend Betru Admassie, general manager of telecommunication, to donate to the project some empty crates and boxes. With that and the Eth$1,000, I built a two-room clinic and a two-room house for a health officer to live and I asked the Ministry of Health and Minister of State Ato Eshete Mekonnen to equip the clinic and provide a health officer.

But I found out the health officer could not cope with the patients who came to the clinic. It needed a medical doctor, but to bring a medical doctor to the clinic the need for an access road became very obvious. So I started to think of how to raise funds to build a road. The distance from the main road to the school and clinic is 22 kilometers and raising funds to build this was not easy. I thought in terms of the problems facing the whole region, which was completely devastated during the Italian occupation because it was the stronghold of the resistance movement.

It was a good theme to exploit for raising funds by saying it would serve the whole region from one end to the other. The starting point from the east is Sembo, a small village 90 kilometers from Addis Ababa on the Dessie Road, and the termination point is in the west at Arerti, a span of 114 kilometers. I prepared an expose of the suffering of the inhabitants of Bulga because they had provided shelter for the freedom fighters. By doing so, their houses were burnt down, every property lost, and those who survived the bombing and poison gas of the invaders migrated to the other parts of the country until they returned to their devastated land after the enemy was thrown out. No government aid or any assistance was provided to rehabilitate these poor people to whom every Ethiopian owes his freedom. So I established an association to finance and build the Sembo Arerti Road project and within a month of its establishment, Eth$12,000 were raised. With this fund in hand, I made arrangements with the highway authority to undertake the buiklding of the road and I would cover fuel and overtime expenses.

Within a month, the construction of the road passed the 22 kilometers mark and access to the school and clinic became possible. I spoke with my doctor friends to see if they would be willing to sacrifice one of their Sundays for voluntary service to those who are badly in need of their assistance. The following doctors and nurses took turns giving free service every Sunday at the Sekoru clinic:

Doctors: Mehretab, Gebru, Shawle, Mohammed, Ide Mariam & his wife, Assefa, Befekadu, Keterew, Gizaw, Ignatovic & his wife Joffrion, Seare, Adugna, Abreham, Birhane Tumelisan, Fekade, Sisay, Fikre, Jemal, Admassu, Sayed, Belachew, Pietros, Mehari, Yayehiard, Paulos, Mikhail, Grebenarov, and Mr. and Mrs. Markos. Nurses: Ejigayehu, Ayelech, Senayt, and others.

In providing transportation for the volunteer doctors and nurses from Addis and back, the committee members - Shibru, Demissie, Taye, German Wolde, Telahun Paulos, Shimels, Negash, Lulsegged, and the author - took turns every Sunday. One of the above committee members left Addis at six in the morning with a doctor and nurse, and reached the clinic at Sekoru about eight. They would find hundreds of people waiting there. Some days it would be 5 p.m. before one finished with the last patients and therefore would not be back home before 8 p.m. People saw what had been done with the little money that was contributed to the trust fund and increased their contributions, which enabled the road construction to progress very steadily. By 1974 when the project activity was interrupted, 60 kilometers of road and two bridges were constructed and the Ministry of Education constructed a six-classroom school at Jarso-Amba.

10

Ministry of Posts, Telecommunication, and Transport

I left with my family in the last week of May 1969 to return home, after two years and ten months as Ethiopian ambassador in Mexico. On my way home, I stayed in New York for three days with my friend, Lij Endalkatchew Mekonnen, who was the permanent representative of Ethiopia at the United Nations. We discussed what I was planning to do back home and I told him of my intention to leave government service to go into farming. He made no comment.

Four or five months later Endalkatchew was called back home and appointed minister of post, telecommunication and transport, two ministries that had been joined together. One day in January 1970, I was out of Addis Ababa to see the progress of my rural development project. When I returned home in the evening, I found a message from Endalkatchew saying that he wanted to see me urgently. He asked me to join his ministry and convinced me that my plan to leave government service and go into farming would not work. Since I had powerful political enemies, he said that I was exposing myself as a good target for destruction by those who were determined not to see me succeed in any way. These enemies would include those who were my partners in business. So he told me my only hope of survival during that regime was to stick to government service, he offered me a position as minister of state responsible for roads, rail transportation, and civil aviation. I thought he was right that I would not have the same moral strength to fight corruption and maladministration when it is a question of self-interest as I would when a question for public service. So I joined his ministry and remained very grateful for his kind and honest advice and in offering me that position in spite of strong objections from his cabinet colleagues, including His Imperial Majesty, who was taken by great surprise when my name was mentioned. He asked

The Emperor's Clothes

Endalkachew whether he was in his right mind in choosing me, a man known to be so stubborn and intransigent. Endalkachew had to argue a great deal on my virtues to make His Majesty agree on the appointment. And I saw in his expression, when I was presented, that it was done against his strong objection. When he offered to have me made a minister of state with the choice of my old department or that of roads, railways, and civil aviation, I wanted experience in new fields and more challenging responsibilities.

Endalkatchew first talked to the prime minister, Akililu Habte-Wold, who had no objection to my appointment. He asked him if they could see the emperor together to request his blessing. The first thing in the morning the next day when the emperor arrived, the prime minister and Endalkatchew followed him into his office. The prime minister first spoke: "Endalkatchew is here to request Your Majesty's blessing for appointing someone to assist him in carrying out the work of his big ministry." The emperor responded positively, asking who our choice was. When my name was mentioned, his expression changed. He said: "He is a very difficult person. Could you be able to control him?"

At this juncture, the prime minister left Endalkatchew alone with the emperor. Endalkatchew argued his case, got the blessing and immediately looked for me to come to be presented to the emperor and for the appointment to be announced. The appointment was announced in the evening news and the well-wishers started to stream to my house for the next two days.

The responsibility of the minister of state for roads, railways, and civil aviation included the following: chairing the Road Transport Administration Board, overseeing railroad management, chairing the Civil Aviation Board, and overseeing airways management. Of these, the most sensitive and disorganized was road transportation administration. With the introduction of the transportation legislation of 1965, the administration of this institution had been divided into two categories: the licensing and control of road transportation operators was to be administered by a Road Transport Authority which was governed by a board composed of members representing the transportation operators, users of transportation, representatives of the ministry of commerce and industry, the police, and a representative from the Ministry of Transport to be the chairman of the Board; the second was urban transportation, issuance of driving licenses, and registration of ownership.

The licensing and control of this category was the responsibility of the Ministry of Transport although it could delegate its powers to the city council while retaining the power to oversee. Before the introduction of the legislation, the administration and control of these activities was carried out by the city or town council of each province and it was one of its sources of income. As soon as the legislation was introduced, the Ministry of Transport, without any consideration of the administrative problem or the political and economic implications for the provincial authorities, saw only the expansion of its empire. The ministry set up offices in every provincial town, only Addis Ababa and Asmara were delegated to carry out partial services of the issuing of driving licenses and registering ownership.

By deciding to carry out the administrative duties and control of the urban and provincial transport activities, the ministry was thus depriving the provincial town authorities of a long-standing source of income. This provoked an outcry from the provincial authorities who took the matter up through the Ministry of Interior to the prime minister's level. However, the Ministry of Transport insisted it was complying with the provisions of the transportation law. So in 1966, the prime minister's office appointed a committee chaired by Bekele Haile, an assistant minister, to resolve this impasse.

The first problem with which I was confronted when I took office was this one. I received a letter from the prime minister's office instructing me to chair the committee instead of Bekele. After studying all of the correspondence concerning this matter, including the legality and efficiency of the provisions as institutions set up by the ministry. I decided to eliminate corruption and improve the services to the public. I gave full delegation to the city and town authorities to carry out the administration, and control the urban and provincial transport activities. The ministry was to see that the service to the public was delivered efficiently and effectively.

So I prepared a memorandum clearly explaining the legal provision to be complied with by the city and town authorities, their obligation to the Ministry of Transport to carry out these services in an efficient and effective manner, and the offices and employees of the Ministry of Transport instituted for this purpose. It was sent to all city and town authorities, provincial governors, the Ministry of Interior, and the prime minister's office. If they agreed to the conditions expounded in the memorandum, the Ministry of Transport would give full delegation. The response was positive and the problem taken care of without requiring the meeting of the committee which had been appointed three years before to resolve it. Now everybody concerned was happy, resulting in an efficient and effective service to the public without corruption. The present vehicle inspection and licensing office at Asmara road in Addis Ababa was built as a result of this memorandum, including the organizational setup, which was accomplished in less than a year of my appointment. The next problem I encountered was a complaint from the road transport operators against the administrator of the Road Transport Authority.

Although this body was governed by the board, the administrator was a government nominee who had its blessing. The incumbent administrator was an educated but bureaucratic young man. He could not get along with the people he was supposed to serve. In the first place, they complained, access to him was very difficult and his office was always closed with a messenger guarding it. When they got to see him after a long wait at the door, he received them with a frown and treated their requests with disdain. I tried to give him a piece of my mind, reminding him that he was the servant of the public and should not consider himself the master of it. I don't think he appreciated it when I had people complaining against him because I called him to my office to discuss the problem and show him how easy the solution was. One only needed to be well-disposed and have sense of responsibility to serve.

What disappointed me and made me lose hope in this young man was when visiting the various offices I found the Road Transport Authority either in shocking disorganization or nonexistent. He had installed himself in a large office, carpeted wall-to-wall in bright blue, beautifully furnished with a high-backed chair behind an impressive writing desk, and a life-size portrait of the emperor beautifully framed hanging on the wall behind the writing desk. I had not seen any other office like it.

The only two members of the organization, one old man responsible for registry, and another old man responsible for accounting, were housed in two dirty little rooms with no furniture to speak of except the simple writing desks and the chairs on which they were sitting. There was not even a shelf for the files; everything was piled up on the floor. It was a deplorable sight.

While I was contemplating a more subtle approach to remove him, he came to clash with the minister and was suspended immediately. It was surprising that an officer who was suspended for incompetence was appointed as the general manager of Addis Ababa Water Authority the day after his dismissal.

I started to search for a competent person to run that important organization and Shimelse Adugna was chosen. His appointment was confirmed by the board and he was given full responsibility for organizing and running the setup. He was given an empty house so he could employ young university graduates to staff the organization and get rid of the corruption for which that service had been notorious. He employed well-known radicals like Walelign, Gebru, and Teka. Less than two months after Shimels' appointment, the organization became fully operational and the demands of the public were met efficiently and effectively. The stream of complaints stopped. Shimels later became world-famous as relief and rehabilitation commissioner.

During the revolution, Gebru was appointed as district governor and Teka as permanent secretary of the Ministry of Transport by the Derg, but both defected and joined the EPRP (Ethiopian Peoples Revolutionary Party). Now when the public realized a just administration had been instituted, those who have been unjustly treated by the previous administration came up with their complaints for redress. One of these complaints was the monopoly given to some groups of road transport operators.

Some minibus operators on the 100 kilometers stretch between Addis Ababa and Nazret had managed to get a license to operate about 80 minibuses in exclusion of other operators. To carry passengers even by free use of the road to Addis Ababa, one must have the expressed permission of the authority. So the other minibus operators from every corner of the eastern and southern sectors lost the right to carry their passengers to the capital. They became feeders of these monopoly holders for 10 years.

The board decided the administration should take appropriate action to redress this anomaly. The road administration prepared a well thought-out schedule taking into account all the registered minibuses operating in these affected sectors so every one of them would get equal access to the capital, therefore abolishing the monopoly. This brought an outcry which berated every section of the government. Minister Lij Endalkatchew was approached by, among others, Ras Mesfin and Archbishop Abune Tewoflos who advised him not to disturb the status quo. He was then called to the palace to answer the charge that his ministry was causing a disturbance of the peace by the action taken against the interest of road transport operators by altering long-existing arrangements.

He explained that it was difficult for him to interfere in the board's decision. So I was called to the palace, as chairman of the board, to answer the charges. The day I was called to the palace, there were about 20 petitioners of transport owners. First, they were asked to read out their petition so I could hear the charges and answer. The main contents of the petition pointed out that they were given an exclusive license by the legal authority to operate transport between Addis Ababa and Nazret. The abolition of that monopoly was going to cause them to lose all the investment they had made. They felt this was deliberate sabotage on the economy of the country.

I simply answered that, in the first place, the board had acted on the basis of a petition by other transport operators who were not privileged like them to reach the palace. (Some of the minibuses operating on that road belonged to members of the entourage of the emperor). I said: "The board found out on examining that petition that you had been operating for the last ten years illegally. Why should you be given an exclusive right to operate on a public road which is built by the taxpayers' money when the other operators are denied even the free use of the road? There is no such law in Ethiopia. If the board's decision is reversed by any pressure, the other party, which is numbered in the thousands and has been denied the use of the road, will come here with its petition charging the authority which gave you the monopoly through corruption and abuse of authority. It will expose who the real owners are of some of

165

those minibuses which enable you to have that privilege. So the board, after taking all of this into consideration, has acted according to the law and re-dressed the injustices committed by the previous administration.''

The emperor then said to the petitioners: "Since it is done as explained according to the law, you go back and comply to that." I bowed and left. Although I had created so many enemies, I was happy justice had prevailed. Previously, transportation matters had not been dealt with fairly. As early as 1948, Ethiopian railway staff had protested against their French management. The government did not support them and they were dismissed. Some of the railway staff had been absorbed into the civil service and one or two had reached the rank of assistant minister.

In September 1973, I had been minister of state for roads and rail transport as well as chairman of civil aviation for two years and nine months. Every status quo in all these areas had been affected with change. The railway administration, which had been the exclusive domain of the French for 70 years, had now been Ethiopianized. The Frenchman, M. Peity, the dictatorial administrator of that organization who was feared by everybody because of his association with the top circle in the government was removed and replaced by an Ethiopian. He lived like a small king with 10 retainers, a big stable of selected horses, and entertained top officials. No one would have imagined his being removed from that position and the administration being changed to Ethiopian control.

The management of Ethiopian Airlines, after 25 years under TWA manage-ment, was now Ethiopianized. Ethiopianization of the airlines took place with-out any ill feeling. Ethiopian control of marine services was achieved only eight years after the federation of Ethiopia and Eritrea, while that of the rail-ways took 75 years.

Endalkatchew's resistance to the pressure of my enemies appeared to be giving way. The undermining of the road transport authority started. Without the board or the chairman knowing about it, Shimels had been transferred with the rank of vice minister to the prison administration. In his place, Ale-mayehu Wolde-Selassie, the young brother of the minister of imperial court, Dejazmatch Berhane Meskel Wolde-Selassie, had been appointed as the administrator of the Road Transport Authority. I came to know all this from Radio Addis Ababa when it was announced and I could not believe my ears. I started to wonder why Shimels would do this without telling me, and how he could abandon the organization he setup and the staff of young radicals and idealists he had hand-picked. Shimels' departure from the ministry was betrayal because his replacement was one whom the more progressive ele-ments wanted to get rid of.

The new position, except for the status of vice minister, had no challenging activity and the pay was 100 percent less than what he had been earning. I could not think of any reason except the incident that took place with the transfer of the administration of weight control on the highway from the highway authority to road transport administration. The Ministry of Transport was responsible for this, but during previous administrations, when the highway authority was considered an efficient and effective administrative setup, the ministry delegated this task to the highway authority.

But lately, the management of this operation had deteriorated into corruption and the excessive weight of the trucks on the highway was causing great damage to the road. The World Bank called for an effective control to this operation as one of its financing conditions.

Now the road transport administration was considered efficient and effective enough to administer this operation. This was acceptable to the World Bank. Shimels had been approached by General Manager of the Highway Authority Aba-Shawl and had agreed, but the matter had to be referred to the board. The board, after discussing the financial responsibilities, means and organizational requirements needed to operate effectively, agreed that the road transport administration could take over the task without the personnel. The highway authority agreed with the board on this condition. But behind the scenes, the highway authority discussed the matter with the minister of public works, Salah Hint, who agreed to raise the matter at the council of ministers meeting. Shimels was called there and forced to agree that the takeover include personnel.

One of Shimels' weaknesses was that he was too obliging to superior authority. When he was asked anything by his superior, his response was invariably yes. When he faced the council of ministers, it never occurred to him to say that his governing body, the board, should be consulted on the matter. To everything he was asked he agreed. When he prepared the budget and presented it to the board, he included the salaries of the personnel which the board rejected. Shimels was criticized for giving way to blackmail against the board's decision. This was definitely the main reason he abandoned the organization. By doing so, he became instrumental in undermining it. The new administrator had neither the personality nor the prestige and capability to motivate the staff and run the organization. It was a setup composed of radicals interested in changing the old order to carry out a reform of the administration. For nearly three years, this group had enjoyed seeing the results of their ideas in practice.

Unfortunately, their leader shimeles failed to stand the test of time and acted as an opportunist. It made one wonder if when he recruited the personnel, he was motivated by his own principles or by the ideas of his superior. When he realized he had committed a blunder that would affect his relationship with that superior and was offered a politically attractive position, he abandoned the organization letting his personnel fall into the hands of their political enemy, the person they were fighting to change.

There was nothing I could do to change what had taken place behind my back, to purposely undermine my own position and ruin everything we had worked for during the last three years. When I saw Endalkatchew and complained bitterly asking him how this could be done, his response was cool and unconvincing, I could read between the lines that he was fed up with me and wanted me to leave his ministry. Something was being cooked up.

The staff, young university graduates, might have thought Shimels was an innocent victim. They could never imagine his opportunism was responsible for all this. He might have told them he was leaving because of a disagreement with me.

One of the group, Walelign Mekonnen, decided to take a drastic step in expressing his bitter disappointment in the failure of the change and reform the group was engaged in through this organization. Since the work of road administration takes the staff into the countryside and remote areas, the organization provided a revolver for self-defense from a would-be attacker. Walelign was scheduled to go to Asmara on a mission and was carrying one of these revolvers. He planned to use the occasion to hijack the Ethiopian airline flight from Addis Ababa via Asmara to Europe.

On 8 December 1972 at about 10 in the morning, Director of Civil Aviation Hailu Alemayehu called me on the phone and informed me there was an attempt to hijack the Ethiopian airline flight going to Europe via Asmara. Apparently one of the hijackers was Walelign from the Road Administration Authority and the other was the daughter of General Mebratu, of the police. Both were killed in the shootout with the security men on board the plane. The aircraft was slightly damaged, but returned to Addis Ababa airport safely. The only casualties were the hijackers.

I immediately left my office for the airport to inspect the aircraft and get more information. I found the aircraft completely empty. There were two bullet holes through the roof and one big hole in the floor made by the hand grenade thrown by the female hijacker. The bullets were from Walelign's revolver provided to him for his own protection by his organization. The attempt to hijack the aircraft took place less than half an hour after the plane took off from Addis Ababa.

When I returned to my office, I found the chief of security, Colonel Solomon Kedir, waiting for me. He asked me how and with whose authority Walelign was employed. I was told: "His record as a security risk must have been quite clear to you from his student days as a radical political activist and his jail sentence of a year. With all this evidence against him, how is it possible that he should be employed in a government organization? For that matter, all of the groups in the road transport administration, like Gebru and Teka, are veterans of student struggle, leaders against the government and, according to Shimels, he recruited them on your order."

I responded to all the charges brought against me by the chief of security calmly: "Whether I ordered Shimels to employ these groups, or as the administrator he had full authority to choose his staff is another matter. These groups are Ethiopians. They are free citizens entitled to work and live. What you are talking about? Their being a security risk is something which I am learning now. Is there any confidential circular from your department to inform us of this? I for one have not seen anything like it. So how do you expect me or Shimels, for that matter, to know Walelign has been identified by your department unless you care to inform us? So trying to find a scapegoat for the failure of your department cannot succeed with me."

Solomon left my office and I went home for lunch. When I returned to the office, the minister wanted to see me. We discussed the incident and I reported to him what went on between the chief of security and I. He asked me to hand him the file concerning the committee for aircraft flight security, of which I was the chairman. He said that from now on, he would chair the committee himself.

Everybody, including Endalkatchew, believed Shimels only acted as a tool to employ all of those groups by my order. The fact of the matter is different. I did not know any of them and as for Walelign, I only met him once. He was a latecomer to the organization. The others were recruited at the beginning so I had the opportunity to meet them on many occasions.

11

Cabinet Resigns (February 1974)

February 1974 marked the end of the last emperor and with him the ordained social order. Haile Selassie had been feared but not loved, accorded the outward forms of dignity but not respected, because all his actions were based on self-interest and foreign values. Many people are mystified even today that a dynasty which had stood the test of time, 3,000 years, could have collapsed without a shot being fired.

Why did the empire not collapse when Emperor Tewodros ended his life in Mekedal after he realized he had been defeated by a foreign power? Why did the institution of monarchy not collapse even earlier? It had been only a symbol for seven decades before Tewodros came to power, with the real power concentrated in the hands of local chiefs.

I believe the monarchy had been undermined long before its overt collapse and that it was the Italian invasion which precipitated the final crisis. In 1924, the regent of Ethiopia, Ras Taferi, who was to become Emperor Haile Selassie, visited Europe and came back with the feeling that European culture was superior to his own. He began undermining the stability on which the monarchy was founded by casting aside everything from the Ethiopian tradition and replacing it with European modernization.

He imitated Europeans in his dress and his way of life. He introduced a standing army in place of the traditional army. The monarchy had always been looked to as the fountainhead of justice, and it was the belief of every Ethiopian that the divine power of justice was embodied in the emperor. This belief ensured the unity and political stability of the nation.

Had Haile Selassie been a wise leader, he could have strengthened the foundations of national unity by grafting onto them any intrinsically valuable

171

foreign elements without destroying the original. Japan had succeeded in doing so and there was no reason why Ethiopia could not have.

Haile Selassie brought about his own downfall and everything that the country held dear in its culture and history with him. The first sign of the collapse of the regime was an army mutiny late in 1973 at Negale. Traditionally, the army was comprised of individuals who were called to defend their country in times of emergency and who followed leaders of their own choice. If for any reason they were not satisfied with their leaders, they chose others. At Negale, the modern army detained their officers, a practice which had no precedent in Ethiopian history.

When this unbelievable news reached the emperor in the capital, he sent the commander of the ground forces to Negale, but he too was detained. Then the commander of the air force, General Abera, was sent. By promising an Imperial review of their grievances, he persuaded the soldiers to release the officers. It was clear the relationship between the soldiers and their officers had been destroyed. News of the events at Negale spread like wildfire and triggered further mutinies in Addis Ababa, Harar, and Asmara.

The cabinet, which was comprised of opportunists and yes-men, lacked the courage to deal with the situation and thought to absolve itself from blame by resigning, thereby abrogating its responsibility to the nation.

Prime Minister Aklilu Habte-Wold called a cabinet meeting on 26 February 1974 which was attended by all the ministers except my boss, Minister for Posts, Telecommunications and Transport Endalkatchew Mekonnen, who was not informed. The cabinet resigned and immediately went to the Jubilee Palace with its decision. In the old days, the Radio Addis Ababa announcement of their resignation would have announced a new prime minister and a cabinet reshuffle, but Haile Selassie was not in control of the situation.

When the country had faced a leadership problem after the death of Emperor Menilek, the solution was brought about by a natural born leader whose origins were obscure, Fitawrari Habte-Georgis. He put Menilek's daughter, Empress Zewditu, on the throne with Ras Taferi as crown prince. But in February 1974, there were no men in such a mold. Haile Selassie had cast aside the traditional leaders and blocked the advancement of men of merit who could have replaced them. Traditional leaders did not believe in amassing wealth for its own sake. They maintained the welfare of the nation by sharing their wealth with their followers. The wealth of the leader was counted in terms of the number of good men who would follow him, not in the number of bank accounts, gashas of land, or rental houses he had.

When it was clear that the emperor could not last, the whole nation heaved a sigh of relief, not caring who replaced him, so long as he went. History gave them every reason to hope he would be replaced by a leader who would return

11. Cabinet Resigns (February 1974)

to the traditional system of values and justice. When the emperor received the resignation of the cabinet, he called the president of the Senate, General Abiy Abebe, and asked him to head a new government. The president agreed provisionally, but asked for time to think it over.

A few minutes after the president left the palace, the emperor's aide-de-camp handed him a note from the army, naming their choice for prime minister, Endalkatchew Mekonnen. Endalkatchew had gone to his office for duty, unaware of the resignation of the cabinet, and that was where I found him.

When I was informed, the same day in the afternoon that his appointment as prime minister had been announced on Radio Addis Ababa, I went to his house not to express the conventional congratulations but to wish him strength from God to carry the heavy burden he had been given. There were many people there in the sitting room of his house to congratulate him but I noticed his wife, Enkenelesh, was sad and crying. It must have been women's intuition. I was also sad because I felt the appointment was unfortunate. Endalkatchew was a very religious man, kind-hearted, and careful to avoid hurting people's feelings. The office of prime minister was going to hand him difficult problems to face.

When the president of the Senate and Endalkatchew presented themselves at the Palace, His Majesty proposed that the president should serve under Endalkatchew as minister of Defense. Both accepted. It was an unusual arrangement and I do not know whether the usual ritual of kissing the emperor's feet was followed. We shall never know, since none of the principals survived the upheaval which was to follow.

On 28 February, a group of air force NCOs (noncommissioned officers) from the air base at Debre-Zeit arrived at Fourth Brigade HQ in Addis Ababa. A committee, which began to detain former cabinet ministers, was formed with junior army officers. Besides the work of trying to form his cabinet, the new prime minister and minister of defense had the added burden of negotiating the release of their erstwhile colleagues.

On the morning of 29 February, the forces committee took their prisoners with them to the Imperial Palace, where His Majesty came out to receive them. There at the Jubilee Palace, one of the officers read out a statement accusing the ministers of corruption and demanding that the emperor immediately set up a committee to investigate the charges against them. The emperor only said: "We will set up a commission to investigate the charges you have stated." The former prime minister, Aklilu, was heard to whisper to the emperor that he should respond since they were his ministers and were answerable only to him. Therefore, there could be no question of an investigation.

When the former prime minister heard the emperor meekly accept that they be handed over to the wolves, he was shocked. He was a fool to think the emperor would risk his own position to protect those who had served him. That would have taken a man of principle. The situation was rapidly deteriorating once it was realized that the very foundation of the dynasty was crumbling away. The trade union movement threatened a general strike unless about 20 demands were met.

The new prime minister was faced with the task of finding an immediate solution to the trade unions' demands if everything didn't to come to a standstill. I felt sorry for the prime minister because he was the sort of person who did not wish to offend anybody and this was a handicap in negotiating effectively.

By now, Endalkatchew had worked out his Cabinet and it comprised the following:

Endalkatchew Mekonnen	Prime Minister
General Abiy Abebe	Defense
Dejazmatch Kebede Tessema	Palace Affairs
Dejazmatch Zewde Gebre-Selassie	Interior
Dejazmatch Tesfa Yohannes Berehe	Mines
Ato Belet Gebre-Sadiq	Land Reform
Ato Minasse Haile	Foreign Affairs
General Assefa Ayene	Telecommunications, Posts,& Transport
Ato Million Nekneke	Social Welfare
Ato Taddesse Terefe	Education
Ato Belachew Asrat	Justice
Ato Tekaligne Gedamu	Planning
Dr Jemal Abdelqadre	Health
Ato Mehamed Abdurhuman	Commerce and Industry
Ato Bulcha Demeksa	Agriculture
Ato Negash Desta	Finance
Ato Kifle Wodajo	Minister Without Portfolio
Ato Gaitachew Bekele	Public Works

When the name of Bulcha Demeksa was announced as minister of agriculture, there was an immediate petition to the prime minister from the staff of the ministry. Ato Bulcha was never allowed to occupy the post, which remained vacant until Lij Mikael succeeded Endalkatchew as prime minister after six months. I accepted my appointment unwillingly. I did not want it, but it was no time to shy away from responsibility, especially when my friend Endalkatchew was the one calling on me. He offered me the post when I was together with Negatu in his office. When I tried to decline, he told me bluntly he expected better from me so I felt I had no choice. The majority of the new

11. Cabinet Resigns (February 1974)

Cabinet were technocrats and all were new to the Cabinet except for the prime minister, the foreign minister, and the minister of palace affairs.

Dejazmatch Zewde had fallen out of favor when he was mayor of Addis Ababa in 1958-1959 and had been exiled as ambassador to Somalia. He was recalled after the 1960 coup attempt because his grandfather, Leul Ras Syoum, had been one of the victims. The emperor thought that if Zewde was appointed as mnister of justice he would become a draconian minister of revenge and clean up the emperor's enemies. Instead, Zewde behaved like a principled patriot and set about the fair administration of justice. When it became apparent that he was putting his nation above his emotions, he was called to the palace after a year and told that his services were no longer required. After two years of enforced idleness in Addis Ababa, he went to Oxford where he took his doctorate and completed the biography of his grandfather, Emperor Yohannes IV. When he returned to the country after eight years, he was again shunted off as permanent representative to the United Nations.

Lij Mikael Imru suffered a similar fate. From the time he returned home on the completion of his studies, he was unable to fit into the system because of his strong principles and refusal to obey meaningless orders without critically evaluating them. As a result, he was shifted from one department to another. During the 1960 coup attempt, his father was named prime minister by the rebels because of his popularity with the public. Mikael at that time was ambassador to the United States. He was recalled and appointed minister of foreign affairs, but such a strong character could not last there under the emperor and after six months he was pushed off to Moscow as ambassador. Tadesse Terefe, because of his past experience in the Ministry of Education, was asked to serve and so left his World Bank post in Washington.

The rest of the Cabinet were men who had established good reputations with the public in various posts, the new prime minister was taking care not to include anybody who had been tainted with public suspicion. At the same time, he tried to maintain an ethnic balance in his appointments and in this he was largely successful.

On 3 March, we were presented to the emperor in the Throne Room of the Jubilee Palace where he was seated with all of his entourage standing. We entered that great hall and stood facing the emperor at a distance. We bowed low and stepped aside to join the prime minister. A few minutes after the last minister performed the bow, an aide-de-camp signaled that we should leave. It must have been the first Cabinet formed in the life of the emperor where he had no say in the choice of the members and where the appointees had not kissed his feet when they were presented to him. I wondered how he felt.

Apart from firefighting strikes and demonstrations, the first task of the new Cabinet was to draw up a new constitution, which had to be submitted to a referendum within six months to pave the way for constitutional government. The committee to draft the Constitution was chaired by the respected historian, Ato Tekele-Tsadiq Mekuria, who had served in various government and diplomatic posts. The committee included former Cabinet Minister Yilma Deressa and Dr. Aklilu Habte, president of the university.

A white paper, which addressed the most pressing grievances on land questions, was hastily prepared by the Cabinet. The prime minister submitted it to the emperor to be sent on to parliament. It was a time of management by crisis. There was a Cabinet meeting practically every day which meant that ministers had no time to spend in their offices solving real problems. The revolutionary spirit of the times was overtaking the speed of bureaucracy.

The army demanded to know what had happened to the investigating commission which the emperor had promised to win the release of his former Cabinet. The Ethiopian contingent to the Congo believed the old Cabinet had pocketed payments made to Ethiopia by the United Nations for the upkeep of the force and asked the new prime minister to ensure that they were paid what they considered was due.

All of the state-corporations came up with grievances in their turn and demanded satisfaction. Two such bodies directly concerned my ministry, the highway authority and the water resources department. They came separately to me with copies of the petitions which they had submitted to the prime minister. I promised them action provided there was no disruption in services.

The management of both departments was accused of nepotism, corruption, and mismanagement. I called the general manager of the highway authority and his chief engineer and without disclosing the details of the petition against them I asked them to do whatever was necessary to maintain peace with those working under them until the committee I was about to set up had a chance to ascertain the facts.

The next day, 5 May, I was called out of a Cabinet meeting and asked to rush to the highway authority offices where I found everybody milling around in the compound except the management, the section heads, and their secretaries. There were two factions in the department, the small group around the managers who were the subject of the complaints of nepotism, and the majority. Despite my warning, the general manager had tried to absolve himself by calling a general meeting of the workers to put the blame on the chief engineer, who objected and resigned.

The workers locked the general manager out the next day and his executive officer, whom they accused of being the general manager's relative and the instigator of most of the trouble in the department. The executive officer quit. I persuaded the workers to return to their posts and appointed one of the engineers to act as head of the department.

11. Cabinet Resigns (February 1974)

I called the general manager to my office and demanded his resignation. He got on his high horse, telling me that he was an Imperial appointee and only the emperor could remove him. I was surprised by his naivete and told him: "If you cannot see the way the revolutionary wind is blowing, I shall have no option but to call the board to dismiss you and appoint a new general manager." He went to the palace and complained to the emperor, who called the prime minister and told him to advise me to take no action against the general manager.

When the prime minister called me to his office to convey the emperor's message, I offered to resign. He said we should go to see the emperor together. The emperor blustered that his only concern was that the general manager was very experienced in the post. However, if I thought I had a competent replacement he could go.

Immediately, the appointment of Hailu Shawl as the new general manager of the highway authority was broadcast on the news. He swept into office, stabilized the department, and completed long overdue projects which had been stagnating. The World Bank had been delaying finance for the Sixth Highway Program, but when they visited the new general manager, they were satisfied that things were going to improve and released the money.

Hailu Shawl had been earning twice the salary of the highway authority general manager as an executive of the Shell Company, but when I was told that he was the best man for the job, I appealed to his national sentiment and asked him to take up the post.

Three months after his appointment, I went with him to inspect progress on the construction of the road from Addis Ababa to Nazret. I was gratified by the hard-working spirit of the staff. The engineer in charge told me: "Because it is the new general manager who has set the deadline for the completion of the work, we are determined to work extra hours so as not to let him down." There was a spirit of revolutionary self-sacrifice throughout the country and there were many examples of it, but I attempt to record only what I witnessed of it personally.

The claim of the Ethiopian contingent to the U.N. force in the Congo for payment of a per diem had by now been investigated and found to have been based on a wrong assumption. On receiving the soldiers' petition, Prime Minister Endalkatchew had immediately set up an investigating commission chaired by an assistant minister for education and including a representative of the soldiers.

When it became clear that the United Nations had not made any payment, as the soldiers were alleging, their representative on the committee began pressuring the other members to reach a finding contrary to the established facts. The committee therefore confused the issue by publishing a comparison of the

177

different rates paid to different national contingents in the Congo, instead of answering its brief unequivocally. The committee concluded that Ethiopian soldiers had been paid less than they should have been. The cabinet instructed the Ethiopian representative at the United Nations to send all the records of financial transactions concerning the contingent to Addis Ababa. They then concluded that everything was in order and the soldiers, whose expectations had been falsely raised, were disappointed.

It was the manner in which this question was mishandled, more than any other factor, that led to the rise of the military junta. The mishandling had originated at the time that Ethiopia was first asked to supply a contingent to the U.N. Congo force. The letter of request clearly pointed out what the obligations of the world body were to be so far as salaries, per diem and transportation were concerned. It stated that if the government was going to send units from its existing forces, then the United Nations would pay according to the existing daily regulations of the nation concerned. However, if the units to be sent were to be specially raised, the United Nations would include an additional salary element. Troops from existing units were to get just a per diem, while troops in specially raised units were to get U.N. salaries.

The United Nations asked for all the relevant documents in advance and the matter was passed from the Ministry of Foreign Affairs to the Ministry of Defense without anybody stopping to think of the financial implications.

Although the troops were from existing units and a per diem list should have been sent to the United Nations, a salary list was sent instead. The response from the United Nations was to ask for a copy of the Ethiopian per diem regulations. No such regulations existed, so a list was concocted based on local traveling allowances and submitted through the foreign office. By this time, other countries had complied with the precise requirements of the United Nations.

One man realized something was amiss, the permanent representative to the United Nations, Dr. Tesfaye Gebre-Igze, who ironically was later to become a victim of the events which the error set in motion. When he compared what Ethiopia was requesting with what was being requested by other countries, he saw it was obviously inadequate for foreign travel.

Dr. Tesfaye sent the list back with an analysis of what other countries were requesting. Instead of rethinking the whole question, the Ethiopian Ministry of Defense merely copied the scales submitted by Morocco and sent them back to the United Nations. The Ethiopian request was for U.S.$6 per day for a soldier. Due to negligence, the United Nations had before it the salary list for home service, which had been sent in error, and found that the monthly salary for a soldier was about U.S.$10. Justifiably, they pointed out the anomaly of asking for U.S.$6 a day and U.S.$10 a month in response to the same request.

11. Cabinet Resigns (February 1974)

A clarification was requested, but the embarrassed officials who had blundered remained silent and there was no further correspondence.

When the contingent arrived in the Congo in the absence of any proper clarification, the United Nations decided to pay the Ethiopians the Moroccan rate. The decision was logical because the second list submitted by Ethiopia was identical with the Moroccan list. However, by now the United Nations had negotiated a reduced rate with Morocco and it was this rate which formed the basis for payments. An advance party of technicians sent by Ethiopia had been paid a higher rate and as they departed, they told their newly arriving colleagues what they had been getting. Therefore, the new contingent assumed this would be what they were entitled. Throughout their stay in the Congo, the troops were regularly paid, but they further assumed what they were getting was an advance on the full amount and they would receive the balance when they returned home.

The greatest blunder of all was that the findings of the investigating committee, which the emperor appointed when the returning soldiers petitioned him for the balance of their per diem, were never properly explained to the aggrieved soldiers. The army felt the time had come to force the government to pay up. Each soldier thought he was entitled to Eth$10,000 and was determined to get it.

The Congo contingent was still serving while others had been pensioned off and were employed around the capital as security guards. Others would later come from Eritrea and Harar to attend meetings at Fourth Brigade HQ about their demands. At one such meeting, a young officer, Major Teferra Tekeleab, decided to make political capital out of the situation. A graduate of Holota Military Academy, he had been a lieutenant in the Ogaden campaign and was known for his bravery. He was well-read and a hot-tempered, committed leftist.

He advised the Congo contingent to appoint an officer to organize a committee of representatives from various units which would force the government to accept their just demands. Naturally, Teferra was chosen on the spot. Teferra organized what was to grow into the "Derg" (military junta). But, lacking tact and patience in implementing his political ideas, he found himself imprisoned with the government officials he had been working to overthrow.

I came to know Teferra when I was detained myself in the Grand Palace. He was brought there from another center of detention two months before my release. By that time, he had been detained for a year and his political zeal had waned, to be replaced by religion, since the only literature we were allowed was religious.

To meet the original objectives of the Derg, it was intended to be dominated by ordinary soldiers. The first representatives were from the Fourth

Division. This nucleus was headed by Colonel Melesse Tessema of the army, a Congo veteran, and Colonel Tsegaye Meshesha of the air force. Leaving them in charge, Teferra went to the Third and then the Second Division to recruit committee members, but when he returned the committee was reorganized. The hundred or so men from the Third Division objected to being led by colonels and insisted that nobody above the rank of major be included. The two colonels in control were told to go back to their units and send back two men to replace them.

The Third Division men, being numerically dominant, selected the chairman and vice chairman of the committee, Mengistu Haile Mariam from Third Division and Atnafu Abate from Fourth Division. During the first month of the existence of the Derg, its overt agenda was to seek redress of the grievances of the Congo soldiers. But all the while, the politically motivated officers of the Derg were meeting with radical intellectuals to plan the frying of bigger fish - the overthrow of the government.

In two months, the Derg arrested all army, navy, air force, and police commanders as well as all members of the former Cabinet. After arresting the last member of the former Cabinet, the first member of the new Cabinet to be arrested was General Assefa Ayene, the minister of posts, telecommunications and transport. His brother-in-law Minasse Haile, the minister of foreign affairs, resigned immediately and was arrested. Around 22 July, the new prime minister was put under house arrest for a week before he was sent to join the others in detention.

Mikael Imru succeeded Endalkatchew as prime minister and a week later, in late August, a hundred Congo veterans turned up at a Cabinet meeting demanding to know the outcome of the committee set up to investigate their complaints.

Mikael told them the report was ready and that it would be presented to them in the afternoon. The veterans knew the report was going to be negative and that Mikael was not the man to bend to threats and change it, so they asked that the report be presented to them at the palace in the presence of the emperor.

The veterans turned up well ahead of the appointed time and the palace was an armed camp. The prime minister was surrounded by his entire Cabinet, but when he tried to present the report without the emperor there, he was shouted down.

The emperor was called to the veranda of the palace to face the unruly mob while the secretary to the Cabinet read the report. When it was complete, the mob began shouting insults at the Cabinet. Losing my temper, I turned to the emperor and told him that since we had fulfilled our obligation as a Cabinet by investigating the complaint and reporting the results, he should not put up with their nonsense.

This provoked the crowd against me with many of them calling for my arrest. I was pushed inside the palace by an aide-de-camp and smuggled out long afterward through a back exit because some determined soldiers were still waiting to arrest me.

The emperor dispersed the crowd by appointing General Aman, the minister of defense, to investigate their complaints further. Just a week later, he was deposed, carted out of his palace in a VW, and held for two weeks in the Fourth Division HQ before being transferred to the old Menilek Palace.

The unfolding class struggle had already succeeded in demolishing the status quo within the military establishment and was transforming the regime's pliant tool into a fearsome weapon destined to accomplish its masters' destruction.

On the morning of 11 September, I switched on Radio Addis Ababa to hear that the king had been deposed and Crown Prince Asfa Wosen had been appointed in his place as king, not emperor. It shocked me because I thought, considering the sensitive situation on the Somali border and the age of the emperor, he would simply be stripped of his power but allowed to remain nominal head of state in order to preserve national unity. That way, for the rest of his days, which surely would not have been many, his international prestige could have been capitalized upon to carry out the reforms we needed domestically. It saddened me that such a golden opportunity for a peaceful transfer of power was lost.

The emperor brought it all upon himself. If he had followed tradition and the examples of Yohannes IV and Menilek, he would have allowed born leaders like Alula and Habte-Georgis to rise up and counsel him, instead of surrounding himself with mercenary ciphers. We have a saying in Amharic:

"ketinish yewale tinish new, anso yasanisal, ketiliq yewale tiliq-new, adgo yasadigal."

This means a man who associates himself with petty fools will remain petty and foolish, but a man who associates with principled men of consequence will aspire to their stature. What we have seen in Ethiopia since the revolution proves the truth of this saying. Yohannes and Menilek were revered and because they were respected and mourned bitterly, the nation remained stable and ensured an orderly succession of power.

It was not that Ethiopia failed to produce born leaders during the time of Emperor Haile Selassie, rather he felt he did not need them. During the Italian invasion when the emperor's army was defeated, he ran away for five years. In all that time, the enemy was fought and defeated by born leaders who emerged in his absence. Let me recount what happened to one such leader, Belaye Zeleke, who was born the son of a peasant farmer in Gojam, but rose to command a thousand fighters in the field.

Belay could not be dislodged from his stronghold by the Italians and went so far as to confer titles up to Ras upon his followers, which was the prerogative of a king. His younger brother asked him: "If you call a man Ras, what does that make you?" He replied: "I am happy with the title I was given by my mother, Belay." Belay means "the very top."

I was a student at Menilek School when I saw Belaye hanged in a public square as a common criminal by His Majesty's regime. A minstrel composed this verse in his memory:

"Teseqele bilugni zinaru new biye,
Teseqele bilugni mewzeru new biye,
Isus Belay norwal tilequ sewye."

This means that when the hanging was announced it was naturally thought it was his bandoliers or his Mauser which were to be hung, but it turned out to be the great man himself.

The great majority of my generation, and that which has followed, have been deprived of the opportunity of learning and growing to respect our own history and culture to which our ancestors attached great value. They were proud to be identified as Ethiopians. The generation which has succeeded Haile Selassie is without history, culture, or foundations. The proof is that Ethiopians, who before were rarely to be found outside their homeland, have become the wanderers of the Earth. There is no room in modern Ethiopia for entrepreneurs or professionals, and those who remain behind are expected to revere posters of foreign ideologists. The emperor was despised and hated by every section of society. Those of all ages were ready for change, but not the bloody revolution to which we have fallen victim.

The emperor created the dearth of responsible leadership which the radical intelligentsia and power-hungry individuals were able to exploit and turn against the people. Such destructive elements were able to use the repressive machinery which the emperor had created. This was the main reason the reforms, which Endalkatchew and Mikael Imru wished to bring about, never had a chance. All this was made possible by the ingrained Ethiopian traditional belief that whoever rose to power would respect and administer justice by not violating human or property rights without due process.

It was this ingrained belief in Ethiopian justice that led all former government officials to give themselves up to the new regime when called upon to do so. It was not that they went willingly like lambs to the slaughter; they believed in the Ethiopian principle that a fallen adversary should not be harmed, let alone killed. It is recorded that the same Italian forces who had behaved like swine were allowed in defeat to withdraw from the field with their arms, under the protection of Ras Mekonnen.

In Ethiopian tradition, it was considered manly to show magnanimity to a defeated adversary and churlish to abuse his weakness. Even in a personal fist fight, a man who struck out at another on the ground would be booed. An opponent had to be given the chance to stand up and show himself able to continue the fight.

The Derg lacked leadership. Contrary to popular belief, it was not the Derg that arrested former Cabinet ministers in late April, but an ad hoc committee under the buccaneering paratrooper, Colonel Alem-Zewde Tessema. It was this incident, which proved that arbitrary arrest had become the order of the day, that led the Endalkatchew Cabinet to submit its resignation to the emperor. There was no point in the Cabinet maintaining a fictitious of orderly government if the army was determined to arrest people arbitrarily.

The army, impatient because the emperor had not made good on his promise to investigate the former Cabinet ministers, arrested them and took them into detention. The Cabinet was in session when we heard the news and we debated the issue as a matter of urgency since it was fundamental to our role as a governing body.

There were two divergent views on what action we should take. The majority felt that if we could not be allowed to govern the country under the law, we should resign. A minority thought since the country was in crisis, we were morally bound to continue trying to contribute whatever we could under whatever conditions. The Cabinet adjourned after midnight on Friday and reconvened eight hours later to continue the debate. By two on Saturday afternoon, we were resolved to resign and broke for lunch on the understanding that we would meet again at five in the palace to submit our resignation.

When we arrived at the palace, we found 30 or so army officers standing in line. We left them there and went into a reception room to wait to see the emperor. When we were ushered in to see him we found that the army officers who had been outside were already in. Before anybody else had a chance to say anything, a Colonel Mulugeta of the Imperial Bodyguard began to speak.

Colonel Mulugeta pledged the loyalty of the entire army to the emperor and to the new Cabinet. He said the army was aware we wished to resign because of the arrest of the former Cabinet but that the arrests had been made with the blessing of the emperor. The colonel said: "If this action has offended the new Cabinet, the ad hoc committee formed for the purpose has been dissolved and no such action will be repeated. We request the new Cabinet to reconsider their decision to resign and we request Your Majesty not to accept any resignation." After the colonel had finished speaking, a major made the same pledge, followed by a captain, then one man from each of the ranks down to that of a private.

The emperor then said: "We have no doubt of your loyalty to us and we are also quite aware that you will not take any action without our blessing." He then withdrew, leaving most of us flabbergasted. As the soldiers left, we withdrew into the waiting room to consider the implications of the incident. How could the army have known of our intention to resign and the exact time we would present ourselves at the palace? Most of us suspected Dejazmatch Kebede Tessema, who had argued strongly against resignation on the grounds that it was wrong to throw the whole burden on the aging emperor.

From the palace, we went back to the conference room of the council of ministers. As soon as we sat down, the minister for finance, Ato Negash Desta, asked for the floor and announced he was the one responsible for the incident at the palace. When he had gone home for lunch, he had found his brother Colonel Alemayehu and, without thinking of the possible consequences, told him the Cabinet was going to resign because the army was taking the law into its own hands. Before he could finish what he was saying, his brother jumped up and rushed out of the house. It was clear he must have gone to inform the ad hoc committee.

When he had finished his statement, he asked for permission to withdraw so the rest of us could decide what action to take against him. However, General Asefa Ayene proposed that since Ato Negash had courageously made a clean breast of the matter, he should be forgiven. It was agreed upon and the plan to resign was allowed to rest.

After the establishment of the Derg in mid-June, another mass arrest took place Prime Minister Endalkatchew, General Asefa Ayene, and Minassie Haile were among those arrested. Once again, we were thrown into a Cabinet crisis. Mikael Imru succeeded Endlakatchew for just a month before the Derg took power and declared General Aman head of the government. Mikael Imru became minister for information and the remaining members of the Cabinet were asked to retain their portfolios. I remained as minister of public works, with the added portfolio of mines.

One of the last public duties in which I was engaged was the land reform committee which was set up soon after the Derg deposed the emperor and declared General Aman head of state and government. The committee was made up of some Cabinet ministers, including myself and various officers of the Derg.

The minister of land reform, in providing the committee with the studies compiled by experts, commented that there were differing views on how land reform could be achieved and the committee decided to call the groups with differing views and let them air their opinions. It was interesting that those who had been educated in the West held the most radical views, favoring the nationalization of land and the reorganization of agriculture along collective lines. Those who had been trained in the East and had been given the opportunity of studying collective agriculture firsthand knew it had one important failing—despite all its apparent attractions, it did not work.

Although the radicals argued that the existing land tenure system was feudal, they produced no examples from Ethiopian society or history to show

184

what they regarded as feudalism in the Ethiopian context. There was no historical comparison they were able to present to justify their advocacy of communal landholding. On the other hand, the opposing group presented concrete examples of historical cases to show that nationalization and communal holding resulted in social injustice, mismanagement, and underproduction. They were able to cite Russia, Poland, and Mexico as examples of countries where agricultural production had fallen when land was collectivized.

This group argued that the landholding system could not be regarded as feudal because it varied from region to region and was rooted in the principle of cognatic descent. The Eastern-educated group proposed that land should be individually held, but that there should be a ceiling on the number of gashas any individual could hold. The excess should be expropriated and distributed to the peasants as rist.

The committee was able to profit greatly in understanding the issues by listening to the two groups: the radicals who were mouthing ideology, and the pragmatists who were basing their arguments on professional and scholarly research and a thorough understanding of the subject.

Just as the experts were divided, so were the members of the committee. The Derg were radical and the Cabinet members were pragmatic. The committee was able to gather a vast body of historical and statistical evidence to show that "Every free born person had the right to claim his share of land and for the individual farmer, the producing class, these rights were embodied in the rist system [hereditary land ownership]."

In reporting, the committee reviewed the communal land system and rejected it as unpractical and inappropriate for Ethiopia. In Eritrea, where land was communally held, the soil was denuded and eroded. In other regions, individual holdings were planted with trees. The traditional system recognized the rights of the landlord and the state to claim a share of surplus production, but only so far as these rights did not impinge upon the more fundamental right of the producer to sustenance. The whole basis of the traditional landholding system was this basic right to sustenance.

Things had worked well as long as the traditional system was maintained. Even when a government official was granted a large tract of land, it was not regarded as his own for exclusive use, he was expected to distribute it among his followers for them to support themselves under the maderia system (land given in lieu of salary).

So the committee, on drafting its proclamation on land reform, took into account the traditional values and moral order and declared: "Every Ethiopian has the right to claim an equal share of land."

The committee, in a majority decision, recommended that land should be individually held up to a certain ceiling. However, if a large landlord could prove the land he held had been developed on a commercial scale and not left idle, he could be allowed to keep the whole of it as a concession.

At the last meeting of the committee, the members from the Derg pressed that they be allowed to present a minority report which they had drafted in collaboration with radicals who were not members of the committee. This proposal was rejected by the committee, which said it had been granted a mandate to investigate the issue to the fullest and to present a possible solution.

I was in the majority group on the committee, but was detained the day before we were to have reported and the Derg promulgated a land reform proposal based on the views of the minority members. The result of the Derg's decision has been the most savage and prolonged famine in the history of Ethiopia.

All privately owned land was nationalized and put under the control of farmers' associations which were chaired by men handpicked by the Derg. In choosing the chairmen of the farmers' associations, the Derg unerringly picked the most destructive elements in each community who succeeded in rapidly causing discord and discontent among the farmers, many of whom revolted and killed their imposed overlords.

The brutal regime of the Derg so undermined the traditional values of Ethiopians that they became as brutal in seeking redress for their grievances. In the subprovince of Bulga, farmers went to the district administrator at Shola-Gebeya. When their demands were refused, the farmers fatally shot the administrator and the farmers' association chairman. A six-man delegation was sent to the provincial capital of Debre-Berhan to tell the provincial governor to collect the bodies of his men, but not to try to bring troops or police unless he wanted an insurrection.

In November, I left Addis Ababa to tour the gold mine at Adola and to see progress on the construction of the road from Dila to Moyale on the Kenyan border. On 13 November, the day after I returned, the evening radio news named the officials who had been found responsible for the 1973 Wollo drought. I was among them, having been charged with negligence.

After the announcement, my telephone was jammed with calls from friends and relatives advising me to run away from the capital. Since my conscience was clear, I resolved to stay put. I felt far from being responsible for the famine and that I was instrumental in revealing its existence. When I went on an official visit to England in December 1973, I came to know that Jonathan Dimbleby had a film of drought conditions in Wollo and I asked the counselor of the Ethiopian embassy, Zewde Mekuria, to arrange for me to see the film. I was so sickened and shocked by what I saw that I asked Mr. Dimbleby for a copy of the film to take home to show to those in power. Mr. Dimbleby was surprised and warned me I would be making trouble for myself with the government. All my life I had been making trouble for myself with the government, whether I

11. Cabinet Resigns (February 1974)

was in or out of it and I begged Mr. Dimbleby to get me a copy of the film. Although I had to leave without it, I told all my colleagues who would listen what I had seen.

I was detained for ten months, ostensibly because of negligence over the drought. My wife was aware of my request to Mr. Dimbleby for a copy of the film because she had been present when I asked an Ethiopian Airlines pilot, Captain Adamu Medhane, to collect the film from him. When he heard of my detention, he wrote her a letter recalling the incident which she submitted to the authorities to absolve me. It was gratifying to know more than 300 people who had benefitted from my self-help projects in Bulga wrote and signed a petition for my release. But my wife was advised not to submit this to the authorities, since the intention of the regime was elimination of leadership it would have the opposite effect of what had been intended.

I had been detained on Thursday 14 November when, at about lunch time, I was called from my office to the former office of the emperor in the Menilek Palace, which was now the office of the Derg. I was informed by a young officer of my detention as soon as I arrived, but was kept there under guard until six in the evening until they could decide in which detention center I was to be held.

At six, I was taken to the basement of the building where most of the former ministers, the two prime ministers and the generals were being held. The partitioned basement had formerly been a store and wine cellar. Above, the former reception hall was now the assembly hall of the Derg and the adjoining throne room had been converted for the military tribunal.

The two basement rooms were divided to segregate the 150 prisoners into two groups. The whole area was ventilated only by the gap above the steel door. A fluorescent light burned day and night. The outside of the building was surrounded by barbed wire and floodlit at night. A temporary guard house had been set up outside the barbed wire. Inside the cage in an existing building, four toilets, four showers, and four wash basins had been installed. At six in the morning, the two groups would be let out separately to use the facilities. The regime never varied and whenever the door was opened the number of guards would be tripled. Bathing at six. Fresh air from nine to ten. Fresh air again from three to four. Bathing at six.

During the morning exercise period, our captors would inspect the two cells. We were provided with spring beds by the Derg and our families were allowed to provide us with bedding, including clean sheets, and food which would be inspected as it was brought. Our families were allowed to enclose a two-line note with the food, but we got to see them only at Easter.

There was no interrogation or attempt at indoctrination. After ten months, I was released. It may seem strange, but I felt no joy at my release, rather concern for those I had left behind. I remembered how I had felt in 1960 when I remained behind as others were released. Conditions in 1960 had been far more humane. In 1974, the prisoners maintained their morale by not being idle a minute of the day. There were organized classes in history, language, law, and religion.

Ten days after my arrest, on Saturday, 23 November 1974, I was to witness the beginning of one of the most savage acts of murder ever perpetrated in my country. Lying in bed close to the door with a cold, I noticed a blanket being draped over the peephole from the outside. Fifteen minutes later, the door opened to reveal Major Getachew Shibesh standing outside with a piece of paper in his hand.

Major Getachew Shibeshi asked for Dr. Minasse, the spokesman of the inmates, to come forward. The major then announced he was going to read the names of a group of people who should come out when they were called. Minasse was to repeat what he said so everybody inside could hear. Twenty-seven people were called out. The peephole had been covered so we could not see them removing people from the adjoining room. We were to discover later that as soon as they were out of our sight they were handcuffed and pushed into a waiting prison van. They collected a total of 60 victims from various places of detention, including those who were in the hospital, and transported them to the main prison compound. There they were machine-gunned.

Three days after my release, I was called to the offices of the Derg. Captain Alemayehu asked me to serve the regime. I told him that after 22 years of public service I had seen enough. He gave me a telephone number at which I could call him if I changed my mind, but I told him—I hope truthfully—that once my mind is made up I do not change it. Belaye Abaye was made the same offer, but chose to leave the country and work for the World Bank. A year and a half after my release, I went to England to visit my daughter. During my stay there, the Derg carried out its second round of liquidations. I was advised by all my friends to stay out of the country.

It took me some time to find out the reason for my detention. I had never been deferential to my supposed superiors and General Aman took my attitude as insubordination. I had failed to change with the changing times. His friend Bereket Habte Selassie was asked to find a reason to have me detained. Bereket was a member of the commission investigating the drought and knew that Mulatu Debebe, the former Cabinet minister who had been in charge of famine relief, desperately needed a scapegoat. Mulatu Debebe told the investigators I had hampered relief operations in my capacity as a minister of state by not providing trucks to transport relief food.

The accusation was unfounded but, in a way, it may have saved my life. Just ten days after I was thrown into detention, General Aman Amdom fell victim to the first of the Derg's massacres and Bereket was forced to flee the country. I was safe in the basement of the Menilek Palace.

11. Cabinet Resigns (February 1974)

It surprised me that seven days after my arrest the general could abrogate his responsibility and allow the leadership of the country to fall into the hands of the very people he should have been most able to understand, since he had been commanding them for so long. He ought to have known they were undisciplined, self-seeking, and aggressive. In the first place, at the time the soldiers in the provinces had been asked to send representatives to Addis, they quite deliberately sent their worst people in order to be rid of them. They assumed that as soon as the troublemakers arrived in the capital, they would get themselves into trouble and land in jail.

The general should have had access to intelligence reports on these people, which would have warned him of their records in the Third Division. He should have taken steps against them at the opportune moment. Since these men had no real support among their colleagues in the Third Division, if their leaders had been arrested by the general's bodyguards and the rest ordered to return to their units in disgrace, nobody would have given them any further support. Instead, when the rabble challenged his authority, rather than asserting himself, the general chose to go off to his house to sulk like a child. He should have seen that by leaving a pack of gangsters in control, he was jeopardizing his life, his close associates' lives, and the future of the country.

Three days after their disagreement with the general, the group thought he might call in the Third Division to deal with them so they embarked on a desperate and drastic plan to protect their position. They sent an armored car at 7 p.m to the home of the man whom they had declared head of state and government just two months before. General Aman was killed in an exchange of fire. This was the day officials of the former government were collected from their various places of detention and taken to the compound of the main prison where they were machine-gunned.

This was the beginning of a reign of terror which has lasted until the present day because the men who filled the vacuum left by the collapse of the Imperial regime have been concerned only with maintaining their power. In their excesses, they have punished the men, women, and children of their own country, driving those who are still alive and willing to oppose them into exile.

189

12

Epilogue

Rereading these personal recollections, I can see that an outsider might find it difficult to understand how, in a generation and a half, a civilization which had stood the test of thousands of years could be destroyed by an anarchistic military regime without a drop of blood being spilled [all bloodshed came after the Derg took power peacefully].

Looking back, not one of us was prepared for either a civilian or a military takeover, particularly by such destructive elements. We had completely failed to appreciate the potentially disastrous effects of the negative developments which took place during the reign of Haile Selassie: the promotion of weak and negative elements in our society in place of the strong-minded and positive ones of former times; and the subordination of Ethiopian culture and values to those of foreign origin.

The old tradition of a monarch's sacred personality and the respect given to the wisdom of experienced leaders had guaranteed that power would not fall into the careless hands of young, adventurous, and destructive persons. It was only a weak-minded, cowardly, and destructive leader who could have carried out the systematic destruction of the very cornerstones on which the foundations of stability and leadership were resting: the monarchy, religious freedom, justice, the land tenure principles, and the sanctity of private property.

The collapse, when it came, was so rapid we were all bewildered by the turn of events. That Aklilu's Cabinet could resign en masse and the resignations could be accepted and announced on the radio astonished us all. It is clear the emperor had lost any will he might once have possessed from the pusillanimous way in which he responded to the Cabinet resignation. A leader with strong-minded responsible men around him would never have allowed such a situation to develop; but if it did, he would have announced the name of

191

a new prime minister and a Cabinet reshuffle and shown the people they could still count on firm government.

Those of us who were opposed to the corruption and maladministration of the Haile Selassie regime had always assumed the emperor would live out his years and then be succeeded by the Crown Prince, upon whom strong natural leaders would be able to impose a system of constitutional monarchy with a strong guarantee of democracy and justice. We were all opposed to the emperor for being a weak leader, but every true Ethiopian was loyal to the institution of monarchy—the symbol of unity throughout the history of our nation. The monarchy was the traditional guarantee of freedom and justice. The thought of Ethiopia without an emperor was inconceivable. It did not occur to us that the symbol of national unity could be so easily and carelessly swept away.

Even after the military takeover, we took it for granted that a positive natural leader would emerge and the imbalances of the previous regime would be redressed. I say we took it for granted because it was difficult for any of us to discuss political developments together since there was no forum. There were no social clubs where we could meet to discuss politics because it was not part of our culture. The only organized institution was that of the army, with an officers club. From our place of work we went home. At weekends, some would stay at home and some would go to resorts to relax, but never in groups.

People who were reform-minded regarded with suspicion even those of us within the system who were known to be like-minded. If we, as senior officials, had tried to open a conversation with them on political matters, we would have been regarded as agents provocateur and shunned. One of our greatest errors was to forget that during half a century of foreign culture domination, a new generation had grown up without learning anything at all of Ethiopian culture, which was rooted in biblical traditions going previous to the establishment of the church in Rome.

It was only people with no knowledge of Ethiopian history who could have been so foolish as to destroy the only institution which symbolized national unity, instead of strengthen it with modern ideas at a time when our Ethiopian brothers in Eritra and the Ogaden were revolting against half a century of misrule and sometimes savage repression. None of us realized that for many younger Ethiopians, the very name of the monarchy was synonymous with oppression, not national unity.

Another factor which made it difficult for us to anticipate that Haile Selassie could be overthrown, as opposed to perhaps being kept on as a figurehead, was the enormous esteem in which he was held throughout the world. We knew the fatal weaknesses of the man, but were proud of the way other nations respected the emperor of Ethiopia.

12. Epilogue

Of course, on the domestic front we were dissatisfied with the emperor's regime and we wanted change, but believed it could be peaceful. When Mengistu seized power, not a single bullet was fired. Everybody, except those who were bloodthirsty, was overjoyed because they thought economic development, which had reached the takeoff point, could continue peacefully. The nation was astonished and shocked when the first thing Mengistu did was to destroy the very foundation of belief in government by indiscriminately massacring former government officials without a pretense of the process of justice.

The mindless adoption of outdated communist practices has made it more difficult for Ethiopia to recover from the present chaos. Under the old system, the people felt a sacred attachment to their religion and to their land principles which the present regime has set out to systematically destroy. In the past, when an emperor declared war against an invader, he called the people to arms to defend their freedom, religion, and their land. The present regime tries to mobilize the people against their brothers, while giving them nothing for which to fight.

The land tenure system has been destroyed by the decree making all the land the property of the state. When soldiers fighting in Eritrea are captured, then released and told to go home, they say they have no homes to go to. Many of them remain to fight against the government. The mass exodus to the West of the new generation is partly due to this lack of security and confidence in the repressive regime. The Eritreans are Ethiopians and many of us would be happy if they were fighting to take control of the central government, following the traditional examples of our forefathers of overthrowing an oppressive regime, to unify Ethiopia. It would be good if there was a strong leader among them capable of ruling the whole country. It is a tragedy that instead they are fighting for the fragmentation of Ethiopia. However, young Eritreans feel no sense of belonging to Ethiopia; they see Ethiopia as an oppressor and exploiter, and who can blame them. Most of us feel the same way about the administration. But the lasting solution is not fighting for fragmentation, but uniting and changing the repressive regime.

The important question we must now ask ourselves is how to get out of the hopeless mess in which our beloved country has been plunged. We must find a way of regenerating the heritage that was handed down to us by our ancestors, for the sake of our children.

It is to be hoped that by now we have come to our senses, after 16 years of destruction, senseless bloodshed, and disunity for which we have ourselves to blame, partly for looking down on our own heritage and wanting to think we were wiser than our forefathers because of our foreign education and exposure to foreign values. We inherited a country with a unique history on the continent of Africa, but what sort of country are we going to hand over to future generation? A land which is fragmented into territories so trivial they are no longer worthy of the name of Ethiopia?

Let us admit that our forefathers were wiser, and the values they set were genuine and the system they created was pragmatic, selfless, more humane and just in its time than the foreign values and systems which we have been trying to apply to solve our political and social problems. We have now seen that our system has not worked, while that of our forefathers endured until the beginning of our time. All the leaders who are opposing and fighting the present regime lack a sense of unity among themselves because they advocate differing foreign ideologies as solutions to the Ethiopian problems, instead of drawing on the rich political tradition and history of Ethiopia.

One thing we must not forget is that 90 percent of our nation was never exposed to foreign culture and education, and that it is an insult to a people who ruled themselves for thousands of years to try to subordinate their traditional values and culture.

It is an undeniable fact that Haile Selassie's regime has made the institution of monarchy hated by a great section of the population. However, Mengistu's barbarous actions and his system of administration have now reversed that feeling. Recent developments in Addis Ababa have amply demonstrated this fact. When members of the royal family who had been imprisoned for 14 years were released, the big crowd which turned up to wish them well, and continued streaming to their residence for weeks afterward, was concrete evidence of a change of heart about the monarchy.

But until now, no single opposition leader has come up with an idea which appeals to the whole nation by inspiring confidence and rallying support. I do not believe there could be any better option than going back to the time-proven values of our tradition, with the restoration of a monarchy as a symbol of our glorious history and heritage.

Our forefathers earnestly believed in and followed the faith of a God who is the creator of everything on Earth and in the Universe, the giver of the law that governs his creatures, the appointer of leaders to emerge from the nation, to administer His law and dispense justice, so as to maintain peace and harmony among individuals and communities. This was the reason for the title of the supreme leader of the nation—"Syume Egziabher Niguse Negest"—which translates as "The appointee of God, King of Kings." The belief in the supremacy of the law was so great it was said its power could stop the flow of a river: "Be Hig Amlak sibal enkuan sew woraj wonz yiqomal."

During the reign of Emperor Yohannes IV, an incident which took place demonstrated the administration of justice reached everyone, including domestic animals. The emperor, who was concerned about the proper dispensation of justice under his rule and had the welfare of his subjects at heart, wanted to

12. Epilogue

establish a means by which each one of his subjects could reach him easily to appeal to him against maladministration of justice. He ordered a big bell to be hung close to his palace so he could hear whenever it was rung by those who wanted to draw his attention.

It happened one day that a donkey was rubbing its back against the pole on which the bell was hanging and caused it to ring. The emperor ordered one of his attendants to go and fetch the person who rang the bell. But the messenger returned alone to inform the emperor he found only a donkey standing by the pole. "Well," said the emperor, "go back and bring the donkey. It might have some complaints to make." Sure enough, when the poor animal was presented to the emperor he noticed it was suffering from a sore back. The emperor gave orders that necessary care should be taken for the sore back of the animal to heal completely before it should be handed over to its owner. When it was handed over, the owner was admonished about his responsibility of taking good care of domestic animals. Such a concern for justice and humanity is one thing which one never heard of or read from the actions of such leaders as Hitler, Mussolini, Stalin, Idi Amin, and Mengistu, all of whom rose from the rabble where the essential qualities for constructive leadership such as justice, magnanimity, kindness, honesty, and courage are rare. They were only known for their indulgence in atrocities and destructions. Future generations will do well to take careful note of the fundamental weaknesses of these leaders in order to avoid repeating such human tragedies and the destruction of civilization.

On the other hand, those leaders who rose from a good family background such as Cromwell, Abraham Lincoln, and Tewodros were reputed for their great statesmanship and constructive leadership as reformers, founders of democracy, abolishers of slavery, and builders of national unity.

A revival of our traditional values and a search for born constructive leaders appears to be the only road leading away from the bleak situation which now faces us. Such leaders can be identified by what they have achieved among their communities through strong character and leadership qualities, positive and constructive ideas, benevolent actions, and a love for humanity and justice.

It is essential that all those leaders who are opposing the regime in Addis Ababa should put aside their petty differences and stand together as a united front in order to be in a position to call a general meeting which will declare a democratic national government of federal states united under a constitutional monarchy. The position of a figurehead monarch should preferably be filled by someone who can claim descent from all of the royal houses of Tigre, Oromo, and Amara.

Such a declaration of government should be followed with the upholding of Ethiopian unity, the denunciation of Mengistu and his regime, and the spelling out of the crimes and injustices committed against the good people of Ethiopia "in the name of the people." There must be a restoration of human rights, religious freedom, justice, and the principle of hereditary land ownership which gave every Ethiopian the right to own land.

Such a declaration of government would have to eschew borrowed language usage and be phrased in simple language which would be understood by the general public. In particular, we should abandon the foreign title of president for the head of states. After all, it was the person and not the title who abused the power, so there is no justification in abandoning the title in order to subordinate our culture to foreign values. If our present opposition leaders could unite and proclaim an emperor, they would rally so much public support the present Addis Ababa regime would vanish overnight.

Index

A

Abate, Atnafu, 180

Abaya, Lake, 90, 91

Abaye, Belaye, 188

Abdelqadre, Jemal, 174

Abdulahi, 144

Abdurhuman, (Ato) Mehamed, 174

Abebe, Abiy: appointment as minister of defense, 173, 174; character of, 95; and Gaitachew Bekele, 118, 120, 126, 141-45, 150; meeting with patriots, 39

Abebe, Daniel, 111

Abebe, Demisse, 54, 66

Abebe, Kebede, 102

Abebe, Ketema, 90

Abelti, 46

Abera, Amha, 48, 114, 118

Abeye Gedam, 35

Abozen, (Ato) Kebede, 87

Abraham, (Ato) Emanuel, 47

Abrha, Tsige, 71-72

Adamsu, 116

Addigrat, 27

Addis Ababa: Bekele family residence in, 12, 65-66, 156-57; Bekele Zewdu visits to, 10; British occupation of, 39; changes in, 155; Italian occupation of, 29; Zewdu residence in, 8

Aden Port Trust, 52, 53-55

Adera, Manbegroh, 71-72

Admassie, Betru, 158

Adugna, Shimelse, 164

Adulis, 134

Adwa, Battle of, 7, 27

Akaki, 109

Aladeneh, resignation of, 5-6

Alemayehu, (Ato) Hadis, 155

Alemayehu, Hailu, 168

Ambatchew, Zewditu, 56

Amdom, Aman, 184, 188, 189

Amharas, non-tribal tendency of, 122-23

Amde-Tsron, reign of, 25

Amlak, Yikono, 134

Andarge, Ras. See Mesai, (Ras) Andargatchew

Anderson, R. K., 76

Ankober, 116

Arat-Killo, 8, 12

Aregai, (Ras) Abebe: appointment as minister of interior, 42; appointment as regent, 35; appointment to

Sidamo, 41; and Assab Port Development Project, 70, 86; and dismissal of Mr. Diesen, 96-97; and 1960 coup attempt, 110; and resistance movement, 11, 38-39

Aregai, Afe Negus, 39

Army, Ethiopian, 23-24, 27

Asfaha, Bitwoded, 57

Asfawossen, Prince. 59

Asfawossen School. See Menelik School

Asferatchew, Biru, 10-11, 14-15, 16

Asmara, 56

Asmara Department of Marine: establishment of, 58-59, 71; attempts to close, 61, 74, 83-85

Asrat, (Ato) Belachew, 174

Assab, 55

Assab Port Construction Implementing Committee, 87

Assab Port Development Project, the, 66-67, 69-71, 85-87

Awash Valley, farming in, 155-56

Awage, Belete, 113

Axum, 133-34

Ayano, Bezabeh, 119

Ayele, Achaye, 20

Ayele, Atkelesh, 20

Ayele, Feleqech, 20

Ayele, Woldeyes, 20

Ayele, Yimegnushal, 10-11, 15-16, 31-33

Ayene, Assefa, 174, 180, 184

B

Bahr-Dar: geography of, 90, 125; subdistrict governors of, 128

Baro River, 91

Barron, F. S., 58

Bascilios, Archbishop Abune, 106, 137

Batignol, 69-70

Begemdir Province, 69, 90

Bekele, (Major) Monaye, 120, 122

Bekele, Aleme-Worq, 18, 19

Bekele, Ayelech, 18, 65, 80

Bekele, Daniel, 122

Bekele, Gaitachew: appointment to Bahr-Dar, 125-41, 143; appointment to Department of Marine, 61-63, 79-82; appointment to Department of Telecommunication, 161; appointment to Haiti, 141, 144-45; appointment to Massawa, 52-53, 58-62; appointment to Mexico, 150, 152; appointment as Minister of Public Works, 174; and Asmara Department of Marine, 83-85; and Assab Port Development Project, 66-71, 85-87; banishment of, 114, 118-24; and Bekele Zewdu, 18, 37; book publication of, 123-24; and Deqe Istifanos conflict, 133, 138-41; detention of, 112-13, 115-18, 187-88; and dismissal of Admiral Hoarve, 74-75; education of, 43-50, 68, 69, 72-73, 149; and Eskinder Desta, 94-95, 96-97; and Ethiopian Students Association in Great Britain, 48-49; and François Duvalier, 145-46; and Lake Tana Inland Water Development Program, 87-89; and land reform committee, 184-86; meetings with Haile Selassie, 44, 52-53, 59-60, 63, 75, 80, 82, 84, 86, 95, 98-99, 111-112, 126, 141, 150, 153, 175; and 1960 coup attempt, 101-12; and Ras Andarge, 56-57, 61-63, 70-71, 72; residence at Cheffa, 33-35; and the resistance

movement, 36-38; and
Sembo/Arerti Road Project, 157;
and Sekoru Medical Clinic, 158;
and Sekoru School, 157-58; and
Wollo drought, 186; and Yimeg-
nushal, 19-22, 31
Bekele, Habte-Mikael, 19, 36, 43
Bekele, Kassa. *See* Bekele,
Gaitachew
Bekele, Melaku: birth of, 18; deten-
tion of, 110, 113, 122; and 1960
coup attempt, 102-3; residence in
Addis Ababa, 65, 66
Bekele, Senayit, 145
Bekele, Simon, 18
Belehu, Shaqa, 35
Belete, Abebe, 113
Belew, Girma, 88, 98, 111
Beleyu, Woizero, 33
Berehe, (Dejazmatch) Tesfa
Yohannes, 174
Beshah, Kuribatchew, 15
Beso, making of, 23
Betru, Alemayehu, 71-72
Biadgeligh, (Fitawrari) Habte-Geor-
gis, 14, 172Biblical heritage,
Ethiopian, 133-36
Biru, Assegedetch, 10-11, 17-18, 28,
29, 34
Biru, Mulugeta: and Biru Asfer-
atchew, 10, 15; death of, 16; and
journey to Shewa, 28-30; and
1960 coup attempt, 107-9
Biru, Tsedale, 17-18, 29, 30
Biru, Woizero Askale, 28-29
Bishoftu, 6
Bitew, Abebe, 61, 83, 84-85
Bogale, Abozenetch, 18, 22
Bogale, Admasu, 18
Bogale, Kegnazmatch, 17
Bogale, Tenagne, 18

Bogale, Zeleke, 93
Bollosso, community at, 28
Brundage, Avery, 154
Bulga, 11, 21
Bulli, Mulugeta: and dismissal of
Admiral Hoarve, 75; and
Gaitachew Bekele, 76, 77, 79, 81;
meeting with patriots, 39; and
1960 coup attempt, 110
Buschi, Commandatore, 73, 88
Bushen, Tesfa, 119

C

Chacha, 38
Cheffa, 33-35
Cheffe Donsa, Italian fortress at, 38,
39
Chis-Isat Waterfall, 90
Clewer, Selby J., 44-47, 119
Coup D'etat, attempted, 101-110
Cunningham, Sir Alan, 39
currency, Ethiopian, 39-40

D

Dadi, (Dejazmatch) Kifle, 120-21,
125-26, 143
Darge, Balamberas Haile, 37
Debebe, Mulatu, 188
Debre-Berhan, 38, 39
Debre-Libanos, execution of monks
of, 135
Debre-Marqos, 116, 127
Debre-Tsigge, 156-57
Defaye, (Ato) Assefa, 87
Deferesu, Asrat, 106
Dej-tinat system, 41, 61, 126, 143
Demeksa, (Ato) Bulcha, 174
Denbegnotch, the, 8
Deneqe, Mekonnen, 82

Deqe Istifanos Monastery, contro-
versy at, 133, 137-41
Deressa, Yilma, 112, 141-42, 176
Derg, the, 25, 177-81, 186
Dessalegne, Abebe, 156
Desalegni, (Ato) Amde-Mikael, 56,
105
Desta, Beyene, 105
Desta, Eskinder, 85, 94-95, 96-97
Desta, (Ato) Mekonnen, 43
Desta, (Ato) Negash, 174, 184
Desta, Shewa-Regged, 139
Dibu, Tsigge, 104, 105
Diesen, T, 91, 96-97, 102
Dimbleby, Johnathan, 186-87
Dinqe, (Ato) Berhanu, defection of,
149
Dirqosh, making of, 23
Dofa-Mikael, 39
Dubale, Deresse, 119
Duvalier, François, 145-46, 150-51

E

Education, Ethiopian church school, 13
Embur Gebeya, 35
Enda Eyesus, Fort, 27
Endeshaw, Wolde, 62
Engda, (Ato) Gebre-Wold, 97
Enjera, making of, 36
Enqo-Selassie, (Dejazmatch) Tse-
hayu, 144
Equba-Igzi, (Ato) Araya, 87, 126
Eritrea, 56, 69
Erlich, Haggai, 14
Ethiopian Students Association in
Great Britain, the, 48-49
Eyasu, detention of, 116
Eyasu, Melake Tsehay, 11, 35, 41
Ezana, King, 134

F

Fasiledes, Emperor, 25, 135-36
Fernandez, Bill, 146
Fiche, 38
Fish, in Ethiopian diet, 92-93
Fisher, Douglas, 44

G

Gaitachew, Heywote, 145
Gaitachew, Tewdros, 12, 122, 145
Gale, (Weizero) Shewa Regged, 39
Galliano, 27
Gambela, 91
Gamu-Gofa, 91
Garadew, Getachew, 115
Garadew, Negash, 54
Gebar system, 8, 9
Gebeyehu, (Colonel) Worqneh, 105-07
Gebre, Kebede, 106, 108-09
Gebre, Tadesse, 113
Gebre-Amlak, Bemnet, 85
Gebre-Georgis, Assefa, 51-52
Gebre-Igze, Tesfaye, 178
Gebre-Mariam, Asefa, 126
Gebre-Sadiq, (Ato) Belete, 174
Gebre-Selassie, (Dejazmatch) Zewde:
appointment to Department of
Marine, 61, 83; appointment as
Minister of Interior, 174-75;
appointment to Ministry of Public
Works, 63; and Assab Port Devel-
opment Project, 69; and Ethiopian
Students Association in Great
Britain, 48; and Gaitachew Bekele,
61, 62; and Judge Maraine, 114;
and Massawa Naval Training
Establishment, 73, 74; and training
of tugboat operators, 72
Gebre-Wold, Mulugeta, 155-56

Gebre-Yesus, Teke, 54
Gebre-Yohannes, Seyfu, 57
Gebremariam, (Ato) Solomon, 141
Gebru, 164
Gebru, Dawit, 113
Gedamu, (Ato) Tekaligne, 174
Gelawdewos, Emperor, 135; reign of, 25
Genete Leul Palace, 53, 82, 102, 126
Germame, 104-07
Ginager: Italian fortress at, 37; raid on, 35, 36
Gizaw, Tesseme, 71-72, 92
Goben, (Weizero) Askale, 39
Gohatsion, 127
Gojam Province, 90
Gorfo, Italian fortress at, 37
Gragni, Mohammed, 135, 136
Gshetu, (Ato) Guessess, 93
Gullaye, Salah, 55
Guther, Max, 129, 130

H

Hable-Selassie, Sebhat, 44
Habte, Aklilu, 176
Habte-Wold, (Ato) Akaleworq, 50, 52, 56
Habte-Wold, Aklilu, 88, 112, 162, 172
Habte-Wold, Mamo, 106
Habte-Wold, (Ato) Mekonnen: and Assab Port Development Project, 70, 71; character of, 82-83, 99; and dismissal of Mr. Diesen, 97; and Gaitachew Bekele, 75, 81; and 1960 coup attempt, 110, 112
Habte-Wold, Tsehafi-Tezaz Aklilu, 126, 133, 144-45
Habte-Yohannes, (Ato) Debebe, 154
Habteyes, Negussie, 127

Haile, Bekele, 163
Haile, (Ato) Minasse, 174, 180, 184
Haile, Nega, 39
Haile-Mariam, Afe-Negus Gebre-Medhin, banishment of, 121
Haile-Mariam, Dereje, 48-49
Haile-Mariam, Teshome, 114
Haile-Selassie, Nega, 102, 140
Haile Selassie Secondary School, 44, 45-46
Hailu, (Ras) T. Haymanot, 116
Haiti: attempted coup in, 146; Ethiopian embassy in, 141-42, 146, 147-48; Haile Selassie visit to, 150-51
Handal, Nibs, 76-77
Hans-Dieter, Hoeft, 68-69, 85, 102, 122
Harlofson, (Captain) 73, 75
Hayilu, Sultan, 71-72
Hint, Salah, 167
Hoarve, (Admiral), 73-75

I

Imru, (Lij) Mikael: and appointment to Department of Marine, 63, 75; and appointment to Ministry of Agriculture, 79; and appointment to Ministry for Information, 184; and appointment as prime minister, 174, 175, 180; and Ethiopian embassy in Haiti, 142; and Ethiopian Students Association in Great Britain, 48; and Gaitachew Bekele, 68, 76, 115, 119
Inqo-Selassie, Kifle, 119
Inqo-Selassie, (Dejazmatch) Tesfaye, 118-19
Inqo-Selassie, (Dejazmatch) Tsehayu, 121, 138-39, 141, 142
Iquba-Igzi, Blata Dawit, 103

Isayiyas, Gebre-Selassie, 110, 111
Islamic heritage, Ethiopian, 135
Italian invasion, end of, 38-39
Iyasu the Great, reign of, 25

J

Jacobsen, Johns E., 76
Jarso-Amba, 30, 159
Jifar, (Aba), 122
Jimma, 119-124
Jobir, (Aba), 122

K

Kaleb, King, 134
Kasa, (Ras) Hailu, 116
Kassa, Asrat: and farming in Awash
    Valley, 155-56; and Gaitachew
    Bekele, 114, 118; and 1960 coup
    attempt, 106; visit to Eritrea, 59
Kebede, (Ato), 125
Kedir, Solomon, 168-69
Kuntze, Hans, 67
Kelkay, Balamberas, 127, 128
Kereyu, the, 156
Kesem River, 31
Khalifa, Eliasa, 72-73
Kidane-Mariam, Blata, 56
Kidane-Mariam, Yohannes, 54
Kristos, Gebre, 29
Kristos, Tedla, 29
Kulo, Italian occupation of, 28

L

Lalibela, rock churches at, 134
Leadership training system,
    Ethiopian, 13-14, 24-27
League of Nations, Ethiopian admis-
    sion to, 2

Legebar River, 31
Lema, Mengestu, 48
Lema, (Ato) Minasse, 70
Lion Cub, the, 48
Little Aden Port Development Pro-
    ject, 53
Lund, (Commodore), 94, 96

M

Maderia system, 185
Magloir, Frank, 147-48
Maichew, massacre at, 11, 28, 62
Manbegroh, 125
Marain, Judge Nathan, 113-14
Mariam, Mengistu Haile, 180
Maritime Services, Ethiopian, estab-
    lishment of, 55
Marqos, Bishop Abune, 137-41
Massawa: Gaitachew Bekele service
    in, 58-62; naval base at, 73
Massawa Naval Training Establish-
    ment, 94
Maza, (Aba), 138
Mehretab, Bereket, 54
Mekonnen, Endalkatchew: and
    Addis Ababa road transport
    monopoly, 165; appointment as
    prime minister, 173; arrest of,
    184; and attempted hijacking,
    169; cabinet of, 174; and
    Ethiopian Students Association in
    Great Britain, 48; and Gaitachew
    Bekele, 80, 161; meeting with
    patriots, 39
Mekonnen, (Ato) Eshete, 158
Mekonnen, (Fitawrari) Gebre-Kristos,
    121
Mekonnen, (Ras) Taferi, 172
Mekonnen, Tedla, 111
Mekuanent, the, 10, 13-14

Mekuria, Kegnazmatch, 28-29
Mekuria, (Ato) Tekele-Tsadiq, 176
Mekuria, Zewde, 186
Melke, Tadesse, 112
Mellisinos, Captain: and Asmara
    Department of Marine, 58-59, 83,
    85; and Assab Port Development
    Project, 70
Menasse, Abebe, 93
Menelik II, Emperor, 2, 6, 24, 25, 27,
    44
Menelik School, 43-44
Mengistu, (Major) Hayle-Mariam, 24,
    25, 193
Menjigso, 17, 29
Mequelle, 27
Merawi, 127
Merid, Mengesha: and Gaitachew
    Bekele, 110, 114, 144-45; and
    1960 coup attempt, 106, 108-09
Mesai, (Ras) Andargatchew: and
    Asmara Department of Marine, 83,
    84-85; and Assab Port Develop-
    ment Project, 69-71; and
    Gaitachew Bekele, 56-57, 61-63,
    70-71, 72; and Lake Tana inland
    water development, 88-89; land
    ownership in Bahr-Dar, 130, 131;
    and Massawa dredging conflict,
    59-60; and 1960 coup attempt, 118
Mesfin, Asfaw, 98-99, 165
Meshesha, Tsegaye, 180
Mexico, Ethiopian embassy in, 152
Mezgebe-Tibebe, Merigeta, 139
Mikael, (Ato) Kebede, 48
Minjar, 7
Modalsi, J., 76-77
Mourning garb, Ethiopian, 33
Mugere, 34
Mulat, Abate, 122
Mulugeta, Colonel, 183

N

Negale, army mutiny at, 172
Nekneke, (Ato) Million, 175
Neway, (General), Mengistu, 102,
    104, 106, 107

O

Olympic Games, 1968, 153-54
Organization of African Unity, for-
    mation of, 2, 149

P

Peity, M., 166
Petros, Abune, 135
Petros, (Ato) Goytom, 115, 126
Port-au-Prince, climate of, 146
Produce, Ethiopian, 20

Q

Qajima Georgis, 6
Qinbebit: Assegedetch Biru trip to,
    17; Biru Asferatchew residence at,
    15; burial of Yimegnushal at, 16;
    climate of, 32; Gaitachew Bekele
    visit to, 18, 30-31, 38; geography
    of, 10, 31, 33
Qitaw, Blata, 114
Quantta, making of, 23

R

Reda-Igzi, Wold-Aregai, 54, 73, 98
Retta, (Ato) Abebe: and Ethiopian
    Students Association in Great
    Britain, 48; and farming in Awash
    Valley, 155-56; and Gaitachew
    Bekele, 49-50, 124
Rist system, the, 156

Road Transport Administration Board, 162-63
Road Transport Authority, 162, 163

S

Segele: Gaitachew Bekele visit to, 30, 38; Italian fortress at, 37
Sekoru, 19-20, 31-32, 157-58
Sekoru Clinic, 158, 159
Selassie, Bereket Habte, 188
Selassie, Haile: and Addis Ababa road transport monopoly, 166; and Asmara Department of Marine, 84; and Assab Port Development Project, 86-87; and city at Bahr-Dar, 130; and Deqe Istifanos Monastery conflict, 141; and dismissal of Admiral Hoarve, 75-76; and Ethiopian education system, 52; fall of, 171-81; and foreign advisors, 92; and Gaitachew Bekele, 114, 123, 143-44, 161-62; and imperial bodyguard pay dispute, 103; meetings with Gaitachew Bekele, 44, 52-53, 59-60, 63, 75, 80, 82, 84, 86, 95, 98, 99, 111-12, 126, 141, 150, 153, 175; and oath of loyalty, 24; and rejection of Ethiopian culture, 1, 2-3, , 26-27, 132, 171, 172, 181-82; and treatment of patriots, 40-41, 42; visit to Eritrea, 59-60, 95; visit to Haiti, 150-51
Selassie, Prince Sahele, 48
Sembo/Arerti Road Project, the, 157, 158-59
Semeneh, 131-32
Senbete, the, 21
Sendafa, 40
Shawl, Hailu, 177

Shena, Italian fortress at, 37
Shewa, 9
Shibesh, Getachew, 188
Shifferaw, Bezuneh, 117
Shimels, Adugna, 166
Shola, Gebeya, Italian fortress at, 37
Sidamo Province, 91
Sidisto, raid on, 36
Sodo, Italian occupation of, 29
Susenyos, Emperor, 135
Syoum, Leul Ras, 175

T

Tadesse, Afe-Neguse, 117
Tadesse, Mamo, 89, 105
Tadesse, Mary, 48
Tafese, Getahun, 44
Tana, Lake, 87-89, 90-91, 125
Teacher's Training College, 45
Tedla-Mariam, 34
Tefera-Worq, Tsehafi-Tezaz, 70, 75, 80, 144-45
Teferi Mekonnen School, 43
Tegulet, 39
Teka, 164
Tekle, Afeworq, 48-49
Tekle Georgis, Emperor, 106-07
Tekle, Grazmath, 29
Tekele, (Fitawrari) Zekaryas, 120
Tekeleab, Teferra, 179
Tekle-Haymanot, Abune, 134, 138
Tekle-Haymanot, 24
Tekle-Haymanot, (Ras) Hailu, 116
Tenaqne-Worq, Princess, 56, 59
Terefe, (Ato) Tadesse, 174, 175
Tesfay, Berhanu, 55
Tessema, Admasu, 54
Tessema, (Dejazmatch) Kebede, 110-12, 174, 184
Tessema, (Ato) Mamo, 154

Tessema, Melasse, 180
Tessema, Solomon, 154
Tessema, Yidneqatchew, 153
Tesseme, Alemu, 98
Tesseme, Alem-Zewde, 183
Tewalde-Medhin, Meharei, 54
Tewodros, Emperor, 171
Tewoflos, Archbishop Abune, 136-37, 165
Tibebe, Meriggeta Mezegabe, 125
Tideneqialesh, Weizero, 29
Tilahun, (Ato) Abebe, 157
Tilahun, Kebede, 71-72
Tinqeshu, (Grazmatch) Woldeyes, 36
Tiss Issat Falls, 125, 131, 139
Tonto Macoute, the, 146
Tsehayu, (Dejazmatch) Inqo-Selassie, 121, 138-39, 141, 142
Turunesh, Emama, 29

U

Udjus, Magnus, 76
U.S. Technical Assistance Fund, 88, 91

V

Vogt, J., 92

W

Walelign, 164, 168
Wodajo, (Ato) Kifle, 174
Woizero, Beleyu, 33
Wolayta, 8, 10
Wolde, Mamo, 154
Wolde-Aregai, Reda-Igzi, 73
Wolde-Gabriel, Beyene, 48
Wolde-Georgis, (Fitawrari) Tesema, 38

Wolde-Georgis, Tsehafi Tezaz, 59
Woldehawarya, Tesfa-Igze, 54
Wolde-Hawaryat, 5
Woldemariam, Kassa, 80
Wolde-Mariam, Shibru, 122
Wolde-Mariam, (Ato) Zewge, 145
Wolde-Selassie, 5
Wolde-Selassie, Abebe, 54, 155-56
Wolde-Selassie, Alemayehu, 166
Woldesemayat, Berhanu, 71-72
Wolde-Tensay, (Aba), 133, 137-41
Wolde-Tsadiq, Amezenetch, 33
Wolde-Tsadiq, Turuworq, 33
Wolde-Tsadiq, Woodnesh, 33
Wolde-Yohanis Nigatu, 114, 121
Woletehana, 7, 8
Wollamo, 8
Wollisso, 114, 118-19
Wollo drought, 186
Wondafarsh, Amde, 115
Wondafarsh, Germame, 115
Worku, Mekuria, 126
Worqneh, Kegnazmatch, 35, 36
Worqneh, (Colonel) Gebeyehu, 103-7
Wor-Tera system, 8
Wosen, Asfa, 181
Wossene, (Dejazmatch) Mekonnen, 15, 29

Y

Yayeh-Yirad, Balamberas Girma, 115-118, 120
Yenjera-Assalafiwotch Denb, the, 7, 8, 27
Yigezu, Tamrat, 115, 119, 120
Yinesu, (Ato) Asrat, 152
Yirdaw, (Aba), 35
Yirfu, Ketema, 105-06, 123, 142, 151, 153
Yisehaq, Afework, 54

Yodit, 134, 136
Yohannes IV, Emperor, 24, 194-95

Z

Zaba-Selassie, 10
Zagwe Dynasty, 134
Zeleke, Belaye, 181-82
Zera-Yaqob, 134

Zerihun, (Ato) Ferede, 131
Zewde, (Fitawrari) Wolde-Tsadiq,
    34-35, 37, 38, 41
Zewditu, Empress, 172
Zewdu, 5, 7-8, 9
Zewdu, Basha, 41
Zewdu, Bekele, 7-8, 10-12, 27-28,
    41
Zewge, (Ato) Wolde-Mariam, 145